PANDEMIC PREACHING

To Father Dan and Mercy Parish
Our Lady of Mercy Parish !

Blessings !

Fr. David Bur

PANDEMIC PREACHING

The Pulpit in a Year Like No Other

David H. Garcia

WIPF & STOCK · Eugene, Oregon

PANDEMIC PREACHING
The Pulpit in a Year Like No Other

Wipf & Stock
An Imprint of Wipf and Stock Publishers
199 W. 8th Ave., Suite 3
Eugene, OR 97401

www.wipfandstock.com

PAPERBACK ISBN: 978-1-6667-3050-0
HARDCOVER ISBN: 978-1-6667-2212-3
EBOOK ISBN: 978-1-6667-2213-0

Scripture texts used in this work are taken from the *New American Bible*,
revised edition © 2010, 1991, 1986, 1970 Confraternity of Christian Doctrine,
Washington, DC.

Table of Contents

Introduction

I NEVER IMAGINED WRITING this kind of a book. It began because of the coronavirus crisis and lockdown in March 2020. It was a dark and fearful period for us all. There was confusion and changing information about what we were facing, but it certainly looked bad.

Churches were closed quickly and people started to watch Mass and services via livestream. I received several requests from friends who had attended past Masses I celebrated, asking if I would share homilies with them for each Sunday. At first I resisted, but soon I warmed to the idea because it would help so many like myself who were facing a new and uncertain time. This book of homilies and reflections grew from that moment.

Initially the email list was ten or so, including my five sisters! Soon it grew to over 120, with many recipients forwarding the homily to all their email list, literally thousands. I received comments from all over the country thanking me for these weekly moments of hope during a dark time.

I love the Scriptures! There is always a new insight, a new way to look at things in light of Scripture. As a priest I have tried to help people fall in love with Scripture, as I have. I hope my writings here will help in that task.

I have always loved to preach as a priest. It is a passion. I try to prepare well and put myself into each homily. I have been greatly blessed with many experiences in my priesthood which speak to me about humanity and God's ever-present action in our lives. I am an avid reader of newspapers, magazines, and books. I am always listening to the news. I am a bit of a news junkie! I try to pay attention to the human story in all these sources. I find Scripture speaks to all these moments of life and illuminates them for us. I urge you to pay attention to the stories of your life as well as the stories of others around you. God speaks all the time!

My approach to a homily is basically what Jesus did in the Emmaus story. First, understand what is happening in the lives of the people. Second, shine the light of Scripture on those experiences. Third, leave the hearers with the questions: What are my marching orders from this? Where do I go? What do I do?

Maybe these reflections will do that for you.

Thanks to the many readers of these homilies who gave me thoughtful feedback that improved what I was trying to do throughout the year of writing. Thanks also to Sr Theresa McGrath, CCVI, of the University of the Incarnate Word, who proofed the text and offered great suggestions and much support.

At this writing, the virus is slowly retreating in this country and other parts of the world. However, it still rages in many poor areas. It will not be over until it is over for all our sisters and brothers in the world. Our task in solidarity is to do what we can to make that happen.

The last homily in this book fittingly quotes the request of people to the disciples: "We want to see Jesus." That is the deep desire of every Christian. I hope these writings will help you on that journey.

David Garcia
San Antonio, Texas
May, 2021

3/29/20 Fifth Lent

Untie him and let him go free.

Ezra 37:12–14; Rom 8:8–11; John 11:1–45

THREE YEARS AGO, I lost five priest friends within thirteen months, four of whom were mentors and priests I admired, while the fifth was a classmate friend of many years. Eight years ago I lost three members of my family within six months, my mother, nephew, and great-nephew. Those were very hard moments of grief for me and forced me to think of my own life. Confronting the death of those close to us hits home because we must then think of our own death. When will I be in that coffin?

The coronavirus pandemic is an extraordinary moment for us all. We are worried and fearful because it has no cure as of yet and no vaccine to help us avoid it. It is easily spread and can be fatal to some. For the first time in almost everyone's memory, we must follow community quarantines and completely adjust our normal day-to-day routine. This has not happened in such a fashion since World War II. All this is to limit the risk and the number of illnesses and deaths. Nevertheless, despite trying to do what is best for our own health, this pandemic scares us.

In such a time, where can we turn? Our faith, and certainly this season of Lent and Easter, tell us not to see death with fear but with hope, with faith, and, most of all, with joy. That is why, when people tell stories at funeral wakes, they so often relate funny anecdotes. It is a way of letting go of the loved one with the joys of his or her life.

I remember visiting one priest mentor, Father Larry Stuebben, a few days before he died. He knew death was coming. I remember telling him what a wonderful priest he had been and what a wonderful life he had lived, and I thanked him for showing me how to live priesthood. He answered me so simply as he said, "God has been good to me." What a simple moment of total gratitude to God! What a great way to end your life, giving thanks to the One who brought you into this world in the first place. I left Father Larry with the thought that he was already tasting the resurrection.

Today's gospel story about the Raising of Lazarus is found only in John; yet it seems to be the last major story which then leads to Jesus' death. Why was it not mentioned in the other gospels? John's gospel emphasizes theology and signs. This is the ultimate moment of theology. This is the ultimate sign: life and death and faith in God. This is not a story of resuscitating a corpse but about the giving of life to the world. Jesus is the resurrection and the life, sent by God. To believe in him is to have life.

Jesus is told, "The one you love is sick." How often we have been told this about loved ones and we respond. However, sometimes one we love is sick and no one knows or suspects it, or we cannot be with them. They are alone in their illness. The coronavirus is one of these moments when those who are seriously sick in hospitals cannot have their loved ones visit them due to the infection risk, and some have died alone. The sick in first-century Israel were often rejected and required to leave the community to live in the bush or in caves. The alienation and isolation were as bad as, or even worse than, their illness. Jesus especially reached out to the sick of his day, who were not only suffering physical pain but also rejection and humiliation. His healing was both for the body and to restore the person to the community of relationships. Keeping the community of relationships strong is the healing needed for us today in this pandemic.

This gospel story speaks to the coming passion, death, and resurrection of Jesus. At the death of Lazarus in Bethany, Jesus is deeply moved and troubled, as he would be later in the garden of Gethsemane, near Jerusalem. Lazarus's tomb is a cave with a stone that is rolled back, and the grave cloths are removed. This is the dress rehearsal for Jesus' own death, burial, and resurrection. The ultimate price of Lazarus's life is Jesus' death, as this leads the religious leaders to decide Jesus must be eliminated. One cannot give life without dying in some way.

Jesus asks where Lazarus has been laid. He is told, "Come and see," which was the original invitation to the disciples to follow him. Now it is the invitation to Jesus to move toward his own death. The deep moment of emotion about his friend and his own impending death brings forth an intense human response. Jesus weeps.

Lazarus represents the faithful Christian, the one Jesus loves, for whom he weeps. The raising of Lazarus symbolizes the resurrection of the Christian. The story is filled with symbols of Christian life. Jesus was acquainted with grief. He cried as he went to see the tomb. He felt the loss and the suffering of his best friends.

Jesus had waited days before he went to Bethany. Lazarus is already dead four days. This is longer than any other person that Jesus had recalled from death, which shows Jesus' power over physical and spiritual death. This story and the dialogue go back and forth from physical story to spiritual story. Disciples accompanying him to Jerusalem are symbolic of following him, while carrying their own crosses. Jesus lifts Martha and Mary as well as his disciples to a higher level. This requires faith. Jesus opened a breach on the other side of death through which all those who believe in him can follow him. It is the opening to eternal life.

Each story in our recent Lenten Sundays moves toward gradual belief: Samaritan woman, transfiguration, man born blind, and now Lazarus.

I presided at the funeral of a woman who died after a lengthy illness. She was surrounded at death by her brothers and sisters. One brother spoke at the funeral and said that during the final days with her, they told her, "We are with you. We will walk with you as far as we can; then you will need to walk the final way on your own to where you are going." What a wonderful final moment of loving accompaniment! When Father Larry, on his deathbed, said to me, "God has been good to me," I knew he was already on that beautiful final walk to new life.

Maybe that is what must console us as we try to confront death, suffering, and pain. Maybe that is what we must consider during this time of the coronavirus's fears and uncertainties. Overall, God has been good to me. Look at who God has put in my life, even if just temporarily. When death, pain, and suffering happen, I have always had others around to console, comfort, and accompany me. Now is the time for me to be there for them and others in whatever way I can.

The last thing Jesus says in today's gospel is, "Untie him and let him go free." What a powerful, loving command! That is our hope; that is our joy. Jesus wants us untied and free! We can face what comes tomorrow with his words and with the faith that only he can give.

2

4/05/20 Palm Sunday

Are you the King of the Jews?

Isa 50:4-7; Phil 2:6-11; Matt 26:14—27:66

THREE YEARS AGO, WE marked the one hundredth anniversary of the entrance of the United States into World War I. That Great War caused much anxiety and fear in this country. As now with this pandemic, we had never been in such a situation. The war also caused terrible discrimination against American people of German origin. German was the second language of the United States at that time as one in ten Americans was German or of German descent. Many in this country began to question the loyalty of German Americans. They were abused verbally and physically. A German was lynched in Illinois. The same nativist sentiment happened during World War II with the interning of thousands of Japanese Americans for no reason except their ethnic heritage. People later recognized these wrongs and felt the United States had learned its lesson about blaming loyal Americans for what happens in the country of their ancestors.

Sadly, it seems some have not learned the lesson. In the age of the coronavirus in our country, Asian Americans are being subjected to discrimination, name-calling, humiliation, and verbal and physical abuse. Chinatowns in major cities were avoided and boycotted almost from the first sign of the virus beginning in China. Some officials blamed the Chinese for the pandemic, while medical leaders and the United Nations rightly did not. A congressional candidate recently ran an ad saying, "China poisoned our people." Will we learn anything new

5

from this latest crisis? Do we always have to be suspicious? Scapegoat and blame an entire group of people when a disaster which frightens us occurs? Why the cruelty? What causes this to happen?

With Palm Sunday and Holy Week, we enter into the most solemn moments and mysteries of the Christian faith. Each day this week we are asked to place ourselves inside the story and walk next to Jesus. Reflect on how he lived this week. Experience it for ourselves.

The narrative of Jesus' passion shows human cruelty at its worst. It is a story of immense suffering, chaos, fear, aloneness, and death. We need to look at how Jesus goes through his suffering, humiliation, and, finally, his death. Perhaps we can learn something from the attitude he chooses as he is being so terribly and unjustly treated. Jesus is suffering physically, but the denials, betrayals, and abandonment by close friends devastate him spiritually and emotionally. Maybe in the midst of the inhumanity, our hearts will be touched enough to never be part of such treatment of anyone. It may also help us see others in this pandemic through the eyes of the suffering Jesus.

To truly enter the story, we need to place ourselves there and to ask ourselves: Which one of the characters am I? Could I have been Judas, who wanted money over friendship? Or Peter, who denied he knew Jesus because of personal insecurity? Or one of the other disciples who ran and abandoned him out of fear? Could I be one of the religious leaders who had demonized Jesus so much because he did not toe the party line, that the only way to defend their way of life was doing away with him? Could I have been Pilate, facing an innocent person, but yet, because of political or social pressure, made a decision that cost another person her/his life? Any of us might have been any of them. These human situations, emotions, and reactions happen every day in our lives, even if the consequences are not so dramatic. Holy Week puts us in the sandals of those who were there so that we might live the story. At the end of Holy Week, we need to ponder its lessons for our lives.

Matthew's Gospel is written for Jewish Christians who had recognized Jesus as Messiah and were suffering hardships, alienation, verbal abuse, and even physical violence from their fellow Jews who had rejected Jesus and suspected his followers were traitors. In the passion narrative Matthew shows how Jesus is betrayed by one of his own, denied by his closest friend, abandoned by all his disciples and left alone to face condemnation and death. The early Christians identified with the story through their hardships. In some ways we all feel these emotions during our present difficulties, especially being alone in sickness or social distancing. Jesus faced similar situations with dignity, strength, and even compassion.

Peter's denial comes when he is identified and stereotyped as coming from another area, namely, Galilee, a suspect place for people of Judea. Galilee was a mix of people due to many foreigners, non-Jews, who settled there. Galileans had an accent that was clearly different, and were not considered pure Jews by the rest of Israel. It was a place denigrated by Jerusalem: "Can anything good come from Nazareth?" (John 1:46). Peter is confronted, "Certainly you are also one of them, for your accent betrays you." It was in this context of sin, a context of prejudice, that Peter himself sinned. One sin often creates moments for more sin.

Matthew adds the words of Jesus during the Last Supper, saying that this is his blood poured out for many "for the forgiveness of sins." Matthew sees Jesus' death as connected with atonement for sin. Jesus, throughout the gospel, lives a life of forgiving love, teaching others to do the same. A recurring theme in the gospel is that Jesus frees people from sin, heals them from their suffering, reconciles them to the rest of the community, and offers his life for humanity. Some could see this even in their weakness and sin. Peter ultimately accepted forgiveness when Jesus, in one of the resurrection appearances, asked him three times if he loved him. Judas, despite seeing Jesus' ministry of reconciliation for three years, in the end, tragically, could not accept it for himself. It is significant that the disciples call Jesus "Lord" in the gospel, while Judas calls him "Rabbi," a term used in the gospel by unbelievers. The challenge today is to believe enough to live the reconciling work of Jesus in the midst of the chaos and insecurity of a spreading virus that has no cure. We must be believers!

Who is Jesus? Jesus' identity as the true representative of God is important to Matthew. People constantly speak about it: Pilate, the high priest, the soldiers, those at the cross. Matthew shows how Jesus' true identity is named over and over. Pilate asks, "Are you the King of the Jews?" Jesus answers "You say it." Pilate names him twice King of the Jews; soldiers mock him saying, "King of the Jews"; the inscription on the cross reads: "King of the Jews," and the crowd taunts: "Let the Messiah, King of Israel come down from the cross." Finally, a non-Jew, a foreigner, after Jesus' death says, "Clearly this was the Son of God." The curtain of the old temple, closed to all but a few, is now torn, giving way for the new temple which is Jesus, open to all. To name Jesus is to accept his saving ministry and replicate it. Can we take this moment of personal and communal crisis to name Jesus and live his saving ministry to others rather than being selfish, blaming, demonizing, or ignoring?

What will we learn this Holy Week? How do we live as disciples of Jesus today, in the time of the coronavirus, in the midst of uncertainty, anxiety, and even panic, in a time where everyone is suspicious of everyone else, and anyone might give me the virus? What allows us to still live reflecting the Jesus of the Passion?

This week walk with Jesus, see how he was mistreated and misjudged. Who is receiving the same treatment now, and are you participating in that? Our faith teaches us how to die before we die. I have seen that in various role models in my own life—people who lived life by sacrificing themselves over and over for others, who embraced moments of suffering and finally death with a spirit of gratitude toward God and giving to others.

I remember as a young priest being called to a home in a poor neighborhood in my mostly Hispanic Westside parish. The family was gathered around the bed of the elderly grandfather who was unconscious and dying. I said some prayers with them, and after that, his wife, the grandmother, took his frail arm and made the sign of the cross over each family member present. Through her, he gave a final blessing. What a powerful moment for that family, and for me! His life had blessed them many times and now this was his final gift through the one who had lived by his side faithfully for many years. Instead of feeling sorry for herself, the man's wife created a blessing for others. Small yet powerful acts of blessing are what make our lives the lives of disciples of Jesus. Let us figure out how to bless others at this difficult time.

The passion narrative poses the questions: "What motivates people to turn against another, to see in the one who is different a threat? Why belittle, blame, hate, or want to hurt someone else?" This country was relatively peaceful in the twentieth century until a world war twice interrupted our daily lives, causing fear, suspicions, scapegoating, and prejudice to rear their ugly heads. War and violence cause other forms of hatred to spin out of control. The coronavirus has been likened to a war we are fighting. The virus is the enemy, not any person or any one group of people, no matter who they are. The heroic attitude of the medical community, the first responders, and those working in essential services like grocery stores, drug stores, and delivery services, are risking their own health in order to serve and save. That is what we need to focus on and imitate. If anyone can give you a deadly virus, the good Samaritan story tells us that anyone can also save your life. There are many small acts of kindness and self-sacrifice happening all around us during this time of trial. We need to lift them up, support them, and do what we can to reconcile, to give hope and healing. Think about that when you see an Asian American this Holy Week.

Jesus willingly gives his life. This is the story of Holy Week. This is what makes it holy. Touch the story this week by being holy, by imitating the healing, reconciling, serving, and sacrificing of the one who showed us what it truly means to live for and give one's life for others.

3

4/9/20 Holy Thursday

... you must wash each other's feet.

Exod 12:1–8, 11–14; 1 Cor 11:23–26; John 13:1–15

I WAS ASSIGNED TO San Fernando Cathedral in San Antonio from 1995 to 2008. The cathedral, being in the center of downtown, attracted all kinds of people at all hours of the day. Among the regular visitors was a homeless man with a scruffy beard and dirty, tattered clothes. His name was Adam, which was appropriate since, remembering how God created the first Adam, the name means "dirt." It was obvious he never bathed, so no one could sit anywhere near him. He would sit in a pew for hours on end, sometimes reading the newspaper. Periodically something remarkable would happen. Someone, I never knew who, would kind of kidnap him for a day, bathe him, shave him, give him a haircut, and wash his clothes. He would return looking and smelling like a completely different person. Then people could sit near him. Then he could be part of the community. It was amazing how a simple washing would transform his relationship to everyone. Whoever did the service helped not only Adam, but in reality all of the community that gathered at the cathedral. Washing, an act of service and compassion by an unknown good Samaritan, made him a part of the people and a part of the table fellowship at Mass.

During this coronavirus outbreak, one thing that is repeated often is to wash our hands thoroughly, over and over. Our hands can be the source of contracting the virus or giving it to another. Washing, as well as other precautions, allow us to get out into the community for groceries, medications, or other necessities. Washing and sanitizing hands is critical for first responders, medical, grocery, drugstore, and delivery workers, and so many more people who need to interact with the community. Washing allows them to serve others safely.

Jesus was all about that in the gospel reading of Holy Thursday. In John's gospel, read at the Mass of the Last Supper, remarkably there is no mention of the institution of the Eucharist. We do not read the words of Jesus over the bread or the cup. Instead, John passes over that part of the supper and gives focus to the washing of the feet. For John it is the foot-washing, the cleansing, the act of humble service on the part of Jesus that demonstrates what Eucharist is all about. It must have been an astounding moment for the disciples. In those times in Israel people entered homes after walking in sandals or barefoot on dusty roads. Washing feet was important as a gesture of welcome and hygiene. However, the master, the teacher, the leader, never washed feet. This was always reserved for the slave to do, and not even the Jewish slave, but the very lowest person, the gentile or non-Jewish slave.

Pope Francis also has astounded us every Holy Thursday since becoming pope. He gives us an example of Jesus' teaching: he has washed the feet of all kinds of people, including Christians, Muslims, Hindus, prisoners, the young, elderly, refugees, and homeless people. In doing so, he has lifted up people in the community who have been rejected, excluded, or even demonized. Having their feet washed by the pope put the spotlight on them and placed them in our midst to be looked at in a new way, as people Jesus loves and serves and as people who should be welcomed. It is in the receiving of the Eucharist that we are called to be one in service with Jesus who came to serve and not to be served.

After he finishes washing their feet, Jesus asks the disciples, "Do you understand what I have done?" He asks this kind of question only one other time in the gospel. He really wants them to get it. This was a crucial teaching right before Jesus gives his own life. Do we get it? Do we understand that to gather around the table at Eucharist we are called to wash each other's feet, to humble ourselves in serving others, so that all feel welcome in the community and the community reaches out to all? Humble service is the outcome of gathering around the table at Mass and receiving the Eucharist. It is a requirement, not an option.

We need to wash feet, to not only humble ourselves in service, but to help others put their feet in the right direction, just as we have served. It is in the receiving of the Eucharist that we are called to be one in service with Jesus who came to serve and not to be served. Our feet ground us, they connect us to earth and to each other. That is how we meet each other, how we move towards each other, how we move through time and space. People on their feet all day long at work know the sacrifice. Refugees who walk hundreds, maybe thousands of miles for a better life, or to save their family, do it on their feet. People, during this pandemic, are now standing on their feet in lines for hours to get food for their family. Volunteers work on their feet, giving out food and supplies to the needy. Feet are sacred in many ways. To serve others is to wash feet. It is to support them and to help connect them to the rest of us. Washing is what happens at baptism. It is the washing that puts us on our feet as Christians to begin that journey to the Lord.

Another dramatic moment of foot-washing happens sometime before the Last Supper, when a woman washes the feet of Jesus with costly oil. This story is in all four gospels in slightly different ways, but with the same meaning. Her action is criticized by those at table as a terrible waste. Jesus defends her action as helping prepare him for his death and burial: "Leave her alone . . . She has done all she could" (John 12:7). Listen to that: "She has done all she could." What a powerful description! Have we done all we could in the current pandemic crisis? Can we find ways to do what we can, especially for others in need? Those who criticized the woman could not see what this was about because they had not yet done what they could for Jesus or for others. Do what you can!

The Last Supper also was about table fellowship, which was so important. Jesus taught the disciples over and over throughout his ministry how to be in fellowship at the table. He taught what all our mothers taught us from our youngest years, namely, table manners. There are six stories in the gospels where Jesus multiplies loaves and feeds people. Those six times Jesus teaches table manners. Much of what Jesus taught was at the table. Everyone deserves a seat at the table. Feed the hungry. Sit with those not like you. Don't judge others around the table. Share hospitality with those in need. Extend friendship to the stranger. Serve the poor. There is always enough for all if we try. Jesus' miracles feed people. The setting for a meal was key.

Table was family. I know this was true for me as a child, where I have so many memories of sitting together to eat and talk about our lives with family. There was also always room for one more. As we say in Spanish when an unexpected visitor arrives at mealtime, "*Hay que hechar mas agua a los frijoles!*" ("Just add more water to the beans!")

The importance of table fellowship and manners when eating together is why Judas betraying Jesus at table was so painful. Judas is always referred to as one of the Twelve, the inner circle, the closest friends. It was a family member who betrayed Jesus at table, an insider, one Jesus loved in a special way, one he had lived with for three years. The Passover meal of the Last Supper commemorated Israel's freedom from slavery, a freedom given by God, which the Jewish people remembered as they gathered at table. Yet, it was here that Jesus would be betrayed and sold into slavery and death. Jesus says, "it is one who is eating with me now." The Passover meal was so important. It was loaded with meaning: reconciliation, unity, spirituality, religious faith, and tradition. That is why the moment of betrayal was so tragic. It breaks our hearts to reflect on it since that table, as all of our family tables, was a place of trust, sharing, and familial bonds. The gospel shows that even within the eucharistic community betrayal is found. Our challenge with the pandemic fear today is not to let greed or thinking only of ourselves betray our eucharistic community. I may not be physically sitting at Mass these days, but I must continue to live the manners that come from the table of Jesus' body and blood.

Holy Thursday is a reminder of the food and nourishment that God gives. It is not only food for keeping the body alive, and it is not just about us. It is a call to keep the body of Christ alive, and to make service—humble, loving service—our food and our nourishment. It is letting Jesus wash us, love us, and serve us so we can do the same for others. What are your ways of washing feet today in the midst of this extended virus crisis? How are you practicing the table manners Jesus teaches at the Last Supper?

Let us wash our hands a lot these days and weeks. Every time we do, let it remind us of the one who washed feet and taught us how to be at table with each other.

4

4/10/20 Good Friday

Then he bowed his head, and delivered over his spirit.

Isa 52:13—53:12; Heb 4:14-16; 5:7-9; John 18:1—19:42

A FEW YEARS AGO, Pope Francis visited the Central African Republic to open the Holy Door for the Jubilee Year of Mercy. That country then was in the midst of civil war, and surely the pope's security detail was having great anxiety with his choice of where to go, but he went nonetheless. In Mexico the same year, he chose to visit Chiapas, Morelia, and Juarez, all potentially dangerous areas where drugs and border violence had taken many lives. Again, I am sure the papal security was very concerned. Why couldn't the pope just talk about these problems from a distance? Why did he physically have to be there? Did he have a death wish? Was this a form of suicide? Why was he risking his life this way? There are so many ways someone or a group could have taken his life. Thanks be to God no one harmed the pope, but it certainly got the attention of the world and helped us better understand what it means to place our lives on the line for those most in need. A good reflection for Good Friday!

The coronavirus pandemic has thrust upon us the thought that a deadly virus could infect anyone. It can and has taken many lives. It has forced us to reflect on the fragility of life and how little time we actually have to do what God has sent us to do. We have to now live our lives with a conscious attitude to do what is needed to limit the spread of the illness in our community. This is literally a question of life and death.

Many in our community know someone who is sick, or a friend whose family member has contracted the virus. You might know someone who is sick. It forces you to think about your own life, its meaning, and how the shadow of death is always part of our living.

I think Pope Francis was, first of all, showing us what the Year of Mercy was about, namely, compassion. Compassion is accompanying someone in her/his suffering and pain. It is helping to carry the burden so they do not feel alone. The greatest suffering that a human being can have is the sense that they are in deep pain and no one cares. The pope showed us, by risking his life, that compassion is truly the willingness to give one's life for the other, especially the most vulnerable. If, God forbid, someone were to hurt the pope, it would not be a taking of life, but a giving of one. That is what he is all about, and it is the only solution to a world where so many millions experience pain and suffering because of violence and poverty. It is also disproportionately the poor and people of color that are contracting the coronavirus globally at a higher rate than others.

It seems this is what John is trying to tell us in his eyewitness account of the passion and death of Jesus. Again, as last night at the Mass of the Last Supper, we read the Gospel of John. Again, John, as last night, is different from the Synoptics, the other three gospels. Last night, John emphasized the foot-washing over the actual institution of the Eucharist emphasized by the other three. Today, John shows Jesus in charge of the passion, instead of being the suffering servant. He knew they were coming to kill him. He could have avoided it, left town, gone into hiding; there were any number of ways he could have escaped the horrific moment that awaited him. And yet, he confidently moves forward to his death. He accepts his passion, goes to meet the ones who come to arrest him, answers the high priest in such a bold way that he is slapped by the guard, carries his own cross, and announces it is finished. Jesus chooses to do all this. His life is not taken from him, he gives it over. He chooses to give life so we can receive life. He chooses to die but then is raised to new life. This is the new covenant, a self-giving that never ends. Jesus is not a victim. He is confident of the outcome. He freely shows compassion and gives life to the very end.

John constantly uses the theme of light and darkness. Jesus is the Light of the World and the powers of darkness are at battle with him. As Judas leaves the Last Supper, the gospel simply states, ". . . and it was dark" (John 13:30). When Judas and those coming to arrest Jesus in the garden arrive, in the other three gospels they come with swords and clubs. In this gospel they come with torches and lanterns, because they needed lanterns to see in the midst of the powers of darkness that were controlling them.

John portrays Jesus as in charge of his trial. No worldly power has control of him. "You would have no authority if it were not given to you from above," he tells Pilate. Pilate seems to be the one on trial. He succumbs to pressure and fear, and because of that fear makes a decision that he knows is unjust and wrong. It is a lesson that we should reflect on about making decisions in a moment of fear, especially if it causes us to turn against another person or another group of people.

There are so many human stories in the passion account. Peter seems to be acting bravely when he cuts off the ear of the servant to defend Jesus; however, when the spotlight is on him, there is no bravado as he betrays his Master. He ends up as the weak disciple versus the beloved disciple who is the loved one, present at the Last Supper, present at the trial, present at the foot of the cross and the empty tomb. The call of the beloved disciple was simply presence, not abandoning Jesus. He says nothing during the passion. He is simply there. He shows compassion which is a courageous act in the midst of threats, cruelty, fear, and death.

John's narrative of the actual crucifixion is different from the other three gospels. It is the briefest of all the accounts. Again, Jesus is totally in charge. He carries his own cross; no Simon of Cyrene is mentioned. There are no crowds at the cross, no taunting, no mocking, no conversation between Jesus and the other two crucified men. Jesus does not speak from the cross out of need or desperation, but to fulfill Scripture. He gives his mother to the disciple and the disciple to his mother in a dramatic act of compassion. John's gospel does not say Jesus dies, rather he "bowed his head, and delivered over his spirit." Jesus' life is not taken from him; he gives it. He gives us the Spirit with his last breath. He repeats this breathing the Spirit again over the disciples when he appears to them after the resurrection and connects the Spirit with the power to forgive, another key act of compassion.

This moment, the moment of Good Friday, calls us to compassion, to just be there, to see ourselves accompany Jesus, to be next to him, to ask ourselves how we feel in the experience, to let it all just sink in. It is as when we are at the bedside of a loved one taking a last breath and it is sinking in. We don't need to say anything. It is about compassion. The accompaniment and the letting go are intertwined. That might be why saying and walking the Stations of the Cross can be such a powerful experience today. Walk with Jesus.

At the same time, compassion also changes us. Being with another who is in pain, suffering, or experiencing anxiety or physical need makes us realize that life is delicate and very fragile at best. It forces us to truly appreciate those around us and those who are in need. It forces us to realize we have only a limited amount of time to do what needs to be done. We have limited moments to live compassion, limited resources to share; yet it is the call we have been given to imitate the dying Jesus, who showed us how to give life for others.

After Jesus gives up his spirit, the soldier pierces his side and the account tells us Jesus' blood and water flow out of his body. Baptism and Eucharist are given to the church from the cross. The waters of baptism are the beginning of a life in Jesus, a life of giving and service and compassion, which leads us to the table of the Eucharist in thanksgiving and commitment to each other. So many of us are missing the gathering around the table during this pandemic. We want to receive Eucharist and we will return to the table physically sometime in the near future. However, until then we have to be even more aware than ever that we are the body of Christ. How can we live that, give that, love that in the midst of what we are going through today?

Good Friday 2020 asks the question: How can I live compassion in the midst of this pandemic? I can choose to give life. I can be compassionate. I can accompany in the midst of distancing. I can be present to others while I shelter in place. I can carry my cross behind Jesus. I can reflect Jesus, who gives us his Spirit of compassion from the cross on this Good Friday.

5

4/12/20 Easter

…now go tell his disciples.

Acts 10:34a, 37–43; Col 3:1–4; Matt 28:1–10

THIS YEAR EASTER WILL be like none other in our memory. We will not be able to attend Easter Mass. We have not gone to Holy Week services and it has created a void in our experience that we really can't seem to fill. In past years, people who had experienced something like the passion play downtown or the Pesame (a traditional Hispanic service around the burial of Christ and sharing sympathy with the Sorrowful Mother) at their parish would invite others to accompany them to be part of those services together. They would tell their family or friends what they had experienced the year before. They would bring others with them so that they also would hear, see, and experience a similar moment of faith.

Each year the passion play of San Fernando Cathedral is especially dramatic and attracts thousands of people downtown. It was canceled this year. In the past, parents would bring children to be part of the experience. It was like a huge catechism played out in front of the children so they could learn by seeing with their eyes and moving alongside the passion actors with their bodies. The children would ask questions since it all looked so real. I remember once hearing a young child almost in panic tell his mother, "Mom, call the police! Look what they are doing to Jesus!" His mother explained as she calmed him down. The parents have a key opportunity to teach and share faith, which is their primary responsibility. They remember how their own parents brought them when they were children and what it meant. They want to have their children experience it as well. This year parents had to be creative on this day, but their responsibility remained to share with the next generation their faith and what it means to them.

Why would you invite someone to experience the Holy Week story? Could it be you yourself had experienced something very special and you did not want to keep it to yourself? How do you feel when you have some really good news happen to you? Don't you want to share it right away with others?

The resurrection accounts in the gospels are all about the stories of those who had an intense experience of the risen Lord and began to tell others. Most of the time they just could not keep it to themselves. They were the witnesses and they had something fantastic to share.

There is nothing in the gospels that says Jesus walked out of the tomb. Whatever pictures or holy cards we might have seen with Jesus gloriously coming out of the tomb do not appear in the gospel. Today's gospel account from Matthew is a good example. The two women go to see the tomb at dawn on the first day of the week. There is an earthquake, an angel appears, rolls back the stone, sits on it, and tells the women Jesus has been raised. "See the place where he was buried, and now go tell his disciples." Nowhere in the account does Jesus walk out of the tomb. Jesus does not need to walk out of the tomb. The glorified, risen Lord is alive in a new way. He is the same Jesus but also different. Locked doors and stones blocking the entrance to a tomb will not prevent him from appearing to those who will be the witnesses that he is alive.

I did a silent retreat years ago in Louisiana. The grounds of the Jesuit retreat house were beautiful. There was a cemetery at one end, where the custom there was to bury people above ground in individual mausoleums. Each day of my weeklong retreat, my director asked me to meditate on gospel passages. On my last day he gave me the passage on the empty tomb. After reading it, I walked the grounds to meditate and somehow ended up at the cemetery. At one point as I reflected, I looked up and in front of me was a tomb with an open entrance and a white cloth slowly blowing with the wind, uncovering and covering the entrance. It was a stunning moment for me. I witnessed the empty tomb! It was what I needed to finish my retreat. I was there. I saw it. I need to share it with others. That is what I feel the entire experience of Holy Week should do for us. At the end, on Easter, we need to say, "I was there! I will tell others!"

It is all about the witnesses who saw and experienced the risen Jesus. Their telling of their experiences has been handed down for centuries and thus is the basis of our belief in the resurrection. We believe on the testimony of witnesses who were so moved by what they saw and heard that they had a burning desire to share it. The only proof that we have that Jesus rose from the dead is in the witnesses. Witnessing is what Easter calls each of us to do.

The gospels want us to place the greatest importance on this moment, which is similar to the Christmas story, where angels announce what is happening. But it is even greater. Cosmic signs announce the Easter event, while at Christmas a star is the sign. This time an earthquake happens as the women approach the tomb, as at Jesus' death on Calvary when there is an earthquake. Earthquakes often bury people and cause death, but this one announces that the one buried is not dead but alive. The earthquake at the cross opened tombs and people came alive. Resurrection reverses death and brings life. Matthew reminds readers that Jesus was always confident of victory over death. He had predicted his resurrection several times. He turns our reaction to the earthquake from fear to joy. What a great story for us today in the midst of a deadly pandemic!

Another crucial element to the witnessing is those who are first to get the message. An angel interprets the events to the women at the tomb just as angels did for the shepherds at his birth. The shepherds are first to know about the birth, and women are first to know about the resurrection. We see two categories of people who were second-class citizens at the time. The crucifixion, as well as the stories of the resurrection, are filled with women. The people who first see the risen Lord are the women who stayed with Jesus until the end and did not run like almost all the men. The women were at the foot of the cross. They wept over Jesus (Eighth station). They followed and served him. At that time, women were not trusted as witnesses at trial, only men. Yet Jesus chose them to be the first witnesses, to show it is not about one's standing in society or how society looks at people; rather it is about having faith, having the courage to live it, and following close by Jesus on the way to Calvary. Various accounts show that the disciples really did not believe until they actually saw Jesus themselves. Their faith was not yet strong; they had not put it all together.

Shepherds and women were not considered credible witnesses, which is why this is about faith, not proof. The courage of the women brought them to faith before anyone else. Those who follow Jesus on the way of the cross are also part of his resurrection. They see it earlier and more often than others. The first thing they are told is to go share the story with others. At Jesus' birth, the shepherds left the stable of Bethlehem and told their experience to others. In Matthew's account of the resurrection, the women are told by the angel to go tell the "disciples." A few moments later as they are on their way with the good news, they encounter the risen Jesus who tells them to go tell his "brothers." This is a new status for those who believe in the resurrection. They are brothers and sisters of Jesus. Jesus restores the relationship with his disciples which was broken when they abandoned him. They now must tell others and extend the family. This is missionary work.

I remember, some years ago when I was working for Catholic Relief Services, being in Albuquerque one February, speaking to students at a parochial school about global poverty and the CRS food program, Rice Bowl. A fifth-grader stood up and interrupted my talk almost immediately, saying he had something to tell me. He announced that the past Christmas he had told his parents not to buy him anything. Instead, he wanted the money saved to go to buy malaria nets for children in Sub-Saharan Africa. He had read on the internet that a child there dies every thirty seconds from malaria and treated nets can protect them as they sleep. He calculated he had saved the lives of twelve children; twelve children he did not know; twelve children who could never thank him. I was stunned! For a ten-year-old to give up his gifts when all his classmates were excitedly talking about and anticipating getting many things for Christmas was astounding. I asked him to repeat his story to be sure everyone heard his witness. I asked myself later: Where did this kid get this? Was it parents, teachers, coaches, pastors, other mentors? Wherever he got it, he got it! What a witness in such a young disciple of Jesus!

Being missionaries of Jesus also scares us. It is hard to share faith with others. We might be criticized or made fun of. Society in general goes in the other direction from the teachings of Jesus. Yet, it is in the quiet and sometimes not-so-quiet ways we live, speak, and act that we are missionaries of the risen Lord. Twice in today's gospel, once from the angel and once from Jesus, we hear, "Do not be afraid!" The coronavirus scares us all. Easter tells us not to be afraid. Easter people are missionary people, even when hunkered down at home. God is with us. The risen Jesus lives in his people. The church is church when it is in mission, always, everywhere. We can't keep it to ourselves! Let us find ways during this difficult and scary time to spread good news.

There is no real proof that Jesus is alive, that he is raised from the dead, except us. We are the witnesses that are commanded by the angel in today's gospel, "go quickly and tell his disciples." We are Easter!

6

4/19/20 Second Easter

. . . through this faith you might have life in his name.

Acts 2:42–47; 1 Pet 1:3–9; John 20:19–31

DURING THE CORONAVIRUS PANDEMIC, we have been told to stay home or shelter in place and not leave except for necessities like food, medicine, and exercise. This is very hard. We miss not only being with people but we miss touching people, the handshake or the hug, which is something so human. Grandparents cannot cuddle their grandchildren. Best friends cannot be close. Every meeting with a person not in our home could be deadly as the virus seems to be transmitted easily. We stay at home. We wear masks when we go out. We are afraid. We long for a return to the freedom of interacting with others, reaching out to touch or hug, and being out in the world again. It has been a challenge. It tests our faith, and it actually hurts. When can we start again?

Today's gospel talks about the disciples being fearful and sheltering just like us, with the doors locked on the night of the resurrection. They had fled when Jesus was arrested, thinking that what was happening to him would also happen to them. They hunkered down and stayed out of sight. Yet something totally unexpected happened. Jesus appeared. He did not knock on the locked door or come through the window. He did not need to. The risen Lord was the same Jesus, yet different. No barriers existed for him to reach those to whom he had chosen to tell the story.

The disciples had to make a shift in their understanding of Jesus, from their past experience of the human Jesus to their radical faith in the resurrected, glorified Jesus living through the Spirit in the church. They had to go through a radical change of what they thought about Jesus. They had to accept a new life that would include hardships and carrying the cross, yet would be filled with forming a community of caring, sharing, and being the risen Lord to the world.

Today is the Second Sunday of Easter, not after Easter. The entire time from Easter Day to Pentecost is Easter, a long reflection on the central mystery of faith and how we are called to live. The gospel stories for the first part of the Easter season focus on the various apparitions of Jesus after his resurrection. They tell us how a person or a group of people come to believe in the risen Jesus. In some apparition stories we see people finding the risen Lord in a stranger traveling with them: one finds him in a gardener, some find him as Thomas did in the struggles of their doubts, not wanting to believe good news, always looking maybe for the worst. This Easter season confronts us with the question: Even in the midst of a terrible pandemic, how do we find the risen Jesus? How do we reach out to touch Jesus? How do we experience the peace he breathes on us? Where is the good news? Where do we start?

I remember many years ago, in my first parish on the Westside of San Antonio, an area mostly inhabited by working-class and poor Hispanics, I took communion to an elderly, home-bound, Spanish-speaking couple in their humble house. I was impressed by their devotion and gratitude for my visit. After I had finished the rite of Communion for the Sick, the man began to say that both of them were suffering from bad health, had very little, and were barely getting by. Then he looked at me with an almost pleading expression and said, "Can you just share with us some good news?" His request, so simple and sincere, seemed to come from the depths of his heart and close to the depths of despair. It moved me so much that I stayed longer with them, assuring them of God's love and care and that of the parish as well. Good news is what Jesus is all about. Good news is what the church does. I left wondering how many more people live their daily lives in such hardship that all they want to hear is some good news. That is certainly happening now with this virus. Doctors and nurses are getting this question all the time. Sometimes we may not have much to offer but we can at least be, in whatever way we can, with those who are suffering, in their darkness, to assure them they are not forgotten.

The good news of Jesus comes in many ways. Today it seems that the first reading, as well as the gospel, tell us that Jesus and the peace we feel when we know Jesus is alive, come to us in our actions of faith. The Acts reading tells us that the community of believers was of one heart and mind. That certainly sounds very peaceful. Why? Because everyone shared what they had and there was no needy person among them. No one claimed any of his/her possessions was his/her own. Sharing and forgiving. That is quite powerful, yet it seems that was the formula of the early church and why they lived in peace with each other so well. The gospel tells us that as soon as Jesus appears for the first time he says, "Peace be with you." He then says it again. He sends them with the Spirit and tells them to forgive others. So, Jesus links peace with being sent to others and with the message of forgiveness. It makes so much sense!

Thomas comes to believe in Jesus as Lord and God at Jesus' invitation. Jesus invites us to believe in him. The touching of Jesus was important to connect the risen Jesus with the one crucified. It is the same Jesus who was nailed to the cross, but he is different. Sometimes we have to touch the wound, touch where it hurts, in order to believe it can heal. "By his wounds we are healed," reads the First Letter of St. Peter. Thomas's doubt was healed by touching the hurt of Jesus and his own hurt, his disbelief, his cowardice, when he ran in the face of threat. We wound others and others wound us. We sometimes have self-inflicted wounds. Being wounded is a part of the human condition. It is how we care for the wounds, acknowledging them and doing what is necessary to help them heal, that brings us to full health. The coronavirus is wounding our world. We must all work together unselfishly to bring about healing so the community can return to full health and life and start again.

This gospel encounter also gives, in the words of Thomas, the fullest affirmation of Jesus as both Lord and God. Thomas never says he is sorry for doubting, but he does so much more in proclaiming full faith in Jesus, a faith that will cost him his life. It is this same Jesus who then breathes the Holy Spirit on the apostles and sends them out to others, to reconcile, to forgive, to bring peace. It is the breath of new life reminding us of the original spirit of life God breathed into Adam. We are now so afraid of someone with the virus breathing on us and perhaps costing us our life. However, the new Adam, Jesus, breathes new life and helps us get started again to live as the Creator God intended.

John's account is different from Luke's in that more key moments happen on the night of the resurrection instead of an extended sequence of post-Easter events. Jesus appears, gives peace, breathes the Holy Spirit, and gives the power to forgive sins. There is no forty-day period to the ascension or the later day of Pentecost that we see in Luke. For John, it is all in the Easter moment of the risen Lord. This is a single event, the resurrection-exaltation of Jesus.

John concludes the gospel by saying he has recorded only some of what Jesus said and did. This was done to stimulate faith, and through faith to give life. Life is lived in the peace God offers when we accept the Spirit, share faith and what we have with others, and are people of forgiveness. The life of God is peace.

There was a world before the pandemic. It was often a world filled with suspicion, prejudice, discrimination, and a general lack of trust. It was a world where we rarely saw any peace. On any given day, there are over thirty-five violent conflicts happening in the world, conflicts that affect peoples' lives so much they are forced to flee their homes or die. According to Catholic Relief Services there are 65 million displaced persons in the world. Who knows how many other smaller conflicts there are daily between neighbors, gangs, even relatives over a variety of issues?

In the midst of the uncertainty and fear caused by this virus, we might reflect on how we begin anew, how the wounded world can be restored when it is reopened. Can we be better? Is this a new opportunity to get things right this time? Can we truly live in peace?

This Easter invites each of us to be a person of peace, to touch the wounds of our world and begin the healing. Each has to listen to Jesus sending us to forgive and heal others in the power of the Holy Spirit. Each needs to be like the early Christians, thanking God for what we have and remembering it has been given to us not only for ourselves and our family, but also for the common good, especially for those in need. When we truly have that kind of faith, then peace comes to us, to those around us, and to the rest of the world.

There is little doubt that we will make it through this health scare. Yes, there will be more suffering and, tragically, more death. The Easter question is: Can I help bring about the healing of this world, my world, by what I believe? How will I touch the lives of others for healing and to make them better? There will be a rebeginning in the near future, a pushing of the restart button. How do I get it right this time?

7

4/26/20 Third Easter

Were not our hearts burning inside us as he talked to us on the road ...

Acts 2:14, 22–33; 1 Pet 1:17–21; Luke 24:13–35

IN EARLY MARCH I traveled to Costa Rica with two friends, Jeff and Sally Jung. We had a wonderful time visiting San José, other sites and the west coast. At the coast Sally invited us to do morning prayer and reflection on the beach. What a fantastic setting for prayerful reflection! For two days we asked for a shady picnic table from a man who rented beach tents and chairs. He was very welcoming to us and was impressed with our prayer time. He told us later his business was great those days. On the third day we were ready to rent beach chairs and a canopy for shade since we planned a whole day at the beach. He insisted we not pay for the rentals since he felt the prayer was all he needed. He also refused a tip we wanted to give. What a wonderful moment of generosity to travelers who were strangers! It happened from witnessing our faith and prayer. Wow!

I love to travel. Travel is about seeing places, relaxing, and learning. It is also about seeing things in a new way because I meet new people, experience other cultures, and take in sites. I was planning more trips in early March when the coronavirus became a pandemic and all travel became very risky overnight. I miss it a lot.

The virus came to our country through travelers, either returning home from trips abroad or people coming for business or tourism from other countries. The most common form of transmission at first was through travelers. Lately it is close contact or community-spread transmission, but at first everyone visiting or returning here as a traveler was under suspicion. Many had to be quarantined because they could have made others sick.

The gospel story today is also about traveling and travelers. The two disciples are leaving Jerusalem, on the road to Emmaus. They are dispirited, feeling that Jesus, whom they had thought might be the Messiah, is now dead, and with his death all their hopes are shattered. They are suffering, hurting badly, close to despair. They don't want to stay where all this happened. They want to leave it behind.

Luke sets the scene for us by saying the two travelers were leaving Jerusalem to go to Emmaus. Right away we get the message that something is wrong. This is the wrong direction for a disciple. Throughout most of his gospel, Luke depicts Jesus on the way to Jerusalem, and telling his disciples if they want to be his disciples, they must follow him, carrying the cross. Follow him where? To Jerusalem! It is in Jerusalem where we see the culmination of Jesus' ministry, the unfolding of the paschal mystery of his passion, death, and resurrection. So, Luke is telling us these two travelers are going in the wrong direction, especially if they are disciples. How will they turn around? That is the story.

Luke, in many of his stories, wants to involve us, the reader or listener. Often in his gospel, he wants us to identify with a character in the story, so as to insert ourselves into the moment as if we were there. We could then experience more intimately what Jesus is teaching us. In this case Luke identifies one of the disciples by name, Cleopas, but not the second one. Why? Because that one is you! You are the traveler who will see Jesus but not recognize him until the breaking of the bread. You will listen to how he explains Scripture and how it relates to the passion and death of the Messiah. You will be energized by his words and not want this encounter to end. You will invite this strange traveler into your home. You will then realize, at the moment of the breaking and blessing of the bread, that it was always Jesus traveling with you and you just did not recognize him. When Jesus disappears, you and Cleopas will say to each other, "We can't stay here. We need to go tell others what we saw and experienced! Jesus is alive!" What a story! And you are part of it!

The two disciples are joined by a stranger on the road. Why would two disciples who had been with Jesus for years not be able to recognize him? The risen Jesus is the same Jesus who died on the cross, but, as we have said before, he is different. The recognition comes with faith and charity, which happens later in the story. Jesus starts with where they are, namely, asking what they were discussing. He waits for them to tell the story. He then takes their story, their reality, and unpacks Scripture to speak to that story. That is what a homily is about: begin with the reality of a human story, then help Scripture speak to that story, and finally encourage the listeners to respond with faith and action. It all happens in this story.

The disciples are astonished that their fellow traveler did not know what had been going on lately in Jerusalem. They explained their discouragement at Jesus' death. Yet it was this same Jesus who had tried to prepare them for his passion—they simply never got it. They could not believe that the Messiah would die, or be weak, until Jesus shows them that Scripture clearly spoke of a suffering Messiah. They saw Jesus but did not see Jesus the Messiah because they could not accept the passion. Only seeing the risen Jesus and recognizing him in faith would do that. They had tried to teach Jesus that death is not part of the Messiah, but he educates them, showing how it had all been foretold by Scriptures for centuries. Ultimately it had to be a matter of faith, which they reached fully after the resurrection.

It was in the generous offer of hospitality that the beginning of their recognizing Jesus happened. Hospitality was a key value of the Christian community. This was shown in the sharing of possessions and especially in the sharing at table. We see Jesus in the action of our charity. They begin as hosts and Jesus ends up as the host. Their generosity, "Stay with us," means Jesus' abiding presence is desired. Their transformation begins when they show concern for a stranger on the road. Jesus is present in generosity and concern for others. Who are the strangers on the road for us today? Maybe they are those suffering disproportionately from the pandemic. If we are generous with them, we can discover the risen Jesus.

Emmaus prepared the hearts of the disciples for the recognition of Jesus in the breaking of bread by the word they heard on the way. Especially, they heard the word as they were in pain and had lost hope. The story has the elements of our Mass, the word and the Eucharist. During the Easter season we remember that the Eucharist is not a past event, but it brings the paschal mystery to the present. We make present the risen Christ for each generation. The story told the early Christians who had never physically seen Jesus that they had Jesus truly in the word and sacrament.

A big part of our common loss as Catholic Christians during the coronavirus lockdown is not being able to gather in church, hear the word, and receive communion in the Eucharist. We miss it a lot! Seeing it livestreamed on the internet or television is acceptable, but not the same. Our faith needs to be strong at this time to realize we are not abandoned, that Jesus is truly in our midst. When we witness our faith by actions, words and attitudes, as Sally, Jeff, and I did on the beach, generosity and charity flourish, which are gifts of the risen Lord and make Jesus present.

This powerful Easter story should console us as we struggle with the pandemic and all its consequences, like illness, the tragic death of someone we might know, the quarantine, the disruption of our lives, unemployment, income loss, and more. When so much seems lost, Jesus, the risen Lord, is there to give us the gift of himself and his Easter joy.

Luke uses the whole twenty-fourth chapter to show how the disciples slowly realized what Jesus' death and resurrection meant and how they were to share it. It is a transition from the story of Jesus to the story of his witnesses, which will be told more fully in Luke's second book, called the Acts of the Apostles.

We are all travelers. We are moving through life in various ways. We often move in the wrong direction. Right now, we are trying to make sense of the tragedy of a pandemic that is affecting the whole world. It is discouraging and disheartening as we share our feelings and experiences with each other on the road. Yet all around us are works of charity and hospitality: volunteers feeding the hungry, medical teams working overtime with the sick, public servants going above and beyond the call of duty, parents tutoring children, and teams reaching out to the homeless. The story of Jesus we read in the gospel is unfolding in front of our eyes.

The struggles of this crisis and the hopeful responses we see all around us can be a moment to go deeper and discover that Jesus is with us. We can be transformed by this painful experience. We can reverse course, return to Jerusalem as disciples, and let others know what we now know.

8

5/3/20 Fourth Easter

I know my sheep and my sheep know me.

Acts 2:14a, 36–41; 1 Pet 2:20b–25; John 10:1–10

As this coronavirus pandemic has developed, we have been listening to many voices coming at us every day. Some come from medical experts, some from media people, some from politicians, some from our family and friends. To which do we pay attention? Maybe the question is: How do I listen to, how do I judge the voice that speaks to me? In the case of this crisis, listening to and following the right voice could mean the difference between life and death.

Jesus, in the gospel today, calls us together as the Good Shepherd. He overcomes the barriers we place between us by becoming the sheepgate, the way to gather together through him and with him. Gathering together is something that we are sorely missing in this time of self-isolation.

Jesus used the image of a shepherd because shepherds were very familiar to the people of his time. In those days, one of their most difficult jobs was to protect the sheep at night. They gathered the various flocks in one place to jointly keep them safe overnight. One shepherd would lie down to sleep in front of the entrance to the flock, to be the guard. In a real way, the shepherd would literally lay down his life for the sheep. The next morning, each shepherd would call his flock. They would recognize his voice because they knew who cared for them and they would follow him to the pastures.

Years ago, a young cousin who lived on a farm outside Victoria, Texas was raising a lamb for the county fair. After months of daily care, feeding and grooming, she and her dad took the lamb to the fair for judging and then sale. She had more money than ever from the sale and was enjoying the rest of the fair until she experienced what we might call seller's remorse. She had grown attached to that lamb and wanted it back. Her dad tried to reason with her but to no avail, so they went to the large pen where all the lambs were being kept. Her dad told her there would be no way to ever get her lamb back as they all looked alike. She however began to call her lamb and within seconds her lamb was there. The lamb knew the voice of the one that had cared for and loved it.

Jesus is that Shepherd for us, the Shepherd who gives his life and knows his sheep. He loves us and has given his life for us. We need also to recognize his voice and follow him.

Jesus leads us out as his flock to create the world. But he is more than just a shepherd, because he is actually the gate. He is the way to enter a new space, where we do what he calls us to do. He knows each of us. He cares for us personally. It is Jesus' voice which calls us to greater concern for each other and for building a community of trusting relationships so all can benefit. As Jesus knows and cares for us, so should we know and care for each other. That is the space where he wants us. We need to create that space even in the midst of a pandemic.

In this crisis we are not sure whom to listen to and follow. What will we learn from this time of fear and uncertainty? Can we be a better society on the other side of this? Or will we retreat back into our own ways of ignoring others and only caring for ourselves? On Easter Sunday Pope Francis said, "This is not a time for indifference, because the whole world is suffering and needs to be united in facing the pandemic."[1]

In the gospels there are many miracle stories about Jesus healing the deaf. What is the point? Jesus challenges the deafness of the religious leaders who refused to listen to him. Clearly, he wants us not to be deaf to his voice, to faith which calls us to love God and each other. Are you deaf or are you listening? Faith demands that we listen.

What does it mean to truly listen to another? All of us need to develop listening skills. We often do not listen to the other, but just wait to say what we want to say. To really listen is to be fully in the moment, to put yourself in the shoes of the other, to pick up key points and let them

---

1. Pope Francis, "Urbi et Orbi," para. 9.

know you did, to practice active listening, which is to repeat back to them what you heard them say and let them verify if that is what they meant. Active listening is to develop a curiosity, to open our minds, to desire to grow, to really know another. To listen well is to suspend judgment of the other, to resist the temptation to demonize those with whom we disagree, and to try to discern and understand with an open heart. When we actively listen, we not only learn but we form community.

There are many voices in our lives. Which one is that of Jesus? When we listen to Jesus, we enter through him, the sheepgate, to a new world. We are transformed. To enter through him is to know him enough that I can follow his lead in my life. If I am transformed, I can also help transform others, and make the world a better place.

This pandemic has reminded us how interdependent we really are. I wear a mask more to protect others than myself. That might be a template for me going forward. We are seeing and hearing the fragility, the fear, and the courage of others. Is the voice of Jesus our shepherd in those examples? If we listen and learn, perhaps we can become our best selves as we get through this pandemic together.

During this time, let us enter more fully into prayer and reflection on Scripture, to listen to the voice of Jesus, our Shepherd. Let us commit ourselves to be active listeners and to create the community he calls us to become. Even during these difficult days, we can find ways to learn from and support others in our community while we await the time when we can do even more. Today, listen to Jesus, our Shepherd, calling you. Listen to others actively. Become a listener. You will be different. You will be better.

9

5/10/20 Fifth Easter

Do not let your hearts be troubled.

Acts 6:1–7; 1 Pet 2:4–9; John 14:1–12

EVERY MORNING, AS PART of my prayer, I pray for many people, beginning with my parents. I always pray they rest in peace. Lately, with the coronavirus crisis, I think of them and wonder how they would have dealt with it. My parents were born in very challenging times, 1916 and 1918, the time of the Great War and the Spanish Flu. They lived through a pandemic, the Great Depression, World War II, and much more. They sacrificed so much for their country and their community. They dealt with other crises of family and work. Yet somehow they survived their journey, grew through it, were different because of it, and gave their children faith, education, culture, and values. They did amazing things! I give thanks every day for them.

Today's gospel is part of the Farewell Discourse of Jesus to his family at the Last Supper. He has just washed the disciples' feet, and now he tries to let them know he is going away. As we read on Holy Thursday, John's gospel does not speak about the institution of the Eucharist, where Jesus breaks and blesses the bread and the cup. John's focus is the washing of feet to show that Eucharist is service. He also adds the lengthy last discourse to emphasize what Jesus' life was about and how his disciples would continue his ministry. The opening words today, "Do not let your hearts be troubled," seem to be aimed at us as we go through troubling times of a pandemic with no end in sight. Can we really accept Jesus' words for us today in the midst of so much anxiety?

Jesus speaks of leaving, which the disciples do not understand. Throughout the Gospel of Mark the questions repeatedly are, "Who is Jesus?" and "What does it mean to follow Jesus?" The focus is on the who and what of Jesus. However, in the Gospel of John the question becomes "Where is Jesus?" In the beginning of the gospel the first disciples ask Jesus, "*Where* are you staying?" to which Jesus answers, "Come and see" (John 1:38–39). Pilate asks the same question, "*Where* are you from?" (John 19:9). Mary Magdalene tells the disciples on Easter, "We do not know *where* they have taken him" (John 20:2). So, John wants us to ask the "where" question, "Where do I find Jesus?" It is a good and difficult question for us that needs our continual attention and reflection.

John's answer in the gospel is that finding Jesus does not refer to a physical location, but rather inner communion that comes from belief in him and the Father. When Jesus speaks of many mansions in his Father's house, he does not mean specific places but rather a profound union with him that is in the present and deepens in the fullness of time. So, the question of *where* does not refer so much to the end place, but to the journey, which is experiencing more and more the inner communion with Jesus. We are invited on that journey all our lives. We need to be aware of the importance of staying on the journey, constantly seeking Jesus along the way.

A few years ago, I walked the Camino de Santiago in Northern Spain with a couple of friends from my parish, Robert and Lori Valdez. We were on a 1,000-year-old path of pilgrims on the way to Santiago de Campostela to visit the Basilica of St James. This journey has been walked by millions of people over the centuries. I began to understand during the five-day walk that a pilgrimage is not just arriving at your destination but the process of the journey. It is sometimes hard and tiring. It is sometimes confusing, as you are not sure exactly which way to go. It sometimes forces you to reflect on your life as you walk long stretches in silence. It is in the movement, the process of going through time and space, that you understand how much you are changed by the journey. The pilgrimage is a microcosm of your own pilgrimage through life. We are all going through a period of movement now with this pandemic. How will we be changed by it? Can we be changed for the better?

So, it is how you live on the journey that is more important than all that you accomplish in life. The end result is not what you have accumulated, or where you live, or how many honors you have received that are so important, but how you have gotten there, how you made the journey. Jesus says he is the way. Did you travel with him, looking for him, acknowledging him, sharing him, doing what he did for others? That is living the inner communion Jesus invites us to in the gospel today.

Jesus is the way to the Father. That unity we experience in the liturgy. We have missed the community that gathers every Sunday in church. We are eager to return soon, even with restrictions and precautions. John's community had been expelled from the synagogue, where they had worshiped all their lives. Religious prejudice had hit them. Most Jews saw them as traitors following a fraud, namely, Jesus, and had told them not to return to community worship. This was devastating to them, just as the closing of churches has been to us. They had grown up with the synagogue as the heart of their faith, the place to encounter God. So, John is showing with this long discourse of Jesus that it was not being in the place of the synagogue that was important, but rather the way they lived their lives in communion with Jesus. We are "living stones" that form the church as Peter says in the second reading. You carry and build church with you on the way.

Yes, the gathering in church for Mass is the most important action we take each week. It will be important to return. The gospel today tells us that the returning is part of the pilgrimage—the going and the coming—the journey, to strengthen us to keep walking despite the challenges, anxiety, and suffering. Being in the gathering is an important part, but not the only part, of living in communion with Jesus. Jesus promises us a way to God through him and the result will be doing greater works than even Jesus did. That is what he says.

We are now going through the journey of this virus. It is a hard and difficult journey. We see tragedy and suffering and sacrifice all around us. Yet, faithfulness to the journey must be our focus. We should not just want to get to the end of this virus and then say we are back to normal. The journey, the pilgrimage we are on demands we be different as we move through this. It demands we be transformed by union with Jesus. It demands we do the works of Jesus and even more.

The question is where? Where are you going? What has this time told you about where your life is heading? Has the journey these past weeks and months helped you see what is really important in life and what you need to do? If not, it is never too late.

Jesus is in this journey of the pandemic, in the blisters, in the suffering, in the sacrifices, in the person behind the mask you see at the store, in those serving the public in so many ways at great cost, in those in line for emergency food, in those next to you at home that at times annoy you. Can you see him? Walk the walk and appreciate what it can do for you if you take the time to fully enter into the pilgrimage. When we do get to the end of this, and there will be an end, we will be able to look back over the process, the walk, the journey, the pilgrimage, and say we have done what Jesus asked us to do and even more.

10

5/17/20 Sixth Easter

I will not leave you orphaned.

Acts 8:5–8, 14–17; 1 Pet 3:15–18; John 14:15–21

ONE OF THE DIFFICULT results of being in the time of the COVID-19 pandemic is the impact it has had on nursing homes and other facilities for the elderly and sick. Most of these facilities are closed to any visitors, no matter who they are. This means people cannot visit their elderly parents. They might be able to see them through a glass door or window but they cannot be beside them, touch them, or hug and kiss them as they want. Nursing home residents have also suffered disproportionately contracting the virus and have a higher rate of deaths. Nearly one-third of all deaths from COVID-19 in the United States have been nursing home residents or workers.[1] In so many ways, this pandemic has caused many to lose a parent sooner than they expected. It has created many orphans. It has also made many appreciate more than ever what their parents gave them.

In today's gospel from John, Jesus speaks to the disciples as a parent, the only time in all the gospels he does so. He says clearly, "I will not leave you orphans." This is the continuation of the Farewell Discourse, unique to John, that we saw last week where Jesus spoke about leaving the disciples and returning to the Father. The question—Where is Jesus for us?—came from this reading. However, Jesus promised that even though

---

1. Richtel and Abelson, "Nursing Homes Confront New Covid Outbreaks," para. 9.

he would leave, he would still be with them. In today's gospel reading, he goes deeper by saying he will be with them through the Spirit.

What Jesus is saying is that the Spirit will be with us, helping us remember and do what Jesus did. The Spirit inspires us. When we imitate Jesus we are not left alone. He is in us, living in us, directing our thoughts and actions.

So many times, when my family gathers, we remember my parents and tell stories about them. We laugh at times and we remember what they said, how they lived, what they believed, and how so much of that is still in us. Many times people tell me I remind them of my father, not just physically (I am not bald—yet!), but in terms of how he was, his way of speaking, sense of humor, and so much more. The voice of Mom often remains in my mind and heart. I always think of my mother and what she told me and taught me, how she modeled behavior for me. Remembering what our parents taught us and following it, in many ways is keeping them alive. Our parents are still with us. Their spirit is strong in us. I am not an orphan.

Jesus tells us, "You are in me and I am in you." As long as we remember those words, Jesus lives in us through the Spirit. Jesus begins to speak of the advocate being sent by the Father to care for us. Jesus has been the first advocate, always praying to his Father for his disciples while he was on earth. In this gospel, he is preparing the apostles for his leaving to return to the Father, but he is saying he will not leave them alone. They will not be orphans. The Spirit will be the advocate, will speak up for them, will take action on their behalf, will guide them. Jesus speaks about keeping commandments so that we can work with the Spirit. The Spirit is the advocate for us and we need to advocate for each other and all the earth. When we keep in mind the need to cooperate with the Spirit in our lives, great things happen.

Jesus then connects observing his commandments with the way we show we love him. This will result in love from the Father and love from Jesus and Jesus revealing himself to the disciples. The only other time Jesus talks about disciples loving him is when he asks Peter after the resurrection, "Do you love me?" (John 21:15). The love Jesus is speaking about is not only friendship or even spousal love, but more like the love he has for the Father, a total identification with the Father. It is not about keeping rules, as in commandments, but complete unity and sharing the same desire. I want what God wants. I want to see as God sees. In a sense it is a mystical experience, as in the Eucharist, in moments of creativity or wonder, in overwhelming love.

Everything Jesus did in his life was to try to entice humans to fall in love with God. In fact, that is the mandate Jesus gives: love God, love the other. We do it through loving Jesus. It is a matter of the heart, willingly invaded by God. Like a long-married couple who almost grow to look like each other, can you look like God, who is love? We know we will never be God, who is transcendent, but we seek the God who is also imminent, close by. Jesus promises a relationship with the Father like the one he has. Just as God sent the Spirit to advocate for us, so we are called to advocate for each other and for our earth, the great gift God gave us.

Soon the churches will open again for Sunday Mass. We have missed Sundays and all the gathering, communicating, and seeing of each other that goes with Mass. I think we will return with a new appreciation for receiving the Eucharist and being a community of believers.

Of course, we return with some trepidation, with some restrictions like masks, social distancing, and receiving communion in the hand. These precautions and others will be part of worship for some time. However, they are a small sacrifice to be able to celebrate Eucharist again. We will be learning to live with some risks for a long time until there is more control over this virus. If we are responsible and remember that each of us needs to live our daily lives caring not just for ourselves but for others, then things will be much better. We will be loving God in the way we love each other.

Every time we receive Eucharist, we invite God inside of us in a special and unique way. Now we are called again to look for God not only in others or nature, but inside of us. We find him when we begin to see things as God sees, and want things as God wants. Despite the troubles of today, that will change us and that will change the world.

11

5/24/20 ascension

. . . why do you stand here looking up at the skies?

Acts 1:1–11; Eph 1:17–23; Matt 28:16–20

THIS IS GRADUATION SEASON, a time when students excitedly cross the stage to receive a diploma or degree while their family looks on proudly. It is something to which the graduates look forward and work hard to achieve. However, this May it is not happening, at least not in the traditional sense. The coronavirus, which has changed much of our recent life, has also affected school ceremonies. Students will still graduate and receive their diplomas and degrees; maybe sometime in the future there will be a crossing of a stage, but not now.

This year many students are entering a world that they did not expect, one with less opportunity, fewer jobs, and a lot of anxiety. Yet, they have been studying for years to move into a career and begin to accomplish what they feel they have been called to do. They did not go to school to stay in school, but rather to prepare for how they will make their way in the world. In short, ceremony or no ceremony, it is time to get going.

That is what today's first reading and gospel are about. Ready or not, the apostles are told by Jesus to get going with the conversion not just of Israel, but of the whole world. You don't quite hear something like that in a commencement speech!

The readings from Acts and the gospel are two distinct versions of the story of the ascension. This happens often in the New Testament as each evangelist stresses different themes. Luke's version in Acts separates the resurrection from the ascension by forty days, symbolic of Moses and the people of Israel wandering in the desert forty years, as well as Jesus fasting in the desert forty days. Luke concentrates on Jerusalem where everything happens, including the coming of the Spirit. Jerusalem is where Jesus dies, just like the prophets, and it is from there Jesus sends forth the disciples. The apostles want the restoration of Israel; they want the glory. However, Jesus says there is much to do first. They need to follow the Spirit. This is a time of witnessing. Here, the Spirit is not a one-time event but an ongoing presence. There is no time to waste in stargazing, as the angels tell them, in looking up to heaven. Jesus is coming back, but there is need to spread the word now. The graduation ceremony is over before it began as the urgent work of missionary activity is what they need to do now.

Matthew's Gospel is different from Luke's. The disciples do not experience Jesus on the day of Easter. Matthew has them going to Galilee to a mountain where Jesus had ordered them to see him. Mountains are important in Scripture. The mountain is considered the place where heaven meets earth. Important things happen there. Moses receives the commandments on a mountain. Jesus gives his most important teaching in the Sermon on the Mount. The mountain is where the transfiguration happens. Mountains are places of authority. On this occasion Jesus is in his full authority. In Matthew, this is the first meeting with his disciples after the resurrection. In this scene the resurrection, the ascension and Pentecost are all one event.

This is the final sending by Jesus. The apostles are now to go into the world and preach. They have crossed the stage.

I remember, when I was approaching my final weeks in the seminary before being sent out to the parish and to ordination as a priest, I found myself all of a sudden doubting if I was ready, if I knew enough, if I was holy enough to do what needed to be done as a priest. I was filled with a kind of anxiety for some weeks. What finally came to me in prayer and meditation was a sense of peace that told me this was not really my work, but the work of Jesus. If he called me, he would not abandon me, just as his words in the gospel today assured the disciples. I would never really be ready, but the Lord would make up whatever shortfalls I had if I just had faith in him and the Spirit working in me. Could I allow myself to be led and supported by the Spirit? I have found that through service, gratitude, and generosity, Jesus works through us and makes up for our shortcomings. It is like the student remembering his or her favorite teacher or coach who has taught them all they can, and now must see them leave the classroom and put it all into practice. We are never completely ready, but it is time to go.

The gospel makes it clear and gives us all hope. Jesus says "I am with you until the end." This is the assurance of the presence of Jesus. Jesus is in the preaching. Jesus is in the witnessing.

The apostles are commissioned to go to the ends of the earth, to transform it, by transforming people's hearts, to care for each other and for the earth. This was greater than Jesus' own ministry, which he said was to the lost sheep of Israel. Now it is to everyone. God the Father, Son, and Spirit are with us; therefore, we have a responsibility for all the earth. This pandemic has affected the whole world. We will only be OK when the whole world is OK. We must care for people in every corner of the planet. At the same time, the pandemic, as bad as it has been, did have a temporary good effect by reducing climate-polluting emissions, maybe as a reminder to us of our responsibility to care for people and the environment. As Jesus told the disciples, this mission is to the whole world, and not only to people.

The command of Jesus to the disciples was to preach, baptize, and keep hope in his return. This is called the Great Commission: just as Jesus did the mission of the Father, so the disciples must do the mission of Jesus. Baptism is the key. It is the immersion or plunging of the believer into an incorporation with the Father, Son, and Holy Spirit. This is the summary of the whole gospel, that we are called to be part of God, to do God's work of love, and thus to continue the transformation of God's creation. We are baptized to keep Jesus' commandments. Jesus made clear what his commandments were, namely, to love God and to love our neighbor. This is the good news we proclaim in the name of Jesus: God loves us and we must love God by loving our neighbor.

I have always loved the scene in the first reading today of the moment when Jesus is taken up to heaven and the apostles stare intently at the sky. Two angels appear and ask them what they are looking at. They say Jesus will return one day. It is clear: quit stargazing, get to work! Jesus never came to stay in the world as he was. The graduates never went to school to stay. It is time to move on. None of us ever gets to stay anywhere long. That is not what we are about. We need to keep moving, as Jesus has given all of us much to do.

The Feast of the Ascension challenges each of us with the question: Have I done enough since I walked across the stage? Have I truly lived my baptism by using my talents, abilities, gifts, and experiences to be a witness, to help transform the world? Have I lived a life of gratitude and generosity while offering service? These weeks and months of the coronavirus have given us all a lot to ponder. Maybe it has been a wake-up call, much like the angels in the reading from Acts today telling the disciples, "Why are you looking up at the sky?" Even as we do what we can to stay healthy, there is much we can do to touch the world with the love of Jesus through words and actions, especially to reach those people and places most in need. It is also a time to make plans for my post-coronavirus life.

It is never too late to complete our mission. We have crossed the stage!

12

5/31/20 Pentecost

Peace be with you.

Acts 2:1–11; 1 Cor 12:3b–7, 12–13; John 20:19–23

ONE OF THE LASTING impacts of the COVID-19 pandemic on us has been a shared sense of vulnerability. Anyone can get sick and suffer the worst consequences of this disease, which has no cure and no vaccine as of this writing. This makes us live with a certain sense of anxiety. Life is tenuous. If we are to survive, we must work together, which is why wearing masks, social distancing, and other precautions are so important. As Americans, this common insecurity is new to us, yet for many people in other countries, to live with fear, anxiety, and insecurity is a way of life.

Many people live in violent societies where even leaving the home can be a huge risk. Others live with grinding poverty, not knowing if they or their children will even eat today. Some are refugees with no place that will welcome them as they travel through dangerous areas. We do not have these threats every day as millions do, yet as Catholics we are called to live in solidarity with them and be brothers and sisters to them in whatever way we can. We may not speak their language, follow their customs, or look like them, but the pandemic has reminded us of our shared responsibility to care for the well-being of the other. The virus can travel back and forth all over the world. We need to be sure everyone is safe, not just Americans. We also need to keep communicating with other people and nations as they are fighting the same pandemic; we can learn and benefit from shared experiences. To listen and try to understand people from different races, countries, and languages, especially at this time, may make the difference between life and death. It is also the key to peace in the world.

The Pentecost story in today's first reading from Acts speaks of many diverse people, who speak different languages, all understanding the preaching of the apostles. Luke lists the many parts of the world those people came from to underline that the message was understood by everyone, regardless of where they were from or what language they spoke. It also meant that the message was aimed at the whole world.

Pentecost is a day to remember the Spirit working in us and in the world. The images used in the reading included wind and fire. The Spirit was unseen as wind is unseen, but both have power to move things. In Hebrew, the word for wind and spirit is the same. Fire is also powerful, as it both helps us in many ways and can destroy. Finally, the result of the wind and the fire, which represented the Spirit, was communication, the ability to speak, to listen, and to understand. This last gift ultimately changed the world.

In the first book of the Bible, God's Spirit hovers over the formless waste to bring forth the earth. The unseen Spirit creates all life. Wind and fire were present on Mount Sinai as Moses received the Ten Commandments. Pentecost for Jews was the remembrance of that Sinai event. All this symbolism indicates God is creating something new, greater than the Ten Commandments, as this new Pentecost supplants Sinai with the law of the Spirit.

Once again, we see different versions of the story. Last week it was the ascension, and this week Pentecost. Luke, in Acts, notes that the coming of the Spirit happened 50 days after Easter in Jerusalem, while John, in his gospel, has it on Easter Sunday evening. The key for both is that the Spirit is the first gift of the risen Jesus. John has Jesus appear through locked doors. Jesus in this gospel breathes on the disciples twice, first offering them peace, then giving them the Holy Spirit. This recalls the breathing of God into Adam to give him spirit, the breath of life. The Spirit means Jesus has not left, but is with us always. The life we have is that of Jesus through the Spirit.

The important point in these divergent readings is not the historical accuracy, but a theological statement of what God was doing through the Spirit given by Jesus. Jesus gives forgiveness and peace, which are insepa-rable. We know that when we forgive and are forgiven there is a peace not possible before that forgiveness. It always feels right. It always feels good.

Jesus speaks peace twice to indicate God has given full healing, well-being, and blessing to those who have seen the risen Jesus, even as he commissions them to proclaim the news to others. What was destroyed by the sin of Adam is now restored. No one is left out. We can all communicate, talk, and listen.

Pentecost means that for the disciples, and for all of us, the risen Jesus would not just be a fond memory, but would be an active presence through the power of the Spirit working in and through the church, through all of us. Not only did he return to the Father, but he also stayed with us in a new way, so that through his presence we would be witnesses to what Jesus has done and is doing in our midst. To complete his work, we need to learn how to communicate.

I have had the privilege of traveling to some of the poorest areas of the world—Africa, India, Central America, and the Middle East—with Catholic Relief Services. Those trips were transformative for me because I saw not only the worst poverty on the planet, but I heard from people, mostly in languages I could not understand, how much they appreciated the support the American church had provided to improve their living conditions. They communicated their gratitude and joy through song, dance, smiles, and local gifts, even a live goat! I did not need to know their language because they knew how to communicate.

The Spirit is identified with the gift of tongues, so that we can communicate and listen and understand. Understanding each other is the great gift that brings peace and forgiveness, which ultimately gives us the way to live in the world as a community of brothers and sisters.

The Spirit overcomes alienation, which is the opposite of forgiveness and peace. Reconciliation and mutual understanding come from these gifts. The great gift of Pentecost is the ability to listen and understand, to overcome differences in race, in how we think about things, how we see the world, what is important, our attitude, all the things that drive us apart and make us suspicious and resentful of the other. Pentecost is the ability to listen and to understand that the other is also a child of God and always worthy of dignity and respect. It is celebrating the fact that there are many gifts God has given and I do not have them all. Everyone has something to give me and I have something to give everyone, as we are reminded in the second reading from the Letter to the Corinthians. We see that the universal language of God is more important. Pentecost is unity in diversity. Diversity is good. Our differences have always been part of the fabric of humanity and were present from the beginning of the church.

Now, in this time of crisis, we must learn more how to listen to the other. We can listen to each other only if we learn how to listen to God, how to take moments of quiet and see what God calls us to do. Pentecost is listening to the Spirit, which then allows us to listen to each other. Even in a pandemic that is good news!

13

6/7/20 Trinity Sunday

God so loved the world...

Exod 34:4b-6, 8-9; 2 Cor 13:11-13; John 3:16-18

THE QUESTION I HAVE heard from some people throughout these months of the pandemic is, "Where is God in all this?" Some feel that God is either not paying attention to us in our suffering, or that God sent the virus to punish us, teach us a lesson, or get us all back to faith. Where is God?

Today is Trinity Sunday, the day we remember that God has always been involved in the human story. The history of salvation is God constantly reaching out to us, even when we reject, forget, or ignore God. God wants a relationship with us. How do we respond? Let us look at the three readings of today's Mass to give us the road map.

The first reading speaks of the relationship God always had with his people, a God who was involved with them, who wanted to save them. The exodus event was the pinnacle moment. God makes a covenant relationship with the people and they make promises to God. God will love them and save them and they will respond by loving God in the way they love each other.

The Israelites did not have a concept of the Trinity, yet they knew there were many facets to God. Full knowledge of God was beyond any human's capacity, which is why earlier in this text Moses could only see the back of God as God passed by. Today's first reading is part of a large section of Moses and God communicating on the mountain. Remember that the mountain in Scripture is the place where heaven meets earth and very important events happen on mountains. Here Moses is given a glimpse of God, and then God describes himself in these words: "merciful and gracious, slow to anger and rich in kindness and fidelity." Think of each of God's attributes: merciful, gracious, slow to anger, kind, faithful. That is God. Is that us also? We are all called to live life, imitating our Creator who made us in God's image.

We get glimpses of God all around us, especially during this time of crisis with the pandemic, and recently the death of George Floyd in Minneapolis, followed by demonstrations throughout the country and the world. Even the regrettable destruction of property was followed by many volunteers the next day cleaning up and helping those affected. Rich in kindness: a good quality to try to imitate, and we can see those glimpses of God now if we look.

The reading from the gospel of John again emphasizes God as the Savior of the world, which is one of the main themes of the Hebrew Scriptures. God saves the people from slavery in Egypt. Now God sends his Son so that the world might be saved through him. This reading is part of a longer discussion Jesus has with Nicodemus, a Pharisee, who comes to Jesus at night for fear of being criticized by the other Pharisees who opposed Jesus. John's Gospel often contrasts night and day, or light and darkness. Nicodemus comes in darkness and is illuminated with the light of Christ.

The early Christians reading this gospel were going through difficult times, just as we are today. In their case, they were being expelled from the synagogue and persecuted, because they were considered renegade Jews for believing in Jesus. Not being welcome in the synagogue was very difficult for them. Being unable to attend Mass was very difficult for us, even though our story is different. This narrative in John helped the early Christians see that they were sharing in the same rejection and cross of Jesus. God gives his Son for salvation, the giving of life through his death on the cross. God then is revealed through the weakness of the cross, as it becomes the total giving of life for the world. Jesus is revealed as God through the cross. We don't understand this until we understand our own cross and accept it. We then see that the cross is part of discipleship, part of belonging to Jesus, part of the story of our salvation.

For all of my priesthood, after Sunday Masses, when I would stand at the door and greet those leaving, I would often be asked to give people blessings. I know what they want. They want me to make the sign of the cross over them, despite the fact that I just gave a blessing to end the Mass. They want their own blessing. I willingly did it because I knew it meant a lot to them. As I have thought of it, I know that the sign of the cross and invocation of the Trinity is not magic. The cross is still a cross, the symbol of the suffering of Jesus. We are called to embrace that suffering for ourselves, not look for it, just embrace it when it comes despite everything else. We embrace suffering in life, such as we see today, as a moment to unite ourselves with Jesus in giving life to the world.

This pandemic is our moment of the cross, our suffering, which, like it was with Jesus, can be a redemptive suffering, embraced in love and transformed into something that shows love and gives life. Look at all the ways people are volunteering to help others, like the essential workers risking their health to serve, and so many others who are transforming a moment of pain into a saving event. When we understand that the cross is part of life and can be transformed into redemption, then things can change. That is how God loves the world and how we live that love.

The salutation in the second reading from Paul to the Corinthians includes the Trinity. Grace, love, and fellowship are identified with the three persons in God: Father, Son, and Holy Spirit. Relationship is what it is about. Each one of these attributes of God is related to us. We share the grace of Jesus with others when we do the work of Jesus, which is reconciling, healing, including, and affirming. Mutual love, as God loves, is opposed to the spirit of separation and isolation. When we think we can do without others, we make a big mistake. Arrogance is the opposite of who God is. Arrogance says I don't need you. Jesus showed his interest in everyone. We need each other. That is the fellowship which the Spirit gives.

Today is an important day, especially this year. It is a day to praise God, who is constantly involved in our lives. It is a day to remember to look for God in all we do. If we look around us, even in this painful moment of history, we will get a glimpse of God in so many people, in so many ways.

Where is God? Look around you!

14

6/14/20 Corpus Christi

. . . who feeds on this bread lives forever.

Deut 8:2–3, 14b–16a; 1 Cor 10:16–17; John 6:51–58

I GOT A CALL this week from someone who said a relative was asking if they could receive communion without going to Mass. They missed receiving it during the lockdown but were still reluctant to return to Sunday Mass. I have heard a suggestion that there be drive-up communion so people do not leave their car. Some simply do not want to take a risk about being at Mass with other people for an hour. Yet they are hungry for the Eucharist. It caused me to ask myself: What are they hungry for? What is it they miss? What difference will it make when they can receive communion again?

Today is the Feast of Corpus Christi, when we give thanks for the gift of the body and blood of Jesus, who gave his life on the cross for us. The night before his death, he gave us his body and blood in the form of bread and wine to be an everlasting sign of his presence among us.

The first reading from Deuteronomy tells of Moses reminding the people of Israel of their hunger in the desert, and how they were fed by God with manna from heaven. The theme of the exodus was Israel being rescued from slavery in Egypt to feed their hunger for freedom. Nonetheless, the gift of bread is not as important as obedience to God's word, which Moses tells them is the real source of life. Listening to God's word and acting on it gives one true life, and makes one a life-giving person.

Two ways we experience Jesus in Mass are the word and the eucharistic elements of bread and wine. Both unite us to Christ. Both send us out on mission for Christ.

The section of John's Gospel for today is called The Bread of Life Discourse, which is followed by the fact that Jesus did not go about in Judea because opponents were looking to kill him. The gospel makes the connection of the gift of his flesh and blood to his death. Remember that John does not provide an institution narrative at the Last Supper, only the washing of feet, to show Eucharist is service. The Bread of Life Discourse might be a reflection of the eucharistic order of service, with word, commemoration of the passion, and communion. What precedes this discourse is the multiplication of loaves, where Jesus took bread, gave thanks, broke it, and gave it to all those present. Essentially that is the eucharistic formula.

Jesus says in this reading, "The bread I give is my flesh for the life of the world." These words compare to "This is my body given up for you," which is the language of the institution found in the other gospels. John fills his gospel, pre-Last Supper, with eucharistic references. What Jesus gives is now more than just manna, more than just bread multiplied to feed people. This is Jesus' body, flesh and blood. Flesh means the totality of the person, but this is powerless without the life of the Spirit. Baptism gives us life, while Eucharist nourishes that life. Eucharist is indwelling, intimacy with Jesus.

In English, as in many languages, we have ways to describe how we take something into ourselves. We devour a book, drink in a lecture, swallow a story, stomach a lie, eat one's own words—all ways to describe how something affects us deeply and sometimes changes how we act. Today's feast asks us to take in and reflect on how we eat the Living Bread. "Whoever eats this bread remains in me." We must try to understand what it means to remain in him. Paul, in the second reading, talks about participating in the body and the blood of Christ through the bread and the cup. How do we remain in Jesus? "Remain" seems to say we stay with Jesus, we keep living in Jesus, we are with Jesus all day long, in the many moments of life, both easy and difficult. We must constantly work on doing this better. Our lives are not yet in full union with Jesus.

Two years ago, I was in Washington, DC and visited the National Museum of African American History and Culture. It is a powerful place that not only tells the story of the African American, it actually seems to make you walk their history, and experience some of their struggle.

As you enter, you begin by taking an elevator to what seems to be the lowest basement. It is there you start the story with the kidnapping of Africans and packing them, in inhuman conditions, on slave ships, where a huge percentage of them died while crossing the ocean. As you learn this frightful story, you move through the lower levels, which are darkly lit, forcing you to strain to read the signage, always slowly going up a long, wide ramp. You pass through slavery, the Civil War, segregation, civil rights, and up to today, when you finally arrive at the main floor that is fully lit. There you see the great gifts of the African American in education, health care, the military, sports, the arts, and so much more. It is as if you can come up out of the depths, a deep hole, darkness. You are invited, almost forced, to go down, so that you are uncomfortable, uneasy, almost scared, and want to get out. However, you must walk the long journey to the light, to freedom, a journey which is still being walked. When you arrive above, you see what people are capable of, if given the opportunity, and see that they are respected. The overall message of the museum is that we are not done yet: not done yet respecting the dignity of all, not done yet giving equal justice, not done yet providing the opportunity to develop. Certainly, with the events of the last few weeks, we know we are not done yet.

The gospel and today's feast of Corpus Christi say the same thing: we are not done yet in becoming the body of Christ in totality. What is left to do?

We are certainly all going through a very difficult time now. The virus has put a strain on daily living, has challenged our commitment to live in community with others, to be respectful, to care about more than myself and my family. The George Floyd case and the protests have opened once again the question of how people are treated and mistreated in our country and in the world. In this time, can we really hunger for Jesus in us? How do we remain in Jesus? What must we do to truly become the body of Christ?

When we come to the Mass, we reflect on the sacrifice of Jesus and how we are also called to sacrifice. What is it for us? Can it be understanding a shameful history, facing the demons of humanity, seeing how low we can go, how horrible we can treat each other, admitting our sin? Is it poverty, rejection, indignity, disrespect, and, in the time of the coronavirus, not caring about doing what is necessary to limit the spread to others? However, the Mass/Eucharist is also about resurrection, new life, forgiveness, and reconciliation. Through the Eucharist we learn that with the advent of pain and the embracing of the cross come the end of the pain and suffering. Jesus has opened paradise for us. We are not alone, working through all the suffering. The Eucharist we receive is the pledge that Jesus remains with us, that there is something better: new life and total happiness with him on the other side of the suffering.

Every time you prepare to receive the Eucharist, remember what we are called to. We are not done yet. The threat to Eucharist is not seeing Christ in the least. It is our moral numbness, our indifference. We have not yet done what needs to happen to make this world reflect the love of Jesus giving his life for us. God has not given up on us. His Son, in the Eucharist, is the promise, the gift that lasts forever.

The gospel of today's feast says to us, "Do this in memory of me; do this whenever you remember me." That is what we do today and every Sunday. Let us remember through the liturgy of Mass that we are always called to come closer and closer together in Christ, despite our differences.

We are not done yet. Remember me, remember this moment when you face the pandemic and racial issues that are present in our community. Receive the body of Christ. Be hungry to remain in him. That memory will give us the strength to be for each other what Jesus is for all the church.

15

6/21/20 Twelfth Sunday

You are worth more than many sparrows!

Jer 20:10–13; Rom 5:12–15; Matt 10:26–33

JUST WHEN WE THOUGHT things were greatly improving with the coronavirus, we are experiencing a second wave of infections, or more probably the resurgence of the first wave that never was contained. Many people felt that because the stores, restaurants, and other businesses were opening, life was now back to normal. However, it is not. It is scary to live with the possibility of getting infected. Many young people in their twenties are now becoming the next victims of the disease. No one is bulletproof. It makes all of us feel very vulnerable and afraid, just when we thought the virus was under control.

I have found in life when things are going well and life is good, get ready! Something is going to happen to throw everything off. I may have a challenge or struggle I did not anticipate. It is often discouraging, but it is also the reality of human existence.

Jeremiah, in the first reading, is under attack for denouncing the injustices of his time. He often complained to God that he never wanted to be a prophet, but God called and insisted. Jeremiah was always experiencing the ups and downs of emotions and physical threats, constantly calling on God for mercy and justice. He lived with terror and fear. Ultimately, he simply entrusted his cause to the Lord.

Three times in today's gospel Jesus tells his disciples not to be afraid. He has warned them already that they will encounter opposition and persecution when they try to fulfill his mission. He himself is the first example. He was constantly opposed and persecuted and ultimately killed. Jesus tells the disciples to expect the same treatment when they do his work. At the same time, they are not to fear. Jesus tells them that people might be able to kill the body but they cannot destroy the soul.

This segment of Matthew's Gospel is called the Discourse on the Mission and will be continued in next Sunday's gospel reading. In this discourse Jesus is encouraging the disciples to preach with boldness despite those who will oppose them. This is the call to all of us which comes from baptism. We are to proclaim the mission of Jesus to the world. We are to be good news to others. However, expect obstacles, setbacks, and even threats.

We are now fully into the liturgical season called Ordinary Time. The word "ordinary" does not mean something normal. It comes from ordinal, which means a counting. We are counting the Sundays between the great seasons of the life of Jesus. We just finished Lent and Easter Time, where we reflected on the last days of Jesus' life, his passion, death, and resurrection. The seasons after Ordinary Time is Advent and Christmas, which speak of the coming of Jesus and his presence among us. So, during those major seasons we see the great mysteries of the life of Jesus. During Ordinary Time we look at ourselves, the disciples of Jesus, and what we are called to do. What is the mission that Jesus has given us? How do we live it?

Matthew is writing this gospel to encourage the first generation of Christians. After the initial success of preaching and expanding the infant church, the early disciples and followers were experiencing opposition and even violence from those who wanted to stamp out this movement. The message of Jesus challenged people, as it still does today. It demanded of them that they see things differently, which they were unwilling to do. Instead of engaging the message and trying to understand it, they attacked the messengers. This is happening today with the coronavirus pandemic, where health care and civic leaders who are warning us of its dangers, are criticized for urging us to observe certain measures like wearing masks and practicing social distancing. It is also taking place regarding racial protests and demands for reform, where the messengers are attacked because what they are demanding will cause significant change long overdue in our society.

Today is Father's Day. It will be a difficult time to celebrate our fathers. Some have recently died in the pandemic. Several Black Americans killed by police were also dads, which has left children and families in mourning. Many of us lost our fathers years ago. Some come from broken marriages. Whatever the situation, although it will be hard to celebrate this year, we need to be grateful. Dads deserve our thanks for what they did for us, the way they mentored us, how they provided for us. Even in difficult and fearful times, fathers can be a symbol of the caring and constant love of God.

The early Christians looked to God for support. They were discouraged in some ways and were often afraid. Matthew wants to assure them that Jesus prepared them to deal with these situations. Each of them is important and God knows them and will not abandon them. The worth of the person is without compare. That is also the message of Black Lives Matter. Jesus indicates that if God cares even for the tiny sparrow, how much more will God care for us? God knows us, even things we do not know about ourselves.

At another crisis moment in our country, President Franklin Roosevelt told the nation at his first inauguration, "The only thing we have to fear is fear itself." With that, he rallied a discouraged people to start the long march out of the Great Depression. Fear can paralyze, but when it is named and confronted, it can be overcome.

For the Christian, fear must give way to hope. The cross is the prime example of this. Even though Jesus had been in terror and agony the night before his crucifixion, he not only embraced the cross but forgave his murderers while he was dying. The fear of death for Jesus was robbed of any power it had over him with that spectacular gesture of reconciling hope. Reconciliation is what we need to defeat the virus and to defeat racism. Reconciliation forgives, cares for the other, is generous, and restores community. We must persevere and not give up hope. Reconciliation is always possible, even in the deepest moments of suffering.

Recently my family did a Zoom conference call with all my sisters, most of their children, and many of their grandchildren. We had wanted to celebrate the high school graduation of two of my great-nephews and one great-niece, especially since no one except parents were allowed to attend the tightly controlled ceremonies. We even included other great-nephews and nieces who were graduating from kindergarten and middle school. To see how proud they all were of their accomplishments and to hear their future plans, especially of the high school graduates, made me proud of them. However, it also made me anxious for them, knowing they will encounter so much, so quickly in their young lives. Hearing them speak of their futures gave me great hope, despite knowing they will inevitably face huge challenges and even suffering. I am confident their firm foundation of faith and family will make the difference in their lives. Hope was evident in their faces.

The readings remind us that God is always actively present in our lives. That is our hope which overcomes our fear. When we keep faith in God, especially in troubling times and under threat, there is no doubt God will protect and restore what God loves. Life in Christ is eternal, even if the body suffers and dies.

Despite the darkness that comes at various moments of life, we must live in the confidence that God gives us what we need. We are called to life and a future filled with hope here and in the hereafter.

Do not be afraid. Remember: You are worth more than many sparrows!

16

6/28/20 Thirteenth Sunday

He who welcomes you welcomes me...

2 Kgs 4:8-11, 14-16a; Rom 6:3-4, 8-11; Matt 10:37-42

THE VEXING THING ABOUT this coronavirus that has caused such suffering and death around the world is that it is new. It is called the novel coronavirus because it is a new strain of the virus family of diseases that had not been identified previously in humans. Because it is new, we have had to learn about it as it spreads among the population, which is why medical personnel are treating sick people with the virus differently today than when it first started. Also, we get updates on how to defend ourselves and what to expect as more is known. It is a constant learning process that is a matter of life and death. We will probably never know all there is to know about it, but the more we learn, the better off we will all be. This is also a moment to learn more about ourselves and how we relate to ourselves and others in a crisis.

Lifelong learning is what the gospel is about today. This part of the Gospel of Matthew is a reflection on discipleship, called The Apostolic Discourse or the Discourse on Mission, as we noted last week. We are in Ordinary Time when the readings call us to look at our lives as followers of Jesus. Matthew uses the word "disciple" seventy-two times in his gospel, and the word "apostle" only once. Disciple connotes a learner-follower, who is studying from the master. Apostle means one who is sent. Matthew wants us all to realize, even though we are sent to bring good news and to be good news to others, we are still always learning. We will never know it all.

In these hard and polarizing times, it is a big challenge to maintain family ties while living out our values. The quarantine, economic damage, social unrest, mental stress, and fear have caused tensions within households and families to run high. Jesus speaks of family relationships in the gospel. We must learn how to live and love family while being faithful to Jesus. How do we stay true to the message of Jesus as our primary focus while loving family as much as we can?

In the early church, new Christians were often expelled from their families who thought they were betraying the Jewish faith. Jesus talks about leaving family to follow him, and only then is one worthy. This would have sounded radical to the people who heard it from Jesus. For the first-century Jew, one's entire identity came from family. The clan was their world. To be cast out of family was a form of death, to lose one's identity. The disciples are being asked to take on a new identity and to make new familial relationships based on faith in Jesus.

In one family there may be many different opinions, attitudes, and actions. These are highlighted in times of stress. These differences are the cross we need to embrace, a cross Jesus speaks of taking up in order to be worthy of him.

One cross is the sacrifices we need to make to protect each other in the pandemic. It is clear that wearing a mask and maintaining distance reduce infection and protect others as well as ourselves. Refusing to do even these limited actions goes against Jesus' mandate to receive and care for the other as if that person were Jesus. It requires consideration and patience. Are we willing to do that much?

How do we make the connection that our faith is a work in progress? It is not one moment and then finished. It is a process with which we must continue to engage in order to grow. I recently had a call from someone trying to arrange a baby's baptism. The parents are not active members of a parish. The godparents are not married in the church and do not attend Mass. Wanting to baptize a baby is a good thing, to be affirmed, but is there an intention of truly raising the child in the faith by modeling active participation? I have seen this many times in my years in ministry. Paul speaks to this in the second reading to the Romans by reminding us that we were baptized into the death of Jesus so we might live in newness of life. This is an ongoing process, death to self and new life in Christ. Death means the many little sacrifices we make daily. It does not happen just once, but over and over as we struggle to be lifelong learners. A child needs to see in parents and godparents what baptism means.

All the sacraments are moments to deepen and learn more about our faith. Confirmation is not the end of learning about faith. In reality, it is an ongoing step of fully living the faith, which requires a commitment to lifelong learning. One does not receive the sacrament of marriage and think they know all about marriage. Also, a priest is not ordained and then thinks he knows all the theology and pastoral practice he will ever need. There is much to learn from that day forward. Just ask anyone who has lived married life or been a priest for any period of time!

The lifelong task of learning to live the faith is what the Christian must be about constantly. We need to be aware of what gifts we will receive in the process of sharing the good news. When we share and live the faith, inevitably we will learn more if we are open to learning. Even though we are sent, we are also receiving as much as we give, and maybe even more. This has certainly been a constant theme of my life as a priest. I always learn more and receive more from others than I can give. The key is to be aware of those gifts we are being offered. When I think of others as having nothing to offer, then I am the one losing out. Jesus makes it clear at the end of today's gospel, there is a reward in both the receiving or acceptance of another as well as in the giving to another, especially those most in need.

This is not easy work; therefore, we always need to learn more about Jesus' life and teachings. He warned his disciples that there would be opposition and a cost to doing his work, but there would be new life in him. There is an urgency about being sent, but it is in the receiving that we see God and Jesus. Receiving others is a form of giving ourselves to them, welcoming, helping, supporting them.

Jesus mentions specifically that we need to receive prophets and the righteous. Prophets were not people who predicted the future but who reflected on the present and condemned the injustices they saw. They were considered teachers, but often without students, as many were not open to hear what was wrong; rather, they were comfortable with how things were. However, there were many righteous people at that time doing good works. There are several examples of this today as many are following Jesus' call by responding to the pandemic at great personal sacrifice; for example, donors have expanded their giving; food banks have received a 623 percent increase in gifts.[1]

---

1. Howes, "Food Banks See 623% Surge."

Finally, the gospel today ends with Jesus saying there is a reward for giving a cup of cold water to a "little one." In the arid and hot climate of Israel, a cup of water meant life or death. When Jesus speaks of a little one, this might indicate it is in the small gestures that we receive God, and many small generous gestures will merit a reward. Think about the next small gesture you can offer a person in need, because there is so much need right now.

We have gone through a lot lately, and surely more lies ahead. What have you learned?

17

7/5/20 Fourteenth Sunday (Ordinary Time)

Come to me all you who are burdened. . .

Zech 9:9–10; Rom 8:9, 11–13; Matt 11:25–30

IT IS SHOCKING THAT the coronavirus has surged astronomically in the past month in so much of this country and is making a comeback in other parts of the world. This is not over by a long shot. Here in San Antonio the Metropolitan Health Director managing the response to the pandemic has resigned, seemingly because the burden of leading this overwhelming crisis was just too stressful. It is certainly understandable as she and her staff have worked nonstop without a single day off for five months. It was a burden she could not bear. It is hard to blame her.

The ongoing pandemic has caused huge burdens on everyone at every level of society throughout the world. It has sent many to the hospital and has killed many people. It has challenged our resources, limited our movements, curtailed what we can do, where we can go, or whom we can visit. Just when it seemed things were improving, we are much worse off than when it began. It is a heavy burden to carry and it will not end soon.

The gospel for this Mass speaks about carrying burdens. It tells us that Jesus invites those who are burdened to go to him. It is interesting that Jesus promises he will give those who accept his invitation rest, but invites us to take on his yoke. A yoke was the way oxen did work in the fields. So, it seems strange that Jesus tells us his yoke gives us rest, but in fact it does. To take Jesus' yoke, Jesus' work, is to be free of all that oppresses and burdens us, the anxieties, anger, revenge, hate, fear, arrogance, and the petty and not-so-petty ways we hurt each other. Resting in Jesus is being in right relationship with each other and appreciating God's goodness. That yoke we can carry. That yoke can make a difference.

There is also another aspect to taking on Jesus' yoke. We must do it in humility, accepting what comes with it, which is often difficult. Right now, we need help. We can't do this by ourselves and we need to be humble enough to admit that. Humility is the recognition of who we are, what we have, who we are not, and what we don't have. We are all getting a huge lesson in humility right now. We are not in control of this pandemic. It is causing suffering, death, and is putting limitations on how we live as we adopt new actions like wearing masks, distancing from each other, staying home, and such. This is all very humbling. We can fight it and be angry, cynical, strike out, be stubborn or selfish, and not protect ourselves and others, or we can live through this time in humility. We can learn from it and develop attitudes of greater compassion, thoughtfulness, and care for others that hopefully will stay with us long after the virus subsides. Even locked up at home in solitude can be a moment to humbly listen to God as the many holy monks and hermits have shown us for centuries. Learn something from this time. Are we humble enough to take Jesus' yoke?

About eighteen months ago I lost one of my best friends, Father Jim Barlow. He was retired at the time he died, but had been suffering numerous illnesses, including Parkinson's. He continued as a pastor until he was unable to actively minister anymore. With the various illnesses, he could not do what he wanted to do. I remember numerous conversations where his frustration was so evident. I would sympathize with him, wishing there was something I could do, but there was nothing possible. In the end, he accepted what was happening in humility. It was out of his control. He had accepted the yoke of Jesus. The gospel he selected for his funeral Mass was this one we read today.

Jesus comes in the spirit of the lowly and gentle. He avoided power, the idea of the Messiah as a powerful king. His power was in his way of life, the way he touched people's lives and healed them, the way he inspired, and what he taught. People's expectations were of a king, a powerful political and military ruler, but Jesus was different. Jesus simply tells us in the gospel reading that he has come to serve. He will help us carry our burdens. He will help us carry our yoke.

At the back of San Fernando Cathedral where I served thirteen years as rector, there is a large crucified Christ, called the Cristo Negro, the Black Christ. It is a replica from a famous sixteenth-century sanctuary in Guatemala that was brought to our cathedral forty years ago.

Below the Christ is a bulletin board where people post notes, pictures of loved ones they are praying for, locks of hair, *Milagros* (charmlike medals representing body parts one is praying will be healed), hospital bracelets, and other mementos. It is their way of entrusting their prayers for someone or themselves to Christ. I would often observe all kinds of people, but especially the elderly, entering the cathedral to pray in front of that image. When they began, they looked bent over, often tired, sad, sometimes anxious or fearful. They looked as if they were carrying the weight of the world on their shoulders. They would pray, leave a memento there, and sometimes seemed to be in a lively conversation with the Black Christ, almost as if demanding that he help solve their need. Inevitably, as their time with him ended, they would stand up a little straighter and seemed to leave the church with much less of a burden and much more peace. There was a power in what had happened. They had agreed to take on the yoke of Jesus. It made all the difference. I always prayed I would have the kind of humble faith I constantly saw there.

Jesus is the revelation of God. However, to fully grasp that revelation, we must approach him in humility, openness, and lowliness. That is why Jesus' message was received by outcasts, sinners, publicans, and others rejected by society. These are the little ones Jesus talks about. Their acceptance of Jesus was not compromised by status, pride, a know-it-all attitude, or being judgmental of others. They knew who they were and who they were not. They took on the yoke of Jesus, and it gave them strength to carry their own burdens and to see how imitating Jesus was the way to full life. To study Jesus, learn Jesus, imitate Jesus, is to take the yoke, knowing that it is light because there is a companion on the way with us, namely, Jesus. As St. Paul says in the Letter to the Romans, the same Spirit that raised Jesus from the dead also dwells in us and gives us life. Our faith gives us great hope!

If part of taking the yoke of Jesus is to have him carry our burdens as we seek to imitate him, then we need to look at how we help carry each other's burdens. On this Fourth of July weekend, as we face an uncertain time, with the virus out of control in most of the country, and racial turmoil at a critical reckoning, what will it mean to carry burdens as Jesus does for us? What we do at this moment will define our country today and going forward. It will happen in the little things. A woman I know, who cleans homes for a living and is a single mom of a teenage boy, contracted COVID-19 this week. Two families who know her have come forward to take groceries and some money to help her and are committed to continue until things improve. No one asked them to do this; they picked up the burden and helped carry it. That is Independence Day, a day to instill a spirit of gratitude for what we have and the willingness to be generous to those in need. That can define us all.

Listen to Jesus today and decide how you will respond: "Come to me, you who are burdened."

18

7/12/20 Fifteenth Sunday

He it is who bears a yield of a hundred- or sixty- or thirty-fold.

Isa 55:10–11; Rom 8:18–23; Matt 13:1–23

SINCE THE CORONAVIRUS CAME roaring back a few weeks ago, it seems everyone has been trying to blame the failure to control it on someone else. Some blame our government, either at the state, local, or national level. Some blame health care and medical officials. Some blame young people for being in bars or at gatherings without masks or social distancing. Some blame people who came here from other countries. There might be blame enough for everyone. There was a great failure and someone failed us.

Failure has always seemed to be something very bad. You failed. Something is wrong with you. You should be ashamed of yourself. We lost the ballgame. Someone failed: the coach, one of the players, the coaching staff, the referees? Someone will be blamed for the failure.

This negative attitude toward failure seems to be ingrained in us. Could we ever consider turning that attitude around, and see failure not as a total loss but rather as an opportunity to grow, to be better, to learn? How do we learn from failure or seeming failure?

There have been numerous examples of supposed failures that became spectacular successes. Albert Einstein could not speak fluently until the age of 9, was expelled from school, and later refused admittance to a polytechnic school. He won the Nobel Prize in Physics in 1921. He often

said, "Success is failure in progress."[1] Abraham Lincoln failed in business, had a nervous breakdown, and lost his first run for president. His
comment: "My great concern is not whether you have failed but whether
you are content with your failure."[2] Michael Jordan missed more than
9,000 shots, lost 300 games, and missed the game-winning shot 26 times.
He said, "I have failed over and over again in my life. And that is why I
succeed."[3]

All of these remind me of being at a funeral last year when the son,
in his eulogy, quoted his deceased father's saying, "In life there are no
failures, only lessons to be learned."

If you look at Jesus' life and read the gospels, you might say he was
a failure. Few people accepted his teaching and most rejected him at the
end. He suffered a humiliating death, and his ragtag group of disciples
did not make much progress at first. Yet Jesus was the most significant
person in human history.

Today's gospel is the parable of the sower and seeds. It is a parable
of failure turning into fantastic success. In the reading, Jesus sits down
to speak, the posture of a rabbi teacher. Matthew wants us to hear the
teaching of Jesus speaking with authority. Three out of four groups of
seeds sown were failures. They ultimately did not bear fruit. Jesus was
saying that most people would reject his message. However, to those who
hear Jesus and respond to his words, there is a rich reward. If we listen to
Jesus and respond, there is no limit to what we can accomplish, even if
we fail numerous times!

We have to hear the parables of Jesus not with our head but with
our heart. Our heart is where we will learn deeply and then be moved to
action. We are not the seeds that are just hearing Jesus for the first time.
We have been baptized, raised in the faith. We have heard about Jesus all
our life for the most part. St. Matthew, the gospel writer today, wants us to
listen and then ask ourselves, "What are we supposed to do about this?"
Matthew knew of the power in these stories. Think of many stories you
have heard, or maybe seen on television, that moved you, that made you
want to do something. Certainly, the stories we are hearing more recently
of so many African Americans unjustly killed by some police have moved
this whole country to do something. It is long overdue.

1. Andal, "10 Famous Failures to Success Stories."
2. Andal, "10 Famous Failures to Success Stories."
3. Andal, "10 Famous Failures to Success Stories."

For early Christians listening to this reading, these seeds that did not give any harvest represented people who never took Jesus' word seriously, or maybe they started to follow Jesus then stopped or were overwhelmed by other concerns. We see the same today. Are you taking Jesus seriously in your life? Are things seeming to all go wrong now? Sometimes the world is crashing down on us and we can't see what to do. The good seed took time to sprout and grow, but it finally did.

Jesus was not a farmer, and he was not teaching farming or how to get a better crop. What he knows is how things are when God is in charge. It is about the abundance God can produce. A sevenfold harvest would have been terrific, tenfold almost miraculous. Jesus says up to a hundredfold! The parable is all about hope, especially when things are hard. The early Christians faced persecution constantly but did not give up hope. For a person of faith, this time of living during a pandemic is also about hope, hope in the Spirit of God that unites us to confront this emergency together.

Taking root and growing to give a harvest is not about you, or even how well you do things. It is about being faithful to the mission of Jesus which you received long ago and to which you must respond again today. Mother Teresa said, "God didn't call me to be successful, he called me to be faithful."[4]

God's goodness is always greater than sin. So, there is always reason to hope, room to grow. God's love extends to those who are the seeds that do not grow or stay. We must do the same. Never give up on ourselves, never give up on others. We can overcome this virus. We can overcome this racism. We can overcome the pointless divisions that are created in so many ways. We can overcome the bad things in our world. Pope Francis once said, "Stop complaining and act to change your life for the better."[5]

In 1987, I was in charge of preparing an outdoor Mass site for the visit of Pope John Paul II to San Antonio. Three days before the pope arrived, everything was pretty much prepared when a freak tremendous wind hit the site and tore down much of what we had built for the backdrop of the altar. Thankfully no one was hurt but the place was in ruins. Within hours of the disaster came offers of help from all over the city including contractors, machinery, and people who were willing to help replace what was lost, all at no cost. Everything was finished just in time.

4. https://catholic-link.org/images/god-has-called-me-to-be-faithful-mother-teresa/.

5. AFP News Agency, July 14, 2017.

The Mass was wonderful except in our haste we had forgotten to shade the altar area from the mid-September Texas sun. The very white Polish pope was beet red when I escorted him to his trailer to take off the vestments after Mass. I was mortified seeing him tired, sweating, and sunburned. I blurted out in Spanish, "*Como se siente Santo Padre?* (How do you feel, Holy Father?)" He stopped in front of me and slowly responded, "*Todavia vivo* (I am still alive!)" He said it with a sly grin. Talk about never giving up faith; there it was in front of me!

Your faith is part of this never-give-up attitude despite challenges and failure. Never give up your faith no matter how many tell you it is useless. Never give up turning to Jesus. Never give up on God, no matter how many things go wrong in your life and in the world. Never give up on the Holy Spirit who is constantly active in your life.

This time in our lives is a huge challenge. Things do not seem to be getting better. All around us are sickness and conflict. Blame is being thrown in all directions. There is the temptation to just give up and retreat into my own world and only care for myself. Don't yield to that! Our faith is stronger than that. If we all dig deeper into our faith, we will find ways to help each other overcome pandemics, racism, and every other challenge in our world.

There is an over-the-top harvest waiting for you!

19

7/19/20 Sixteenth Sunday

Then the saints will shine like the sun in their Father's kingdom.

Wis 12:13, 16–19; Rom 8:26–27; Matt 13:24–43

EACH EVENING WHEN MAYOR Ron Nirenberg of San Antonio announces the coronavirus cases for that day, he also gives the number of people who passed away, describing age, sex, and if there were underlying conditions that may have complicated their COVID-19 illness, leading to their death. Then he asks all those listening to remember these are people, not statistics. They are mothers, fathers, grandparents, children, relatives, and friends loved by many. They were part of our community and now they are gone. We grieve, pray, and keep them in memory. It is an important daily reminder that this virus is not just an inconvenience; it is the life and death of human beings.

We need to remember people are suffering and there does not seem to be an end to it. We are so impatient with this virus. We want it to just finish, go away, stop inflicting itself on the world. We want to get back to our normal life that we enjoyed prior to the pandemic. Some of the impatience manifests itself in resistance to wearing masks or hosting parties without attendee limits or social distancing. This has deadly consequences as more are being infected, and sadly more are passing away, including many younger people.

The impatience is showing itself even within the family where we live. We love them, but they are wearing on us. We find ourselves snapping at each other, arguing, and criticizing more. It is hard to have patience and wait a year for a vaccine before we can get back to normal. Is patience possible under these circumstances?

All three parables in today's gospel deal with patience. Jesus speaks of it as key to the reign of God. He tells these stories as ways to understand the reign of God, not the kingdom of God as the term is sometimes used. Reign might be the better word as it describes a way to live and not just a place to live. It is an ongoing reality. These three stories are similar in that each calls for patience, but a patience that is not static; rather it is active and ongoing. God will do what God wants in God's time. We just need faith and patience.

Matthew's thirteenth chapter has seven parables. Last Sunday, we heard the first about the sower and the seeds. Today there are three more, and next Sunday the final three. People liked to hear stories in Jesus' day. That was their social media platform. It was powerful because it came from the storyteller and then would be mostly passed on by word of mouth. Jesus was a master storyteller. Each story had something to hook you and make you think in new ways.

Matthew was speaking to a frustrated early Christian community. They were being persecuted without end and were suffering. At the same time, they were enduring persecution, and they were being hard on each other. They had the tendency to try to expel those they felt were not perfect Christians. We also are frustrated now and critical of family members who don't do what we think should be done. We want them to be a certain way, our way. Jesus told the story in part due to his struggle with Pharisees who always judged others and were quick to condemn. They considered themselves the elite, better than others, and opposed Jesus for reaching out to the lowly and the rejected. Also, in the parable, evil wins at first as the weeds are allowed to remain, just as evil seems to conquer Jesus when he dies; but that is not the end of the story. There is much more.

We often have a tendency to judge others right away, deciding who is right or wrong, good or bad. However, we are not God. Jesus tells us that God's way is to have patience, to actively wait. God loves us with all our imperfections, is patient with us, and calls us to do better. Our temptation is to condemn, but our role is to reconcile. We are called to help transform the world by transforming ourselves, and, in the process, help transform those around us.

The first parable speaks of weeds and wheat growing together. We live in the midst of a church and world that have both good and bad within them. We also have good and bad within us. Even when we recognize the bad, there is no need to judge ourselves harshly. We have time to change. God invites us to new life. We just need the will to do it.

The next two parables on the yeast and the mustard seed focus on small things that can make a big difference. Patience is also part of this. A small amount of yeast can transform the flour into bread with time. The story talks about three measures of flour, which is about fifty pounds. That can feed the entire village. Small acts can make a big difference for good. Every person helping in his or her own little way during these hard times of the virus and unemployment is making a difference. They are the yeast that, little by little, can feed a village.

A mustard bush was actually considered a weed. The story allows the bush to flourish and birds to come to nest in it. Birds in this story are not the beautiful winged creatures we love. They are considered an enemy, since they eat crops. The mustard seed is rejected because it is an invasive species no one wants, which gives shelter to birds that destroy crops. However, in the story, God wants what no one else wants. God wants the rejected. The otherwise unwelcome are made welcome, and the misbegotten find a home. The stories help create an image of the reign of God: we all live in solidarity. There is room for all.

Patience is tolerance and action. I need to learn to tolerate what I cannot change, especially differences in people, but I act to make things better when I can. A tiny bit can make a difference. Our role is to do the little things that make things better for all. The world is imperfect. I have to admit there is good and bad in me. God is a merciful judge, helping us bring out the good. We must work little by little through our faults and failings to live the reign of God.

The reign of God is not some big show. It is small acts of love, kindness, tolerance, and compassion that form a way of living by simple people who are filled with faith and come together to live the gospel and form community that makes a difference. God looks to the little things we do to change others and the world, one person, one kindness, one act of love at a time. That is how we live out patience, and how we will survive this pandemic.

Last Sunday, as I finished Mass at Mission Concepción, a parish member who had not been at the Mass came in very distraught. He told me his wife of fifty years had just died an hour before at their home. It was not COVID-related, as she had been sick for a year. He asked tearfully if I could pray with him and the family over her body. I followed him to his modest home and we spent some time in prayer and silence, amidst tears. I stayed just a few minutes, but he and the family were so grateful and more peaceful as I left. I was moved by their faith. God does much through our small efforts. I have learned that over and over.

Every time we hear or read the Scripture, we acknowledge our littleness before the God of patience and mercy. This virus seems to be raging out of control, and it is testing our patience profoundly. However, in so many ways, little things, small gestures and actions, can make a difference. A baby born in a little town called Bethlehem, in a small insignificant country far from the seat of power, changed the world. Patience means we are called to grow in small ways, even through a pandemic with all its restrictions. These ways can make a difference, and will help us to understand better what it means to live in the reign of God.

20

7/26/20 Seventeenth Sunday

The reign of God is like a buried treasure...

1 Kgs 3:5, 7-12; Rom 8:28-30; Matt 13:44-52

THIS PAST WEEK CONGRESSMAN John Lewis of Georgia passed away from cancer. He had worked with Dr Martin Luther King Jr throughout the civil rights struggles. He continued his fight for justice through a long career in Congress. As a young person he had to sacrifice so much for what he believed. He was among the first to integrate schools, soda counters, and stores. He suffered insults, spitting, harassment, violence, and physical injury. He made a difference because he believed strongly in what he was doing and was willing to sacrifice a lot to accomplish the goal of racial justice. He was not perfect. No one is. However, he showed us what it means to totally sacrifice our life so that all can live in dignity as God created us.

Two of the parables of Jesus in the gospel today challenge us to reflect on what is worth giving our lives for. Matthew tried to encourage his readers, who were suffering persecution for being Christian. They had found the pearl, they had found the treasure, and that treasure was the reign of God. Matthew had been sharing parables about what the reign of God was so the struggling early Christians would understand what a gift they had. They had received the most precious gift of all, faith, to be disciples of Jesus. That faith called them to live in the reign of God. Matthew was telling them they would need to be wise enough to recognize that it was worth everything they had, even their life, to nurture and keep it.

Jesus gives us stories of what people will do when they value something, namely, sell all they have. Many of his parables were exaggerated somewhat to make a point. He challenges us to decide what we will hang our lives on, what we will value, what will be the ultimate way we live, what will get us enthused. Sometimes we find that living according to these values requires sacrifice, for example, having less money, living a simpler life, experiencing more struggle, or encountering opposition; however, that is our call as followers of Jesus. Selling all we have means making the sacrifice, knowing that there is a higher good. Jesus calls us to put God and our sisters and brothers first. He connects this challenge with the judgment day when the good and the bad will be separated. Thus, the choice we make about values to hang our lives on is the choice by which we will be judged.

In these stories there is also a sense of urgency. If we don't seize the opportunity, it may pass us by. We are challenged to take a risk for something greater now. This seems to be happening with the continuing protests in our country around systemic racism. It needs to be addressed now. It can't wait any longer. The issue for the first Christians is the same for us today, namely, what to value in this world. What should be worth the most to us: money, possessions, power, prestige? Or is it a right relationship with God, which is demonstrated by how we treat others and our world?

In the first reading, King Solomon asks for the gift of an understanding heart to discern the difference between right and wrong. Notice he asks for an understanding heart, not an understanding mind. This was not analysis, but rather compassion. This was the treasure. This was the pearl of great price Solomon was seeking. However, God gives him the gift of understanding to know what is right, not necessarily what is wrong. Why? A right relationship with God and our neighbor is at the center of an understanding heart. That is what God is speaking about. When we do right by others, we do right by God.

A nationally published article[1] recently spoke about how the coronavirus pandemic was overwhelming the Rio Grande Valley of Texas, one of the poorest areas of our country. The vast majority of people there are Latino, with many serious health issues, such as diabetes and heart disease. They are more at risk for complications from the virus. The article spoke of a woman with the virus giving birth to a baby and not being

---

1. Dickerson, "Vulnerable Border Community Battles Virus."

able to hold the newborn for fear of transmitting the virus. More babies now are contracting the virus and some have died. That baby is her pearl and treasure, a gift from God. She wants to give everything she has for that gift, yet she will have to wait in faith until she overcomes the virus. She will need to sacrifice for her pearl, her treasure. She was willing to do it, but it hurt so much not to be able to be close to her newborn, the treasure she had carried inside her body for so long.

We also have the pearl of great price. God has given us life and has put us in a community with others. Do we appreciate it? God calls us to do right and to do it now. How do we live it, even if it means suffering and sacrifice? Today each of us must sacrifice repeatedly to fight the spread of the virus. We do it for ourselves and we do it for others. We stay at home as much as possible. We wear masks and practice social distancing, even though it is inconvenient. We sacrifice a little of our freedom so that all may live healthy lives and be the community God calls us to be.

St. Paul, in the Second Letter to the Romans, reflects on our call as he tells us that all things work for good for those who love God. In the midst of so much suffering and sickness today with this pandemic, can we focus on that call and believe that things will work for the good? What am I willing to do to make the good happen in my life and in my community? How will I help spread the reign of God?

What is really important for us today? There is a story John Lewis told about his childhood. His family raised chickens and he had to take care of them. He would preach to the chickens and they would actually look like they were paying attention, unlike Congress! He also shared that, unlike Congress, the chickens would then take action and produce something, namely, eggs! In John Lewis's life the highest priority for which he sacrificed his life was human rights for all, especially people of color. Constant action in this regard defined his life and actually brought him satisfaction and fulfillment.

This time of pandemic and of racial reckoning is challenging us to ask ourselves serious questions. What is our pearl of great price? The parable is really not so much about the sacrifice but about the great joy in finding what we discover—about ourselves, about our world, about others, and because of all those, about God.

21

8/2/20 Eighteenth Sunday

Give them something to eat yourselves.

Isa 55:1–3; Rom 8:35, 37–39; Matt 14:13–21

MANY CATHOLICS HAVE SAID they miss attending Mass during these months of the pandemic. They are fearful of assisting in person due to a health condition or simply because they feel afraid of being in a public space with others for an hour. Even though the parishes take every precaution to be safe with deep cleaning, mask requirements, and social distancing, some do not feel ready to return. Often what people say they miss the most is receiving holy communion. It is very frustrating for them. They are hungry for the real presence of Christ. That has made a huge difference for them for as long as they can remember.

Recently I was speaking to longtime friends, a San Antonio couple, who are retired and have medical conditions that make them very cautious about the coronavirus. They told me they are not ready to attend Mass yet. They feel the need to be very careful. Yet they very much miss receiving communion. They told me they decided to volunteer to be in the trials for one of the vaccines being developed for COVID. This is a way they feel they can help others during this pandemic. I was impressed. Even though they miss the Eucharist they are still fulfilling the work of being the body of Jesus for the world. They can be God's gift to others.

Today's story of the feeding of the 5,000 is repeated in one way or another six times in the gospels. It is the only miracle story told in every gospel, which means it is a key to understanding Jesus and his ministry. It shows that Jesus met the real physical needs of people. This was especially true in Jesus' many instances feeding people who were hungry. The huge number of people fed by Jesus' miracle is a sign of God's abundant mercy and love. The abundance is also seen in all the leftovers. God gives even more than what is needed. Jesus did not perform this miracle to impress, but to show the compassion of God for people.

The pandemic has caused feeding programs at schools to be closed or reduced greatly. Many low-income families have depended on them to give children at least some nutritious food every day. This has stressed the food banks and food pantries as they need to provide more food to make up the loss to the children. Many people have stepped forward, volunteering to assist in this feeding, reflecting the compassion of God and continuing Jesus' ministry.

The feeding stories in the gospels are also very clearly related to the gift of the Eucharist. Each has the same wording as at the Last Supper, when Jesus said the blessing, broke the bread, and gave it to the disciples. These same words are in the gospel today. Matthew wants us to see that Jesus' body and blood are real food and real drink, which nourish us and send us out on mission to do the work of Jesus. We see that the work of the church includes helping people meet their physical needs as Jesus did. We can see this not only in the food pantries at parishes and convents, but also the Catholic hospitals, nursing homes, and other centers caring for people. Jesus cured the sick and fed the hungry. The church followed his example from the beginning. Without many of these church actions, the impact on people at this time of COVID would be much worse.

Food was always seen as God's gift to people. God promises the people of Israel a land of milk and honey. Adam and Eve are given fruit trees in Eden. God provides food for Moses and the people for forty years in the desert. In the Gospel of Matthew, Jesus is the new Moses, who feeds people in the desert. Jesus, however, gives food that lasts forever.

In this part of the Gospel of Matthew, we move from parables about the reign of God to the church and what the disciples will build in their mission after the resurrection. John the Baptist's death causes Jesus to withdraw, and a new phase of his ministry begins, which emphasizes God's providence, and the healing of sin, sickness, and hunger. Jesus is beginning to be known because he cares about the physical as well as the spiritual needs of people.

The gospel story says Jesus was moved with pity for the people. Pity in this sense reflects more of a deep, gut-wrenching compassion for others. Jesus probably was already feeling deep sorrow and shock at the execution of John the Baptist, knowing that this was a prelude to his own passion. This deep compassion of Jesus ultimately inspired the apostles and should also inspire us.

In today's story, at first the apostles see a problem of hungry people and want to get rid of the problem. Jesus tells them, "you give them some food yourselves." They feel inadequate to the task since they only have a meager amount of food; but with Jesus, whatever we have will always be enough if we follow his commands. Jesus has spent the whole day, despite his grief at the loss of John the Baptist, ministering to the needs of others. Now he asks the disciples to do the same. They are to imitate his generosity and give all that they have, even though they feel they have very little to give.

Jesus did not multiply the loaves. There is nothing in the gospel that says that he did. Instead, he blesses, breaks, and gives the bread to the disciples. It was in the act of sharing on the part of the disciples that they found they had enough, and even more than enough. They fed the entire crowd until they were satisfied and had baskets of leftovers, to emphasize God's mercy and abundance. Miracles happen when we are generous, even when we feel we have little to give.

Bread is the sign of the Eucharist where we are fed. Also, the Eucharist is a challenge to help feed others. Matthew emphasizes that it is the disciples who bring the problem to Jesus, then offer the food, and then help distribute it. This shows the role of other ministers. This is part of the multiplier effect, when more people get involved. The loaves are multiplied in the act of distributing them. When we share what we have in the name of Jesus, no matter how little, it is multiplied. We all have something to give in service to others. Discipleship requires generous action on our part.

Some time ago I traveled to West Africa with Catholic Relief Services, the international relief agency of the United States Catholic Church. I saw beautiful, welcoming people everywhere we went. At the same time I learned that many, especially in the rural areas, live in extreme poverty and do not eat three meals a day; sometimes not even eating every day, but rather every other day. I was shocked to learn this, but glad that CRS was addressing hunger by helping the people develop better agricultural methods to feed themselves. This has been greatly complicated during the pandemic since so many vulnerable people live day-to-day. CRS, in our name, is responding to this need and developing new ways to help during these times. We are making a difference fulfilling Jesus' ministry of feeding people.

Every time we gather at Eucharist, we come together because we trust what Jesus said. We trust that he wants to give us what we need. We accept that belonging to this community means serving each other, not as problems, but as people we care about. Is that our reputation? Can we be trusted to be who we say we are?

Today's pandemic and its effects are testing us as never before. People have so many needs in this environment. In the midst of this struggle, we need to listen to Jesus' words, "you give them some food yourselves."

22

8/9/20 Nineteenth Sunday

It is I. Do not be afraid!

1 Kgs 19:9a, 11–13a; Rom 9:1–5; Matt 14:22–33

DID GOD SEND THIS virus as a punishment for our sins? Did God send this virus to make us return to church? Did God want to test us? Is there a message from God in this pandemic?

Many times, during this coronavirus, people have spoken about God testing us, or God sending these kinds of disasters to see how much faith we have, or to punish us for our sins, or to get us to return to church. This kind of thinking is common. It seems as if every time there is some unexplainable catastrophe, people tend to blame God. They find one line somewhere in the Bible to verify their theory and then tell everyone about what God means by this event. People have spoken about it since March when the pandemic hit our country.

Do not believe any of these theories.

Do not blame God for what is happening. Throughout human history these types of events have happened. We need to take responsibility to deal with them to protect everyone, especially the most vulnerable.

Don't blame God, but keep the faith and look for God in what is happening.

The gospel story today is the very famous moment of Jesus walking on the water in the midst of a storm that is threatening the lives of the disciples. Matthew is, in the section of his gospel about Jesus, establishing the church after his parables on the reign or kingdom of God. Matthew is speaking about the church and discipleship and the mission of the church after the resurrection. He was writing his gospel to first-generation Christians. The early church was going through persecutions and much suffering. They were having difficulty understanding why it was so hard to live their faith since it seemed the whole world was against them. They were asking where God was in the midst of their struggles, much as we are asking where God is in this pandemic today.

Jesus tells the apostles to get in the boat and sends them out while he goes to the mountain to pray. Mountains were traditional places of encounter with God because at their peaks they were seen as the intersection of heaven and earth. In the gospel the boat is a symbol for the church. The lake is symbolic of the world, with the boat of the church sometimes on calm waters and many times in the midst of storms. Even though the disciples do what Jesus asked them to do, they are in trouble on the lake. Living a faithful life does not guarantee that everything will go well. The church has seen that throughout its history. We see that right now.

The boat is being tossed by the waves and is in danger of sinking. The disciples are terrified for their lives, much like many of us today. Jesus comes to them in the midst of the storm. They can't see it is Jesus because they have no focus. In the midst of terror all they see is a ghost that brings more terror. Jesus calms them by repeating words similar to what God told Moses. "It is I" is like "I AM" (Matt 14:27, Exod 3:14). The next words, "Fear not," often accompanies theophanies or divine manifestations in Scriptures. We have nothing to fear if we maintain faith in God. We need to hear these words today as well. We are being called to have faith, not to be afraid, and to look for God in the midst of the storm.

Jesus is the Messiah who cares for people. The common understanding in the days of Jesus was that spirits were in the storms and sea, and only a more powerful spirit could control them. Throughout the gospels Jesus is always challenging the spirits and controling them, especially in the healing of illness. He had just prayed, so the power of prayer to get results from God was evident.

Peter recognizes the Lord. He starts with some faith and focus. He says, "If it is you," which is not complete faith, and then tries to go when Jesus calls. Peter starts well, like many of us, but then has doubts when he focuses on himself and the dangers that surround him. He lacks faith, and is rescued by Jesus, who is always there when we call. Jesus then chides them for their lack of faith. Matthew is telling his community that even Peter, who had seen many miracles, had doubts and floundered. If that is true, it is much more so for us.

Having faith does not mean we will not have doubts and flounder at times. We believe, take steps toward Jesus, then lose focus and concentrate on ourselves. It is then that we fail. Paul says God's power is made perfect in weakness. Matthew is the only gospel to use the word "doubt" since for him faith and doubt exist together in the life of the Christian. None of us is perfect. Often doubts enter our minds and thoughts. This is natural. Faith calls us to deal with doubt by focusing on Jesus and taking steps toward him.

Once Jesus is in the boat with them and the waters are calm, the apostles respond with a post-Easter declaration of faith, "You are the Son of God." This is the strongest statement of faith before the resurrection. They are now focused. Don't forget to focus on Jesus.

As I reflect on focus, I think of my own story with my eyesight. I wore glasses through high school and got contacts in my college years, which I used for over thirty years until I underwent Lasik surgery. I could see clearly for the first time since childhood without corrective lenses. Ten years later I began to develop double vision, which usually manifests in children but sometimes in adults. This required that I return to glasses, but after a few years was convinced by the eye doctor to try surgery to correct it. The operation involved clipping eye muscles and stitching the eye. The operation failed completely and I continue wearing glasses today. I was greatly disappointed. My focus never returned. I need help to see clearly and I need patience. It is really a small disability, but also a lesson. Today's gospel tells us we all need to accept God's help to see clearly.

Many moments and circumstances in our lives can give us a taste of listening to the whispering voice of God, as we saw in the first reading, where Elijah experienced God in the whispering of the wind. We need to take the time to do this. Much of our life is spent in the whispering wind, the quiet, ongoing, everyday moments where we need to recognize God is present. If we take time to listen to God in the day-to-day events of our lives, it will help us when we experience difficulties.

Listen to God in the quiet, but don't forget that God also comes in the midst of the storm. We are in that storm now. We are afraid. We think only of ourselves. We struggle with others about what we should all do. It is a serious time that is affecting all of us. Don't blame God for the storm. God did not cause the virus. However, this is the time to look for God in the storm, focus on God and walk in that direction. We will then realize Jesus is really in the boat with us.

23

8/16/20 Twentieth Sunday

Woman, you have great faith!

Isa 56:1, 6–7; Rom 11:13–15, 29–32; Matt 15: 21–28

MY GRANDMOTHER, SALOME CHAPA de Vela, was a woman of exceptional character. Born in 1877 on a *rancho* in the lower Rio Grande Valley, she married and had ten children, one of whom died as an infant. The family left the valley to seek a better life on the Texas coast in Port Lavaca, an ethnically and racially mixed town. My mother told me that one Sunday, at Mass, the priest, under pressure from some of the Anglo members, announced that in the future the Anglos would sit on one side of the church and the Mexicans on the other. My grandmother had suffered discrimination and prejudice in the valley all her life. She was a devout Catholic who had had hosted many priests to her home for dinner for years. She immediately confronted the pastor and said her family would not return to church until all were treated equally. He backed down.

The gospel today speaks of another forceful woman who suffered discrimination and who also caused a man to change his mind. The Canaanite woman was a woman in a male-dominated society, as well as a gentile in Jewish territory, two strikes against her. She has a "troubled" daughter and asks Jesus to cure her. The disciples want to get rid of her, reflecting the then-common prejudice against non-Jews and women. She knows Jesus can heal her daughter, as Matthew wants to emphasize that not one but two women are involved. She recognizes Jesus as the Davidic Messiah, a title not given him until his entry to Jerusalem, and a title rejected by the Pharisees. The title "Son of David" would have recalled

the Jewish tradition that kings were to act as God would act, caring especially for widows, orphans, and foreigners, as well as the natural creation,
which belonged to God as its Creator. Her declaration would have been
amazing to a Jewish audience, Matthew's focus indeed.

Jesus at first ignores her and then even insults her. He was showing
himself to be a man of his time. Matthew is writing for a Jewish audience
and would have set up the scene so they would understand the putdown
but then be more impressed with her faith. They would have remembered
great women of Scripture, like Deborah, Judith, and Esther. The woman
outdoes Jesus in the verbal spar and he welcomes her as a disciple.

The issue for the early Jewish Christians was: Can a pagan circum-
vent the law and go directly to Christ? The woman was simply asking that
the blessings which were overflowing could go also to her. She is lauded
for her faith. The phrase Jesus used to describe her, someone with "great
faith," is only used in Matthew. She was undaunted and persistent even
when initially rebuffed by a detached Jesus. She refused to give up. Her
desperation overcame her human pride. Her sense of humor helped as
well, when she said even dogs, which Jesus had inferred she was, can get
the scraps from the table. Often humor brings relief, joy, and happiness
and makes bitter medicine palatable. Self-deprecating humor can break
through barriers between people and help bring them together. We have
seen many instances of this type of humor in cartoons, YouTube videos,
and other places during the pandemic. These have helped greatly to re-
lieve some of our stress. Humor can build relationships and help form
community. We all need to use more of it these days.

The woman took the initiative and was persistent, much like Mary,
Jesus' mother. At the wedding in Cana it also seemed she was rebuffed by
Jesus when the hosts ran out of wine, but Jesus ultimately did what she
wanted. Her last words in Scripture, "Do whatever he tells you" (John
2:5), are found in that story and are important ones from Mary to all of
us. Both women had a faith that was strong, unlike Peter last week on the
water when Jesus told him how little faith he had. Through her faith, the
gentile woman insists the barriers separating her from Israel are not im-
pregnable. Prejudice and discrimination do not have the last word. Faith
does. Another lesson for today!

This story was around the issue of table fellowship, to which, for
Jesus, all are welcome. The woman insisted even the dogs are welcome
around the table. The early Jewish Christians learned that they must

invite and share eucharistic table fellowship with those who were different from them. The table was where things happened.

There are several examples of other persistent women in the gospels: one looking for the lost coin, one demanding justice from a judge, and another who touched the garment of Jesus, which was forbidden because she was unclean (Luke 15:8, 18:1–8; Mark 5:21–34). These showed women breaking rules because of something greater. They had to get what they needed and showed faith and persistence in doing so.

There is another story about my grandmother that speaks to the gospel today. I call her the first Hispanic feminist, perhaps even the first feminist! At the age of fifty, with nine children ages five to twenty-five, she lost her husband to a heart attack, causing huge stress for the family just as the Great Depression was about to begin. She managed to send four of her daughters to the University of Texas in the 1930s, where it had almost no Hispanics, much less Hispanic women. She had her sons stay home and work so she could support the women of the family in college. She told her daughters that if what happened to her, becoming a widow with family at a young age, ever happened to them, she wanted them to have a career so they could support themselves. Persistence and faith. An amazing legacy!

During this time of pandemic, we each need to reflect on the twin virtues of persistence and faith. We are in this for the long haul. We are so tired of the lockdowns, the masks, the social distancing, and all the protocols involved with staying healthy and also safeguarding others with whom we come in contact. Persistence means we will continue doing what is necessary to keep ourselves and others in the community safe and healthy, even when it means self-sacrifice. We must dig deep, looking for the faith that God gives us, so we can see the other who shares the same table with us and treat them as family. The virus has killed people of color at a disproportionately higher rate than others in our country. How can our faith call us to work so all have access to what they need in order to live healthy lives?

More than 80 percent of the health care professionals caring for COVID patients today are women.[1] Women lead health departments across the nation. In San Antonio, the Director of Metro Health, as well as her assistant, are women; the previous director was also a woman. They are all going to extraordinary lengths to care for people affected by the

---

1. Day and Christnacht, "Women Hold 76% of All Health Care Jobs," para. 1.

pandemic, at great risk to themselves. The care a woman gives is different from that of a man, as we know from our mothers and fathers. Those differences are complementary and important in the healing process.

There are women of persistence and great faith throughout the Scriptures, and all around us today; maybe even a few men too!

24

8/23/20 Twenty-first Sunday

You are the Messiah.

Isa 22:19–23; Rom 11:33–36; Matt 16:13–20

ARE YOU COVID-19-POSITIVE? Do you know anyone who is? "Positive" has become almost an identity today. It marks someone, and there is a protocol for that person from there on: stay home in quarantine or go to the hospital if symptoms are severe. We cannot get near a positive person; we avoid them, even relatives or close friends. This virus is too contagious. When someone has recovered from COVID, they are still identified as carrying antibodies. We look at them with some caution. It is still part of who they are in this new world of ours.

Identity is a big part of today's gospel. Peter's profession of faith is possible only by divine revelation: Peter names Jesus as the Messiah; Jesus names Peter as the rock of the church. Identity for both of them emerges. For the first time Peter is named as the leader and his importance will grow from here. This is key as Matthew convinces his audience—the Jewish Christians—of Peter's authority and how Peter used his authority to accept gentiles in the church. This is something they would have been hesitant about. Jesus makes it clear his church is built on the believing Peter. It is also clear that Peter's authority, and that of all the apostles, is one of service, of laying down their lives for others. Adding to this, we see later the resurrected Jesus saying to Peter, "Feed my sheep" (John 21:17).

This story comes in the middle of Matthew's Gospel, and from here on Jesus instructs the disciples about his death and resurrection. We heard a few weeks ago that Jesus begins to set up the church. Now the founding of the church gets more detailed in that it will be born in the paschal mystery, namely, the passion, death, and resurrection of Jesus. It is not the first time we hear the term "Christ," but it is the first time we hear "Messiah." Immediately following this exchange, it is the first time the title is tied to suffering. From this time forward Jesus teaches that suffering is part of being the Messiah and following the Messiah. The disciples do not get the connection until after the resurrection.

The identity of the people of Jesus' time was not unique, but always in relation to the groups in which they were embedded: family, clan, nation, religion. Seventy years ago, people in Chicago would not be asked what neighborhood they lived in, but what parish they belonged to. I did community organizing with many others on the west side of San Antonio in the late seventies. Good changes improved the lives of the people there. Community organizing has a principle: perceptions of others help to shape a person's identity in the eyes of others and can get things done. It is not necessarily about who you are; it is about who others think you are. If City Hall thinks you have a lot of people and power, then you do and that forces them to deal with you. Politicians' campaigns follow this principle by shaping and branding their identities to influence how people think of them.

Jesus begins this exchange of identity when he asks the disciples who others say he is. Then he narrows it down and asks his disciples the same question. Peter responds with a profession of faith. Jesus makes Peter the rock, not by his own strength but by the faith of the Holy Spirit. Peter will have to grow a lot to be that rock of the church. He will waffle, reject a suffering Messiah, deny Jesus, repent, and weep until finally confronted by Jesus after the resurrection with a simple question, "Do you love me?" (John 21:16). Jesus does not demand an apology, or that Peter get down on his knees, just digging deep into the heart for the love which God places in each of us. Maybe that was a good example of how to bind and loose.

Jesus gives Peter the keys to the kingdom, which refers back to Isaiah, where the keeper of the key to David's house is mentioned in the first reading. Peter's faith is based on the Father's revelation. This is the only gospel to give Peter such broad power and authority, which is where the church bases the tradition of the pope's authority.

The gospel ends with Jesus telling the disciples not to tell anyone about his being the Messiah. Good advice, as the disciples were not ready to tell others about the Messiah, as we shall see next week. They just did not understand at this point what being the Messiah meant.

We do not grasp yet the impact of this virus. We are still learning. How it affects us and how it is cured, much less avoided, is not completely known. Even though that is true, if you have recovered from the virus, medical experts say you can donate plasma that can help very sick COVID patients. You can literally give life. Your identity as a recovered positive patient will truly be positive as you help heal others.

It was only when Peter and the disciples fully understood that they would need to be willing to imitate Jesus' giving of his life that they were then in a position to preach about Jesus and what he was all about. They ultimately gave their lives, as did many more Christians throughout history. That has been key to the preaching of the gospel and converting others to Jesus.

The church is built on rock, a sure foundation against the powers of evil. Peter is given authority, is the leader, the first mentioned in any list, the one told by Jesus in John's Gospel to "Feed my sheep" (John 21:17). This was the new teaching authority, taken away from the Pharisees. This was important for Matthew's Jewish Christian readers since later Peter makes the controversial decision to extend baptism to gentiles.

So, the question is: Who am I? A person of faith, first and foremost? A person that understands what it means to carry a cross? A person who is called by our faith now to make the personal and communal sacrifices that are needed to fight this pandemic and help heal those affected? That must be our identity. That is how we name ourselves today. How can we also call forth the identity of each other as followers of Jesus in the midst of what challenges us?

Your Christian identity cannot come from what you try to do on Twitter or Facebook, or from who people think you are. It can only come as a divine revelation, a gift from God, that you accept with faith and that you give through suffering and carrying a cross. Your identity, if you want it to be, ultimately comes from God, and God gives you the strength to live it every day you accept his gift of faith.

25

8/30/20 Twenty-second Sunday

If a man wishes to follow me he must...take up his cross...

Jer 20:7–9; Rom 12:1–2; Matt 16:21–27

IT HAS BEEN MORE than five months since we first began to take measures to deal with the coronavirus. The instructions and precautions continue in our lives. When we started in March, it was not clear how long the pandemic would last or how we could cope with it or overcome it. Many thought it would last a few months, but now it will be with us for at least a year or even longer. It has been hard to make the necessary adjustments in our lives. There have been complaints and some resistance to the requirements imposed by government and health officials. We have been told all these sacrifices are necessary to control and defeat the pandemic. In fact, here in San Antonio, the numbers are decreasing steadily every day. It is for the good of all that we carry this burden together.

Big sacrifices are the point in today's gospel. Last Sunday, Peter, inspired by the Holy Spirit, made a profession of faith in Jesus as the Messiah. Jesus acknowledged Peter's faith and named him the rock of the church based on that faith. So now it seems everything is set up for the church.

Not so fast!

In Matthew's Gospel today, which follows last week's, Jesus begins to lay out what being the Messiah means, and it is not what Peter and the disciples think it is. This gospel passage begins with "From that time on . . ." marking a turning point. Peter's declaration of faith in the Messiah was a high point in the gospel story, coming in the middle of Matthew's narration. Jesus then immediately begins to let the disciples know what that profession of faith really means. He begins to talk about going to Jerusalem, suffering, being killed, and on the third day being raised. They heard clearly the suffering and death part but seemed to miss or not understand the being raised part.

Peter rejects the notion of the suffering of the Messiah since he believes the Messiah is supposed to be a royal king, a warrior conqueror, immune from suffering and basking in glory. Jesus talks about a suffering servant, one who accepts the cross. It is the paschal mystery—his passion, death, and resurrection—that Jesus makes the foundation for the authority that he bestows on Peter and the foundation of his church.

Just a few lines earlier, Peter and Jesus were naming each other Messiah and rock of the church. Now Jesus has a new name for Peter, "Satan." He calls Peter an obstacle and tells him to get in line ("get behind me, Satan"). A pretty drastic turnaround!

Why bring Satan into this? Matthew wants us to remember the temptation in the desert, where Satan tries leading Jesus away from the cross to the notion of the triumphant king by offering him all the kingdoms of the world if he worships him, which Jesus rejects. The tempter has returned in the person of Peter and Jesus quickly rejects the temptation, just as in the desert. It is not Jesus who needs to change his way of thinking of himself. Peter needs a conversion in his thinking about the Messiah. He has a ways to go. "Get behind me" means get in line and learn more. You are not ready to lead. That is why you cannot tell anyone about the Messiah. Peter is still called to be a follower, but he is not ready to be a leader.

In a way it is hard to blame Peter. He is like us. Who wants to suffer when there is an easier way? We are always taking the path of least resistance. That is just how we are. However, the suffering of Jesus is not just pain; rather, it is redemptive suffering. It transforms the one who suffers and those around him or her. Jesus' life was not taken from him; he gave it. When we embrace the sufferings, sacrifices, and struggles, especially now with the pandemic, knowing that our experience will help others, and in the process transform us as well, then everything changes.

There are no easy ways to follow Jesus. Too much is at stake. It is not enough to confess faith in Jesus. This is about living our lives, following and imitating him. Learn about the power of suffering for the sake of the good of others. That is what it means to take up the cross and follow him.

There are no easy ways out of this pandemic for any of us. We wish we could ignore it. Some try to, and find out the hard way. An example is a local young person who recently died of COVID after attending a "COVID party," thinking it was all a big hoax. There are more examples of those who refuse to wear masks or follow the other protocols to help stave off the threat of the virus because it infringes upon their freedom. Following Jesus means caring for self and others, which means taking on suffering for the sake of others as Jesus showed us. We are certainly seeing that played out during the pandemic. Not just those with the illness are suffering. The caregivers, the workers harvesting food or packing meat, the delivery people, the staff at grocery and drugstores, the food bank volunteers, and so many more are all going above and beyond, working long hours, often risking their own health for the sake of others. It is costing them a lot, and often they are not appreciated or thanked for their service. Our sacrifices can help their sacrifices.

Jesus calls Peter the rock to emphasize his role of strengthening the church. Peter can and will grow, albeit as he stumbles forward. Those who exercise authority will suffer like the master. This authority of Peter is to serve by laying down his life for others. Cross-bearing and self-denial are integral to following Jesus. To carry a cross is not just to endure suffering, but also humiliation, persecution, ridicule, and hostility. The reality of the world is that we suffer. How we suffer as part of following Jesus, as part of sacrificing for others, distinguishes the follower of Jesus from others.

Pope Francis, the successor to St. Peter, is constantly drawing our attention to those who suffer throughout the world, especially the migrants and refugees, who are still traveling at great risk to themselves and their families. The pope asks us to act in faith to help those who suffer the most. He does not give us faith but confirms what God has already given. He just asks us to work and develop what we have and it will be enough.

Every Mass and prayer begins with the sign of the cross, indicating our willingness to carry it. The word "catholic" means "universal," which is why we are called to help people both near us and all over the world, whether we ever see them or not, and regardless of if they are like us or not, or if they ever thank us.

Jesus puts a cross in front of us and asks us to get in line. This is the time to just do it.

26

9/6/20 Twenty-third Sunday

Where two or three are gathered in my name . . .

Ezek 33:7–9; Rom 13:8–10; Matt 18:15–20

THE CORONAVIRUS PANDEMIC HAS affected us all in various ways. It has
limited much of what we can do, but it does not seem to limit what we
can say, and many have said a lot. There have been arguments about the
restrictions placed on us, but the more serious ones have been on the
science side of the virus. It is more serious because we need to work
together to defeat the virus. Even though what the health experts say now
may change in a month or two, they speak from the best information
they have at the moment. This is a novel coronavirus, which means it
is new, never having infected the world before, and therefore it is not
completely understood. Science is constantly learning more about it
every day. It already seems clear that not following the medical officials
earlier may have caused the higher infection rates in various countries.
What is abundantly clear is that our relationships and communication,
our coming together, will be key to winning this battle.

The gospel today is from the eighteenth chapter of Matthew, which is
called the Community Discourse, a collection of Jesus' sayings that form
a kind of rule of life for the Christian community and show how to guide
relationships. This section speaks about striving to come together after
conflict, a situation which often occurs in the community, and also in the
church. Even though the passage says the brother offended you, it really
means the problem is with the community. Matthew, writing for Jewish
Christians, had to deal with conflicts between his community and gentile

Christians. Jews had been taught from childhood not to associate with or trust non-Jews, namely, gentiles. Yet, the church was welcoming gentiles into the faith as we have learned the last few weeks in the readings. This caused tension for Jewish Christians. The two groups were divided and often in serious disagreement with each other. This was a struggle of inculturation similar to today's experience with different ethnic groups and races trying to live together. In his gospel, Matthew tells his readers what Jesus taught about bringing different people and groups together in the community. He suggests a process for them to reconcile, especially where there was conflict which involved the larger community.

Here is what Jesus describes as a process of reconciliation. First, acknowledge the wrong and ask for forgiveness. This may not be an easy step, since often neither side feels it is in the wrong. The gospel, however, indicates someone has been hurt by the other, so it is they who point out their hurt. We do not need to accuse the other, condemn the other, or insist that the other grovel before us. What this process calls for is to simply tell the other, "I have been hurt by your words or actions." Notice how I place my hurt in the first person. I have been hurt. I do not condemn the other, but simply ask the other to understand my pain and to invite the other to acknowledge that his or her actions brought about my pain. The other may not even know that what he or she did caused hurt until I point it out. No one else is involved at this point. This is a private moment which we want to keep private between the two of us. It can be a beautiful, intimate experience of reconciliation if I can bring myself to truly hear the pain of the other and respond to that pain in order to heal our relationship.

Second, put it in the context of witness and prayer. The gospel describes the second step as bringing another person into the process as a witness. One way to look at the witness is typically what happens in a court. However, remember: a witness was what the disciples were called to be, witnesses of the life, death, and resurrection of Jesus, and witnesses to what he did and said. To witness to Jesus is to act like Jesus, who said from the cross, "Father, forgive them . . ." (Luke 23:34). Some conflicts may not have a clear resolution and are only reconciled in prayer, even when the offender resists. Prayer allows us to slowly heal the hurt by not holding it against the other. As Paul says in today's passage to the Romans, "Love never wrongs the neighbor." Time helps. God listens. God heals.

Third, the process is referred to the community of the church. This does not mean that I get people to intimidate the offender, but that through the community I let go of anger and the desire for revenge or to cause hurt, so that I can move on as a follower of Jesus. Heaven will affirm what is loosed on earth, so that the offense does not control the relationship. Often an offense controls how we see each other for years. That is called a grudge, which hinders any possibility for coming together. Only forgiveness and the desire to come together will help overcome this. Forgive, even when the other does not ask for forgiveness. Begin the process, knowing that, whatever happens, you have already begun to forgive and will work on it daily. The whole process is highly personal and highly communitarian. It is also an act of faith.

However, even if the process described does not work, we never give up. Jesus says, "Treat him as a gentile or tax collector," which does not mean to reject the other, but rather treat the person as someone to be converted. Matthew himself was a tax collector. He had been converted by the call of Jesus to stop being controlled by money and its impact on a person. He had his priorities straight.

During the recent Hurricane Laura, we saw several thousand people evacuate East Texas to seek refuge in San Antonio. The reception they received was automatic. They were welcomed despite our ongoing struggle with the coronavirus, unemployment, food insecurity, racial tension, and other issues. Our leaders could have said we can't help anyone else, but they opened their doors and our community stretched even more to assist people in need. This also happened fifteen years ago with Hurricane Katrina, as San Antonio became a national model for how we received and cared for the refugees from New Orleans.

Generous love should always be first, which also means giving forgiveness is automatic. Resolve the conflict by your love, by your reconciling attitude. If all else fails, pray. We pray, not to change the other, but to change ourselves to take on the mind and heart of Jesus.

We have many conflicts in our community, our country, and our world today. Some are current, like the elections we are now facing to determine the direction of our country, elections which are causing heated arguments and, at times, leading people to say offensive things about each other. I heard one partisan refer to the other party as evil. We can never get to that point. Discussions and disagreements are healthy; condemnation and judgment are not. Some conflicts have their origins many years in the past, such as the calls for racial reckoning due to the hundreds of years of racism in our society. There are conflicts also in the church. We have much to do.

The first and most important social teaching of the church is the dignity of the human person. Each person is a child of God and as such deserves to be treated with dignity even when that person does not seem to treat others that way. We are called to begin the process of reconciling or forgiving. We never give up. Only when someone takes the first step and forgives can the process of coming together begin. There is always hope. This gospel assures us the role of the Christian community is to support us if we start.

At the end of this gospel passage, Jesus tells us if two or more join in prayer, God will listen and Jesus will be in their midst.

Sounds like a good game plan.

27

9/13/20 Twenty-fourth Sunday

. . . unless each of you forgive his brother from his heart.

Sir 27:30—28:7; Rom 14:7–9; Matt 18:21–35

POPE FRANCIS HAS SPOKEN at various times about the coronavirus pandemic, asking Catholics and all people to respond to the crisis as one family. If we do, he says, we will work on eliminating the inequities and injustices that undermine the health of the entire globe. His fear is that we may "be struck by an even worse virus, that of selfish indifference. This is a virus spread by the thought that life is better if it is better for me, and that everything will be fine if it is fine for me."[1]

How do we truly think of ourselves as one human family? The first reading and the gospel today speak about how mercy and forgiveness operate in our lives, in the community of humans, and in our relationship with God. Pope Francis declared a Jubilee Year of mercy a few years ago to focus on how indifference prevents us from being that one human family.

Can mercy help us overcome selfish indifference? The first reading from the book of Sirach deals with relationships, the heart of what makes us human. The difference between a life of anxiety, depression, and violence versus a happy, peace-filled, meaningful journey through life is what is discussed. Jesus always talked about his relationship with the Father and invited us into that relationship. That relationship is the key to fulfillment in life.

---

1. Catholic News Agency, "Beware of the Virus of 'Selfish Indifference,'" para. 3.

This section of Matthew today is called the sermon on the church. Matthew wants to teach his community how they should relate to Christ and each other. Sirach is similar to what Jesus says in the gospel today about mercy: how can you expect mercy from God if you do not know how to show mercy to others? For the writer of Sirach, as well as for Jesus, our mercy must always be seen in the light of God's mercy. God is merciful no matter what. That mercy lasts for our lifetime. That mercy is also overwhelming. It is the mercy that forgives often, seventy times seven times. Seven is a perfect number in Jewish thought, so multiplying it is limitless. Therefore, mercy and forgiveness must be offered always, even without waiting for the other to ask.

The parable Jesus shares tells us that to practice mercy requires transformation. To understand the power of the parable, imagine yourself a listener before Jesus and enter into the moment. The listeners were in for a whiplash experience with this story. Mercy was supposed to change the other and yet it did not.

Jews listening to this would have deduced that the story was about gentiles, not them. Remember that Jews were taught the gentiles were not good people. The king and the servants were gentiles. What was forgiven? A huge impossible amount: 10,000 talents, or 60 million days' wages, or more than 230,000 years of work! This, of course, was a deliberate exaggeration to make a point. Ten thousand was the highest figure in arithmetic for the people of Jesus' time. A Jew would never have been trusted to manage that large an account. So, the listeners would have seen the first servant as a member of the rich class, who were rich at the expense of the poor. As the pope said, "Life is better if it is better for me." The thinking of the time was there was only so much to go around and if you had more, then I had to have less. One of the issues in the racial reckoning we are experiencing in this country is that, historically, every time the black community began to get ahead economically, something happened to take that away. The Tulsa race massacre of 1921 is one of many examples.

Those listening to Jesus' parable will have eagerly waited to hear about the punishment for the king's servant, this terrible gentile. The listener places himself or herself in a position of superiority early in the story. Also, selling the wife and children into slavery is forbidden in Jewish law, so the listener is now feeling even more superior criticizing the gentiles. When the king unexpectedly forgives, the superiority of the listener is taken away. There is unbelief that such generous mercy could happen. This will have created a dilemma for the listener, namely, how to think about nonpunishment and mercy.

The second scene in the parable is a vast contrast. There is little debt, but the forgiven servant, now in a position of power, shows only ruthlessness and violence. Both are servants. However, he seizes the other by the throat and threatens him. There is not a king/servant relationship as in the first scene, so there is more equivalence between the two, like many of our own relationships. Now the listener to the parable is judging gentiles as being unforgiving and identifies with the second servant. The king and the listeners are in the same camp. The servant must be punished and it seems as if it will be forever. Think hell. Punishment is now as exaggerated as the original debt. Do you feel how the listener is being tossed around back and forth?

Jesus' story would have shocked the listeners, which was true for many of his parables. This story moved them to understand the unexpected and astonishing possibilities of living in the reign of God. The big shock would have been in the king withdrawing the mercy. If this can happen, then who is safe? However, the listeners are complicit in this, as they demanded punishment. So now, the listener is in the uncomfortable position of being unmerciful, which means the listener is also at risk of not being forgiven. No one is innocent, because the fellow servants and listeners demanded vengeance, no better than the one they reported. They all failed to show mercy.

The parable is a warning that forgiveness can be forfeited. The evil of the final punishment makes the listener and fellow servants complicit, not for intentional evil, but for systemic evil. The problem about systemic racism is that it is so much a part of the system at all levels that none of us feels we intend it or are responsible for it. This is why it continues.

Matthew knows his Christian community is not perfect. It had its prejudices and, at times, ruthlessness and arrogance. Matthew wants a community of care, tolerance, and kindheartedness. We are all in need of mercy, and thus must carry Christ's unconditional love and forgiveness to all. Seven times seventy means always and forever. In the gospel the Jewish listener has to admit he/she is not morally superior to others. We need to admit the same. We are all sinners in need of God's mercy. Matthew's question, which he wants us to ask ourselves as we read his gospel, then arises: Where do I go from here? What do I do about this?

God's mercy is infinite. If we trust in God's grace, then our mercy can also be infinite. The first surprise in the story was the king's forgiveness. His mercy was overwhelming.

It is clear from the readings that we are called to forgive, not only when it is convenient or to our advantage, or when we need something from the other. We are called to an extraordinary mercy, a forgiveness of the heart. It is the heart that changes us and others. That is transformation.

The coronavirus has exposed many things that are not right with our community and with the world. I think the pope is asking us to hear a call to reconciliation in this difficult time, to show mercy from the heart. This does not mean we condone bad actions, nor does it mean we forget. It does mean we are committed to seeing all as sisters and brothers, children of the same Father who created all in God's image.

Many of us can remember when Pope John Paul II visited his would-be assassin and forgave him. It is not for us to judge; we leave that to God! The readings today focus clearly on God's mercy. Now to do it ourselves.

28

9/20/20 Twenty-fifth Sunday

...are you envious because I am generous?

Isa 55:6-9; Phil 1:20c-24, 27a; Matt 20:1-16a

IS THIS WORLD FAIR? We can point to so much that says it is not.

The coronavirus affects all people, rich and poor, every race, every ethnic group, young and old, every country, health insurance or none. In many cases it makes a crisis worse. An article I read last Sunday spoke about another way the virus kills people in the developing world: hunger. Millions live day-to-day on a meager income, namely, what they can earn that day. Millions have lost their ability to even do that, now earning maybe a dollar a day. Their children are dying of hunger.

When I worked with Catholic Relief Services, I visited West Africa, South Asia, the Middle East, and Central America, and saw the struggles of people having enough to eat. I witnessed people living on the margins. I also witnessed the great work of CRS representing us in those areas and serving those most in need. I have been a CRS donor since then. For the most vulnerable in communities where health systems are strained, the pandemic has massively disrupted their stability, income, safety, and access to food. The impacts of the pandemic on millions of refugees and people displaced due to circumstances beyond their control has also been devastating.

It all seems so unfair. Why was I born here and not there? How can I make things fairer for everyone?

In the gospel parable today, things also seem unfair. The laborers hired last and working only one hour in the vineyard get paid as much as those hired first who worked all day. The owner says, "Am I not free to do with my money what I want?" This is a lesson in God's generosity. It makes no sense for us until we see things as God sees them.

In the parable, the first workers were promised a day's wage, which was a normal payment for one day's work, but the rest were just told they would get what was right. For the Jew, since the time of the covenant with God and Moses, to be righteous in the sight of God was to be in right relationship with God and others, with that relationship especially based on practicing charity. The discussion with those hired first included giving what was "right and just." The first workers were treated fairly, while the others were treated generously. We are reminded of the sayings of Jesus, "The last shall be first" and "My ways are not your ways," which is in the first reading. This is the God of generosity, a model for us all.

We don't ever understand God fully, but we are called to imitate God's generosity and mercy. God shows us that all are treated equally, even those who come late. This is a missionary story, a welcome to all, no matter who they are or how slow or late they have been to come. Those who have served long and faithfully are treated justly, while those who came late are treated generously. The main thing that matters is that one is called. The attitude to the call is what is asked for here.

In my experience as a priest, I have come to the conclusion that to live a happy life we only need to do two things. The first is to always recognize what God has done for us and respond in gratitude. That struck me after witnessing the poorest people on the planet. We must live lives of thanksgiving. If we are truly thankful, then we must imitate God's generosity for us by being generous toward others, especially those most in need. To be thankful and generous is to be happy. A happy life is that simple.

This part of Matthew's Gospel, as we have noted the last few weeks, is talking about the community of the church. The vineyard is a symbol for the reign of God, which the church announces in word and deed. Today's reading says that the church is a community that includes even those who come late. It is significant that this parable is bracketed by Jesus repeating his saying, "The last shall be first and the first last," both right before and right after the story. The parable is a commentary on this saying.

This parable shocked people since they heard the opposite of what they thought they would hear. This is a missionary story, a welcome to all. The church is called to be like this. Matthew's community was mainly

Jewish Christians who resented the gentiles coming into the faith. In their mind, these were the latecomers to the faith. They felt the foreigners did not deserve the same privileges. Matthew was setting them straight. Earlier in the gospel Jesus tells us to forgive unlimited times. Jesus also speaks in Luke of the one lost sheep over the ninety-nine, the lost coin, and the lost son (Luke 15). God is generous in ways we are not. God looks for ways to be generous. Do we? God's grace is gift. Can we accept that God is that way? Or will we say, "That is not fair; I was here first."

Jesus was always criticized by the Pharisees for consorting with sinners. Yet over and over he speaks of God searching for the lost. He always forgave those who asked without condemning them. Pope Francis was criticized in his first Holy Thursday as pope for washing the feet of juveniles in prison, including Muslims, rather than twelve seminarians in St. Peter's, yet his action most closely follows this gospel story.

Matthew is trying to help the Jewish Christians, who believed they were first to come to the faith, to welcome the late-comers, the gentile Christians, those so different from them. Who would it be today? Are we called to respond to the immigrant, the refugee, the person of color, the vulnerable poor in Africa, Central America, or Asia?

This story is not about paying fair wages. It is about heaven as a gift, and that God gives it to whomever God wants, even if they don't measure up to our standards. That does not mean that we can do anything we want and expect a deathbed conversion. We may not get that chance. But it does mean that God's ways are not our ways and we need to imitate God's generosity. We need to admit that we expect God to be generous with us, but then we ourselves practice mere justice in dealing with others.

We cannot earn grace; it is a gift. When we realize what we have been given, the best response is to share it. Bill Gates Sr. died this past week. He believed that it was not right for people to pass on their wealth without returning anything to the American system that helped them create that wealth, as well as to those in need in the world. The Gates Foundation he managed for his son, daughter-in-law, and himself has given 50 billion dollars to noteworthy causes, has reduced the effects of malaria, and provided vaccines, better nutrition, sanitation, clean water, and much more in developing countries. I myself saw some of the results on my various overseas trips with CRS.

You don't have to give billions, obviously, but you do have to give. I remember a *viejita* (elderly woman) at San Fernando faithfully giving us one dollar a week, even as her only income was a few hundred dollars a month from Social Security.

The church is church when it is in mission to others. As missionary disciples, we are called to respond to the urgent needs of those who face hunger, malnutrition, and other tragedies during this global crisis, whether they are in line at the local food pantry or in the African bush. As Archbishop of Buenos Aires, Pope Francis would spend his free days visiting families in the poorest slums of the city. What an example!

So many, through no fault of their own, were born where their opportunity to live a dignified life is close to impossible without outside support. We were born with many opportunities to achieve what we have and to get where we have gotten in our lives. Recognizing that and giving thanks by giving is our call to imitate God's generosity.

The world may not be fair, but we can help make it more right.

29

9/27/20 Twenty-sixth Sunday

...tax collectors and prostitutes are entering the kingdom of God before you.

Ezek 18:25-28; Phil 2:1-11; Matt 21:28-32

I WAS READING A story of a COVID denier who threw a party in June for his family, with none using masks or following any other protocols since he convinced them there was no virus. Within a few weeks the entire group that attended was sick and had begun to spread it to others. Several deaths followed. He himself slowly recovered from a long and painful infection. He not only regretted his actions but then became an apostle for convincing other deniers of the reality of the virus and the urgent need to follow all precautions. He published his story, urging people to make the necessary sacrifices now and stay the course. He was going to do what he could to convince everyone to stem the tide and thus spare others the suffering that he and his family had experienced.

There is a difference between a change of mind and a change of heart. I can be convinced logically that my thinking or my position is not correct and begin to change that for myself. However, to change the heart is more than that. It is deeper and involves thinking and acting not only for myself but for others as well. It involves an attitude of charity, of giving or sacrificing for the greater good. It is really to ask myself: What does God want?

The gospel parable takes place in a vineyard like last week. The vineyard is an Old Testament symbol of God's people, Israel, and also refers to the reign of God. It is about using the vineyard for the place where I can live a changed life, as I harvest grapes that will also change into something that gives pleasure to others. We are not talking about getting drunk; rather, we refer to starting anew, always at God's invitation. God brings a vine out of Egypt to start God's people anew in the promised land, just like cuttings were brought from Italy and France to California to begin anew in making wine. Noah is the first to plant a vineyard after the flood, reestablishing the people and starting humanity all over. There is always a chance to change, to start again in the reign of God.

At the same time there are warnings throughout the Hebrew Scriptures about a vineyard that does not give good grapes. This refers to people who were unfaithful, who only think of number one. They bring judgment upon themselves.

The parable is about two sons, one refusing at first to do what his father asked and then changing his mind, while his brother tells the father he will obey and then does not. The context of the parable is Jesus' ongoing conflict with the religious leaders of his time. They condemned him for reaching out to the rejected of society and those who were considered sinners. At the same time, they refused to listen to what both he and John the Baptist were saying about the call to repentance and the reception of the coming Messiah. As we have noted, Matthew is writing for Jewish Christians who were discouraged that only a minority of Jews had accepted Jesus as the Messiah and joined the Christian community.

The story is really about forgiving those who repent, who have a change of mind. Can we accept them, reach out to them, and give them another chance as God does? Can we also admit that we need to repent and change? Why do we so quickly judge and condemn others, thinking we are better, when there is so much we need to change in our own lives? As the second son, we often say one thing and do nothing. I am too cozy, too comfortable, and it would be too much to think about changing. Some silly virus will not affect my nice life.

Matthew moves us toward a more serious commitment, which gets deeper over the next three weeks. Actions are what are needed. We talk the talk, but will we walk the walk? Matthew's question throughout the gospel is, "What do I do with this?" A good way to answer is to follow what Paul tells the Philippians in the second reading, "Have in you the same attitude that is also in Christ Jesus." It is an attitude of service, humility, and obedience in giving his life for us. A tall order, but a serious challenge to each of us who say we follow Jesus.

This parable is found only in Matthew. Jesus is in Jerusalem, before his passion, stirring up the city and confronting Jewish leaders. There is a great deal of tension. The Jewish leaders challenge Jesus' authority. Before this story, Jesus asks them about John the Baptist's baptism, whether it was of heavenly or human origin. They refuse to answer since they had rejected his call to repentance. They give a political answer which is no answer. The issue is not Jesus' authority but how one responds to God's call to repentance and his invitation into the kingdom. They are using the question of authority as a smoke screen so as not to embrace the call to repent, even as they see the results of Jesus calling sinners who do repent.

The first son represents those who come to Jesus, the tax collectors and the sinners who were converted by John the Baptist. Jesus always reached out to them because they knew they were sinners and thus needed to repent. The second son represents the Jewish leaders who say they are faithful and had initially given assent to God's message but yet reject Jesus. It is like when we faithfully attend church but then fail to see Jesus in the face of the homeless, the refugee, the one who does not look or act like us. Those authorities actually witnessed the conversion of the sinners and tax collectors, but were not moved by such things. It was unthinkable to the Jewish leaders that the lower levels of society would enter the kingdom and that they themselves might be excluded. This was intended to urge early Christians to accept people not like them, namely, the gentiles, who were being converted to the church while the Jewish leaders refused to conver.

The second son's "Yes, Sir" reflected the religious leaders' predetermined understanding of God's message, and thus they remained unchanged. They were stuck in their conception of God and unwilling to move from it. It was not a lack of knowledge but of trust in God. God had to fit in with their conceptions of him and not the other way around. They were not open to the constant call of conversion of heart that we all receive.

One thing is a change of mind, but the other is a change of heart. To say the right thing, to honor the request, but then do nothing, was not obedience to the Father's will. The best response would have resulted in action. That is what Jesus is asking us to do.

The story of the COVID denier is a story of not only regretting mistakes, but of learning from them and reversing them to the best of our ability by a change of heart. It is a story of conversion, which demands action to go in God's direction.

Parables are tough stories that often shock or convict the listener. In this case, are you son number one, who realized he was wrong to reject his father's call, needed to change, and then took action to make it right? Or are you son number two, who thought he did not need to change and thus paid lip service, with no intention to ever follow through? Parables force us to write our end to the story. Which are you? What do you do?

We don't ever fully understand God. We must listen to God, respond to God's calls, and then follow through, confident that God always requests from us what is best for us. Working in the vineyard is living our lives to help bring about the reign of God here on earth while we await our final call to live in the kingdom of heaven.

It is the heart that answers God's call. It is never too late to change, be our best selves, answer God, and do the right thing.

30

10/4/20 Twenty-seventh Sunday

The stone which the builders rejected has become the keystone…

Isa 5:1–7; Phil 4:6–9; Matt 21:33–43

ABOUT TEN DAYS AGO, Pope Francis broadcast an address to the United Nations on the fifth anniversary of his historic visit to that body in New York. His theme now was how we must respond to the pandemic. He said we cannot think of returning to the "normal" of pre-COVID times, but must place the good of all people and the environment ahead of maintaining the lifestyles of wealthy individuals and nations. He drew attention to the violence against children, especially unaccompanied migrant children and refugees. The pandemic, he said, can be an opportunity for conversion and transformation and rethinking our way of life.

Pope Francis is asking us to turn our attention to the plight of the poor worldwide. He warns us all of the "globalization of indifference"[1] which affects those of us who live comfortable lives far from the violence, war, and poverty so much of the world experiences. We often are indifferent when the problem is not immediately affecting us. Yet as Catholics, the pope is calling us to be universal in our care and action. COVID-19 on our doorstep and throughout the world is a grim reminder.

Last week, this week, and next week the gospel readings speak about parables of God's judgment. Along with the first reading, today's gospel shows that God does everything possible for us, and yet we ignore or

---

1. O'Connell, "Pope Francis."

even violate God's wishes. We don't give the yield. The dire warning is that there is a judgment coming for all if we do not act.

This vineyard parable seems not to make much sense since it looks like the landowner never learns that the tenants are wicked. He appeals to their honor. Usually in those times, people would sympathize with tenants who were often mistreated by the owners, but not this time. This would have troubled the parable hearers. God always looks for the best in us, gives us what we need, but expects us to treat others as God has treated us, namely, with respect, generosity, and compassion. The tenants did not practice even basic justice, doing what was right, much less imitating the goodness of the owner of the vineyard. They rejected God's gifts by their greed and the way they treated others. The vineyard, in this case meaning the world where we are placed to live and work, belongs to God, not us.

Jesus in this gospel is confronting the religious leaders. The story speaks of the various servants sent by the owner to collect his produce. This refers to prophets sent by God to call the people of Israel, especially the leaders, to repentance and faithfulness. Prophets were usually rejected, and in many cases killed, by those who had no intention of changing their ways. It is clear that the son of the owner is an image of Jesus, who also is killed.

The context of this reading is that Matthew is writing his gospel for a Jewish audience and is very frustrated with the majority of Jews who rejected Jesus. For Matthew it was so clear who Jesus was. Is it clear to us who Jesus is, that Jesus is in the face of the desperate migrant, the person sick from COVID, the poor, those who don't look like us or live near us? I know for myself I have not always recognized Jesus in them. I need conversion too. We all do. This story is a good reminder.

Matthew also writes for Jewish Christians, warning them that they cannot take anything for granted in their new faith. If Israel missed the message of Jesus, they might repeat the mistake by their treatment of the gentile Christians, not recognizing they are part of the kingdom as well. A good message for us is to remember that living in the reign of God is not just Sunday Mass, even though that is critical to our life of faith, but an everyday commitment to give back to God in how we care for and share with others.

There is frustration in listening to this parable. Who should inherit the vineyard? The parable does not tell us the end of the story, just that Jesus asks the question and the listeners pronounce a harsh judgment, which is really on themselves. There is a severe reckoning for them and there will be for us if we do not respond as God wants, namely, that we give back to God from what God has entrusted to us. At the same time, Jesus does not indicate that he agrees with the kind of punishment the listeners feel is warranted. Rather, he says the kingdom of God will be taken away from you and given to others who will produce fruit. It is a warning that we have all we need to accomplish what God has sent us to do in this world.

Just as the parable leaves the questions open ended, so Jesus as Messiah left many questions unanswered through his words and actions. Why did Jesus associate with outcasts, sinners, the poor and those no one wanted? God wants what no one else wants. Since the story has no ending, perhaps we need to finish writing it, which is so typical of Jesus' parables. You write your ending. Are we good and faithful stewards, or are we thieves? Do we care about all our sisters and brothers as God calls us to do, or just ourselves? How do we conduct our daily business, our daily lives? Is it how we can get away with the small and large ways of cheating, lying, manipulating others? How can we be faithful to God on God's terms, not ours?

Three years ago in July here in San Antonio, ten migrants from Mexico and Guatemala died in a locked trailer that had no water and no ventilation as they were transported north from the Mexican border in 100-degree temperatures for hours. Thirty-four more migrants were left in critical or serious condition in hospitals. This human trafficking tragedy is repeated all over the world for more than 82 million migrants and refugees who are forced to flee conditions of war, violence, famine, and grinding poverty in order to have a chance to survive. Many travel with children.[2] Many do not survive.

Our local Catholic Charities faces these situations constantly. This week they put out an alarm that the St. Stephen's Center on San Antonio's west side, where they distribute food to the needy during this pandemic, is completely bare. The need has been overwhelming. I sent a gift. They need much more. Even from our comfortable lives we can touch our struggling sisters and brothers with some of what God has given us.

This gospel tells us we are stewards of each other. We are tenants of this world, which belongs to all. "*Mi casa es su casa*" (My house is your house) is our tradition. God expects us to care for each other. We who have been blessed need to pray and act on behalf of those who are

2. Reid, "Forced to Flee," para. 1.

vulnerable in our world. Even though my action will not completely solve the growing disparity between the rich and the poor, or eliminate the migration and human trafficking that threaten the lives of so many, or soothe all of those who are disproportionately hurt by the pandemic, everything I do can make a difference.

We are never off the hook. We have never done enough. We are tenants in this world; stewards, not owners. What we have is on loan to us. The *dicho* (wise saying) my grandmother would tell us is "*La vida es prestada*," "Life is on loan to you." How will you return it to the real owner?

St. Paul's reading today provides the encouragement we need in the midst of such heavy thoughts. We are not alone in trying to fulfill our call. Think about the good in the world. There is truth, honor, justice, purity, love, excellence, and grace. They may not be everywhere, but they do exist. Look for them and let them give you hope and strength. Focus your prayers, petitions, and thanksgiving on God as you work to transform the world and your world.

Work the vineyard so that you give back to God what you have produced. This is your life's work. It will never be easy, but as Paul promises, the God of peace will be with you.

31

10/11/20 Twenty-eighth Sunday

The invited are many, the elect are few.

Isa 25:6-10a; Phil 4:12-14, 19-20; Matt 22:1-14

A FEW YEARS AGO, San Antonio declined to submit a bid for the new Amazon Headquarters. Many large cities made elaborate presentations and spent big money to try to lure the mega company to their area. Fifty thousand high-paying jobs were offered, which would be a real game-changer for any city selected. San Antonio, the seventh-largest city in the country, did not even try. Some local business leaders criticized the decision not to engage in the competition. However, the decision of our civic leaders made sense. We were not ready then. We still are not ready.

Why is this community not ready? To begin, we are woefully undereducated, with a high school dropout rate that is very high, and a low college graduation rate, resulting in a low percentage of college graduates. We have a poor transportation infrastructure, a small airport, and no light rail. We are the nation's most economically segregated city and have the highest poverty rate. Certainly, the images of hundreds of cars lined up for food distribution during the pandemic underscores this.

As much as I love the city where I was born, raised, and have lived all my life, our reality hurts. We were just not ready. We are still not dressed for this party and we have a lot to do to get this community dressed. That does not mean we are not trying to make progress. We are, but more action is needed.

That is what the gospel today is about. This is the third of a series of parables on judgment. It is similar to last week's reading on the wicked tenants. Matthew has a favorite theme: Following Christ is more than words and excuses; it must involve action. God's reign is not what you expect it to be. There is the invitation and then how we dress when we come to the banquet.

The parable involves a feast for the king's son. In Scripture a feast often refers to the heavenly banquet. It speaks of God's generosity and how we are to respond. Normally the king would invite only the wealthy and prominent people, very much like what would happen today. The custom for those invited was to wait to see how the dinner developed before deciding to go. Who else is going? Does this not sound familiar? However, by saying no, they dishonored the king, which was a great offense. The second group did worse by killing the servants, and the king retaliated and destroyed their city.

Matthew again is employing images for what happened to Israel. Prophets, as well as Christian missionaries, were at first rejected, then mistreated by the Jewish people, who for the most part never accepted the invitation to repent or to follow Christ and share in the banquet. Jerusalem is destroyed by the Romans in AD 70, before this gospel is written. This parable seems to reflect that history.

The story continues as the king breaks protocol and instructs his servants to go out and invite everyone. Matthew writes, "the bad and the good" are invited, indicating that in the church both are present. Actually, there is bad and good in each of us, right?

Matthew is again referring to the conversion of gentiles which disturbed Jewish Christians. This open invitation would have shocked the listeners, as the elite would never eat with the others. In an honor/shame culture like the one the Jews lived in during those days, this was unacceptable. Jesus was always criticized for dining with those who were unwanted by the elites, but he welcomed all to repentance and the marginalized responded more.

The parable gets complicated, as they all do. It is not enough to be invited. One must prepare to participate. There is no room for complacency or indifference. Matthew alone adds this last part where the king goes to look at and meet the guests, a final judgment before they are allowed to stay. Those who accept the invitation have the responsibility to respond appropriately. The silence (indifference) of the one without a garment is an admission of guilt. He/she cannot speak of any actions. Matthew again stresses his favorite theme: actions speak louder than words. The

Christian who thinks "Just because I am a Christian I need do nothing more" is making a big mistake.

Laxity, not paying the price of discipleship, which is carrying a cross, means I am not dressed for the banquet. The wedding garment was a sign of respect for the one who invited. In this case, Jesus invites us.

So, what is the dress? To be clothed with good deeds. As Paul says to the Colossians: "clothe yourselves in compassion, kindness, humility, meekness and patience" (3:12). The wedding garment is the sign of active faith. Membership is not enough; there must be action. It is one thing to invite and allow all to enter; it is another to condone all behavior, which Matthew says they must reject. Those who pretend to be Christian are as bad as those who reject the invitation.

We do not need the garment in order to be invited, but we need it to stay in the banquet. We cannot take anything for granted and must still put faith into action. The violator is thrown out, not into the street, but into the darkness, namely, hell. He/she is like the bad servant who must stay in jail with torture, until the impossible debt is paid, which is forever.

On Holy Saturday, after the newly baptized come out of the water, they are clothed in a white garment, a sign they have to be ready to act, to serve. During this pandemic, we see another white garment which comforts us when we are sick. Doctors wear a white coat, which is a sign of their service and commitment to heal.

The invitation to the banquet is God's free gift to us, but we must respond with good deeds. Sometimes we may not only have excuses for not fully accepting the invitation, but we also may ignore it or demonstrate our indifference by our silence. We at times ignore the needs of others around the world, and even those in front of us, which is what Pope Francis talked about when he used the phrase, "the globalization of indifference."[1]

So, how is San Antonio going to be ready for other invitations? What will we do to prepare? This year, a young man from Mission Concepción, who had been an altar server and volunteer for years, graduated and went to college out of town, the first in his family to do so. The family, very active in the parish, has limited means and covering costs is a struggle. I helped and also reached out to people who responded readily with gifts for him. In the last few years, I and others have found help for several good students from poor families who want a better education. That is

---

1. O'Connell, "Pope Francis."

the beginning of the kind of action that will assist our city in getting ready for invitations in the future.

We especially need to help young people of limited resources to develop their gifts. They are the future. We must work to improve life for all through means like better education, more job training, and improved infrastructure. None of us can be indifferent. There will be more invitations. When we treat each other right, we can all accept the invitation to go to the feast.

There is another feast, however, one more immediate. We are invited to this weekly banquet, the Eucharist. For those who attended today in person, did we come fully clothed, not only with what we physically wear, but also with what we did this past week? Did we come clothed with good deeds?

Full conscious participation in the banquet of the Lord, the Eucharist, is our call. When we live the Mass all week it affects others and they respond. That action then spills out to the world. That is how we attract people to this feast. That is how we make a better world.

Next Sunday, when you prepare for Mass, whether you plan to attend in person or virtually, ask yourself what clothes you will wear. Think about what you did the past week. Those are your clothes. How do they look on you?

32

10/18/20 Twenty-ninth Sunday

…give to God what is God's.

Isa 45:1, 4–6; 1 Thess 1:1–5b; Matt 22:15–21

WE HAVE BEEN DISCUSSING and debating the coronavirus since it first appeared, and more so when it impacted our lives in such dramatic fashion. Now we are in a debate season, not just for the pandemic, but also for politics. Political debates can be both informative and brutal. Each candidate for office is trying to make a case they are the one who deserves our vote. At times they are also trying to tell us the other person is not only wrong in their positions but actually a bad person. Yet as children of the same Creator, we cannot demonize someone because he/ she does not agree with us politically.

Debates during an election season are like sport. You have a game plan and try to trick the opponent with the way you put your opponent on the spot or use a zippy one-liner. Sometimes real issues fall to the side.

The gospels for the next three weeks talk about debates and tricks as well. These are confrontations of Jesus with the authorities in the temple precincts. In the debates Jesus' enemies are trying to discredit him completely. Matthew places these in the temple precincts to show Jesus' authority to teach as the Messiah. For the Jew, that authority is based in the temple. Matthew does this to bring Jews to Jesus and at the same time assure Jewish Christians they made the right choice.

The question is: How do we live according to the gospel, which essentially is to live by the heart rather than the letter of the law? There is a series of four debates of Jesus with different leaders, but especially with

Pharisees, since they were seen as the main Jewish authority. Matthew shows Jews that Jesus has greater authority and his enemies cannot trick him.

The debates are in the form of question-and-answer sessions near the end of Jesus' life. In this story, the opponents of Jesus try to trap him into recognizing a divine emperor. We know they are setting up a trap when they call Jesus "teacher" since it is Matthew's flag for a person of little or no faith. It was a politically charged environment at that time. Does this sound familiar today?

The Herodians are mentioned only here and one other place in Mark. They are supporters of King Herod, who had been imposed on the Jews by Rome. The Pharisees are not happy with Herod, but if they can use his supporters to trap Jesus, they will. We might call this the politics of convenience, not conviction. It has existed for centuries. The trick question is about paying taxes to Caesar. If Jesus supports the tax, he is unpopular with the people and against the Pharisees. If he opposes it, he is a revolutionary, against Caesar and the Herodians. Someone will not be happy with the answer. Either way, Jesus will suffer. That was the point. They did not care about the answer. They just wanted to get Jesus.

Jesus knows their malice. This political trap refers back to the temptation in the desert by the evil one who offers to give Jesus the kingdoms of the world. So, this is more than just a trick question. He is being tempted by the evil one to get involved in political power struggles. The early church, for which Matthew writes, was struggling with regard to how it should relate to the state, namely, Caesar. The church at times supports the state, and at times resists the state. Early Christians resisted bowing to gods or seeing Caesar as god. In some cases it cost them their lives.

Jesus simply says we have to pay for the things the government gives, especially if we are using the roads, security, and other services, but God is overarching, and our allegiance to God must always come first. A priest told me last year that a parishioner in counseling had told him he was a member of a political party first, then a Catholic. I thought, "Tell that to St. Peter at the pearly gates!" It seems like a clear contradiction of this gospel. Election season might be a good time to think about that.

The Pharisees especially hated the tax because it had to be paid with a coin bearing the image of Caesar. They disliked human images, which were prohibited by their law. Additionally, the coin's writing identified the image as "Tiberius Caesar, august son of the divine Augustus," thus attributing divinity to Caesar as son of the divine. That would have been blasphemy for the Jews, and to even own or touch a coin was a form of cooperating in the blasphemy. Yet, when Jesus asks to see a coin, one is produced by them immediately. This showed that they used the coin without any problem. It is compounded by the fact they were in the temple precincts, thus profaning the sacred place with a blasphemous image. I can imagine the one producing it, realizing Jesus has just uncovered his hypocrisy.

Jesus begins his answer. Caesar is paid the coin that bears his image, but we need to return to God what bears God's image, namely, us! Even though the word "give" is used for both payments, the original wording indicates giving to God is really returning to God what God has given us. The response to God must be total.

Our primary citizenship is with the kingdom of God. Are we as careful paying God what God is due as we are paying our taxes? If Caesar is God or if Caesar is the devil the responses are easy, but what if he is neither? Then the answers are not simple and we have to wrestle with them, using God as our guide. What we owe Caesar is to make the country reflect the values of God, not any party or person.

Do we really believe that a terrorist is created in God's image, or a cohabiting couple or a gay person or a person married multiple times? What about a refugee fleeing violence or poverty and trying to seek a better life, or the homeless person under a bridge? It is so easy to think that someone who is not like us is not as good as we are. However, our teaching says they and all other humans are also the face of God. Do you see yourself, with all your baggage, as the image of God? How can you give to God what belongs to God?

Jesus might also have been telling us not to be so dependent on money. To liberate ourselves from the excessive attachment to money is to live in the freedom of God's children. That is especially hard in our country and in our culture, where buying and spending is ingrained in our lifestyle.

Pope Francis said recently of the COVID pandemic, "Having failed to show solidarity in wealth and in the sharing of resources, we have learned to experience solidarity in suffering."[1] Perhaps the worldwide suffering and personally knowing people who have suffered and even died from the virus will help us put in perspective what God has given

---

1. Mares, "Pope Francis," para. 10.

us and our obligation to return what is God's. We need to pray and work for healing from this time of pandemic. I read an article recently[2] that said the word "healing" comes from the word "whole." Healing, then, is a return to "wholeness" not a return to "sameness." We need to pray that we and this world will be healed, made better, and made whole.

St. Paul tells the Thessalonians in the second reading that the gospel is not mere words, but it is power, the power to change our life and help change the world. Every morning, look in that mirror and see that image of God. You know it is not perfect, so it can help you to see others in the image of God as well.

Return to God today what is God's. Can you do it?

---

2. Egnew, "Meaning of Healing," para. 3.

33

10/25/20 Thirtieth Sunday

You shall love your neighbor as yourself.

Exod 22:20-26; 1 Thess 1:5c-10; Matt 22:34-40

ARE YOU HOLY? DON'T answer so fast!

The church is moving toward canonizing the first millennial as a saint according to a recent article in *The New York Times*.[1] He was officially declared "Blessed" by the pope earlier this month, which is the final step before sainthood. Carlos Acutis, who lived in Milan, was just fifteen when he died of leukemia in 2006. He was buried in his Nikes, jeans, and a sweater. He is known as the patron saint of the internet for the ways he used it as an expression and promotion of his Catholic faith. He attended daily Mass from the age of seven. He sought ways to help poor, older and disabled people, and refugees. He would stop on the way to school to chat with people about their problems. He took meals and sleeping bags to homeless people. At a time when young people are leaving the church, he is a great example and motivation for them. Pope Francis said he was an example that "true happiness is found by putting God first and serving Him in our brothers, especially the least."[2] That is holy!

The gospel today helps us understand that really the entire Bible is a love letter from God to us. Jesus is asked to name the two greatest commandments. The Jews had 613 commandments in the Torah and very few Jewish people could recite them all. Matthew writes his gospel for a

1. Fazio, Italian Teenager."
2. Mares, "Pope Francis Says Blessed Carlo Acutis," para. 3.

Jewish Christian audience and was always looking for ways to connect Jewish tradition to the new Christian way of life so that they would see how Jesus fulfilled the law. In this case, Jesus' focus is on love of God and of neighbor. Even though both laws are found in the Old Testament, Jesus is the first to give equal importance to the two.

It is key that Matthew, in having Jesus quote Deuteronomy about loving God, changes one word. The original text said believers were to love God with their entire being—heart, soul, and strength. Matthew used the term "mind" instead of "strength." He wanted to stress the element of understanding and decision that is required to turn the heart over completely to God. We need to always learn more and we need to constantly reaffirm our decision to respond to God's love. Fidelity to a relationship is what this is about.

Because God loves us first—always has, always will—we in turn return love to God, and in loving God we can and must love each other. When we really realize how much God has loved us, then we must respond with a thankful love. The love in thanksgiving that is generously directed at my brother and sister is a faithful love of God. That is holiness. It does not have to be perfect. It just has to keep trying in that direction.

Notice that Jesus does not say this is the greatest commandment among many. Rather he says that the whole of Scripture, the law and the prophets, must be interpreted in light of this commandment. This gives the law of love a singular and ultimate importance.

The big question then arises, "Who is my neighbor?" Israelites understood "neighbor" to be other Israelites. The family and the clan were utmost. The first reading from Exodus says it is not only family and friends, but also those I don't know, like aliens, strangers, widows, orphans, and the poor. This is a consistent theme throughout Scripture. In fact, in Luke Jesus answers the neighbor question with the good Samaritan parable. Your neighbor is not just the one like you, but rather the one in need.

The Israelite was willing to show some compassion to others not of their race. Jesus, however, demanded we give others the same love we give ourselves, a radically new concept at that time. Jesus is saying that if we love as he asks us to love, then everything else will flow from that. Everything. Our entire call as Christians is anchored in love for God and others. This is how we live out our faith. That is being holy!

To be Catholic is to strive to embrace a universal vision of living, that is to love our neighbor as we love God, to live out our faith, which is a global faith, a universal faith. When we share our love with the stranger, the neediest, the one we will never even know, the one who will never thank us, then we are loving God.

There are more than 82 million migrants and refugees in the world today,[3] mostly fleeing violence, civil wars, grinding poverty, or climate change that has made it impossible for them to raise crops. Today, over 25,000 people around the world died of hunger and hunger-related disease that could have been prevented.[4] The pandemic also has added, as of this writing, 130 million people to the list of those who are food insecure.[5] We don't wake up thinking about whether we will eat or not, but 2 billion people in the world who live on less than $3.20 a day do.[6]

Pope Francis wrote an apostolic exhortation, *Gaudete et Exsultate*, in March 2018, on the call to holiness in today's world. A key passage tells us, "We cannot uphold an ideal of holiness that would ignore injustice in a world where some revel, spend with abandon and live only for the latest consumer goods, even as others look on from afar, living their entire lives in abject poverty."[7]

Are you holy? These words of the pope should urge us on as we try to love others and participate in making our country and our community a better place. This means, to the best of our ability and circumstances, involving ourselves in actions that directly help others in need in our neighborhood, our city, our country, and even our world. Since March, this has included all the ways we help each other during the pandemic. During these upcoming weeks this year, this means participating and voting in the election. Yes, voting can be an act of holiness, especially when it is done by keeping in mind the sacred issues to which the pope referred us. Love and holiness are multifaceted.

Pope Francis is outlining many of the challenging issues today that call us to love others and thus show our love for God. He is pricking our consciences to ask ourselves tough questions in our lives of faith.

Holiness, as we can see in the life of young Carlos, is not rocket science. It is being aware of the small ways we can show care and compassion for others around us. It is supporting those who work with the

3. Reid, "Forced to Flee," para. 1.
4. theworldcounts.com.
5. "UN Report."
6. "Covid-19 to Add," para. 9.
7. Kuruvilla, "Pope Francis," .

neediest here and abroad. It is using all the means at our disposal, like the internet and social media, as Carlos did in such an uplifting way. It is finding opportunities during the pandemic to support others, whether in their illness or because of the consequences of COVID, like loss of employment or food insecurity. It is being an advocate to our local and national governments on behalf of those in need. None of this is really very difficult to do, or even heroic, but it is holy work.

To be holy we don't need to go and convert China. How about starting by converting ourselves a little every day? Continuing conversion is our vocation to holiness and we can't be discouraged when we stumble along the way. That just means we are lining up behind the apostles in the gospels who stumbled a lot. The struggle to love God as we love others can be really tough. However, it is the only way to holiness and true happiness.

34

11/1/20 All Saints

. . . your reward is great in heaven.

Rev 7:2-4, 9-14; 1 John 3:1-3; Matt 5:1-12a

2020 HAS BEEN A year we would all like to forget. It has caused an enormous amount of suffering for the whole planet. Over 1.1 million deaths and 44 million cases—9 million in our country alone—have caused grief, pain, and major disruption for many people. It has been a year like no other in living memory, and the suffering continues. Even though some progress has been made in vaccine development and treatment, we have been told to prepare to live under this threat for most of next year as well. What can we do?

Suffering is a part of the human condition. People suffer in so many ways. Suffering can come from outside ourselves such as this pandemic. We can also be the cause of suffering for others, as well as for ourselves. It seems we can never avoid it and we sometimes make it worse than it needs to be. Yet, despite this grim reality, for the Christian, suffering, as difficult as it is, has a redeeming quality. It can be transformative for a person of faith.

Today we celebrate and commemorate all the saints who have gone before us. Many, if not all, suffered a lot in living out their faith. They are examples and inspirations for us as we try to follow in their footsteps. It might also be a good time to recognize those around us who are doing saintly things.

The gospel reading today is known as the Beatitudes. It is placed at the beginning of the Sermon on the Mount, which was Jesus' lengthy teaching about what it means to be a disciple. As has been said before in these homilies, when anything happens on a mountain in Scripture, it is always a sign to pay close attention. The mountain was seen as the place for the privileged encounter with God, the place of God's revelation, the intersection of heaven and earth. Moses receives the commandments on the mountain while Jesus is transfigured on the mountain where the voice of God identifies him as Son. The difference here is that Moses hands down the law given to him while Jesus speaks with his own authority. Therefore, the setting for this sermon and these Beatitudes tells us this is all of the highest importance. Pay attention!

The Beatitudes begin the lengthy sermon. Jesus puts the most important material first. This is Jesus' teaching on happiness. It might be puzzling that those whom Jesus names as happy or blessed are not what we exactly think of as being happy people, namely, the poor in spirit, the meek, the persecuted, the insulted, the slandered. Is this happiness or what?

The word "blessed" can also be translated into "favored," essentially telling us that God's favor is on those who faithfully go through these struggles of life much as Jesus did. Recall the words from heaven when Jesus was baptized and when he was transfigured, "This is my beloved (blessed, favored) son, in whom I am well pleased" (Matt 17:5). Jesus was beloved and favored by God but that did not mean he was spared rejection, persecution, and suffering.

In the Beatitudes, Matthew lays out the conditions for discipleship, a summary of everything Jesus will teach here. Discipleship is about learning and following the master. Matthew, in his gospel, uses the term "disciple" seventy-two times. He uses the term "apostle," one who is sent to announce, once. He seems to be stressing that we are never finished learning about and following Jesus, which is the only way we can ever be in a position to announce him.

There are two sets of four beatitudes that center on the thirst for holiness in our lives, and the struggles that entails. For example, Jesus glorifies peacemakers, which was countercultural since violence and war were so much a part of that time. Jesus finally addresses the listeners directly, driving it home when he says, "Blessed are you, when you are persecuted, insulted and slandered." In effect, by sharing in the suffering of Jesus, especially the rejection he suffered, we live as disciples and merit heaven. Think about that when you do the right thing and people still attack you.

Again, to be blessed is to identify with Jesus and accept suffering as he did. The lesson of the gospel is that suffering is not just to be avoided, but rather embraced. This is not to say we look for suffering. It will come on its own, but it is the way to transformation. This teaching reverses how people viewed the poor, namely, that those they thought cursed are actually blessed. Additionally, by putting the blessings in the future tense, Jesus is not saying when they will happen, but rather that certainly they will happen.

Jesus is speaking of a transformation. This happens through the daily challenges and suffering we inevitably encounter. Jesus teaches us that God cares and does not leave us alone. We are dependent on God and God will come through for us.

The Beatitudes tell us that discipleship is also a community experience, a community effort. There is a theme of solidarity throughout. What clearer example do we have of this than the community effort to contain the virus by our daily sacrifices and considerations of others? We transform the world together. This is the blueprint for sainthood.

Maybe 2020, as difficult as it has been for all of us, has been an exercise in being disciples and finally becoming saints. We must work together to defeat the virus. We must console and care for those who have been affected. We must support all the essential personnel who have been on the many front lines of the pandemic. We must think of the community and not just ourselves. The small sacrifices of masks, social distancing, limiting contact, and other protocols are simply commitments to being a caring community of disciples in a time of need. Pope Francis reminds us that being a saint is really just being your best self.

Everyday life can lead to holiness, like living at home with family, especially during this trying time, or work or school or shopping or other activities. These times, especially while on the internet, are all about finding ways to be kind, something especially challenging when we are under stress.

In the Cathedral of Our Lady of the Angels in Los Angeles, high up on the walls of the main gathering space, hang twenty-five huge tapestries that depict 135 wonderfully diverse saints. Here we see young and old, male and female, people of all races and groups, from all the 2,000 years of our faith. I have been there many times and have always been inspired by these images, all facing forward toward the altar. I was in touch with those who placed them there and was told that, with very few exceptions, the faces of the saints depicted are people of Los Angeles. The artists painted people from every area, class, color, and group in the city. What those artworks tell me is that saints are simply everyday people, like you and me.

Today we celebrate the family of the church. We remember ordinary people who followed Jesus in whatever way they could from their various circumstances of life. We remember the officially canonized, as well as those who were never canonized and yet lived holy and saintly lives and are now with the Lord. We remember to be inspired by and to communicate with them, asking for their strength in order for us to follow their example. We share a bond with them, a relationship called the Communion of Saints.

Today should remind us our quest for heaven is a community project. We don't get there by our own efforts alone; it is by God's mercy, as Pope Francis reminds us. It is also the inspiration of the many official and unofficial saints who have gone before us, and the many people God has placed in our life, like parents, family, friends, and co-workers. Can I look for and appreciate others who are inspirations and support for me now? Can I also be a source of inspiration for others on their road to being blessed?

We can never get enough of God. If we live our lives dependent on God, we will one day also be numbered among the holy ones.

35

11/2/20 All Souls (*Dia de Los Muertos*)

To whom will all this piled-up wealth of yours go?

Luke 12:13-21

Interesting tombstones:
"I told you I was sick!"
"I think I can make it"
"I've done this a million times."
"Do you smell gas?"
"Hey y'all watch this."
"Any day above ground is a good day."
"Here lies an atheist,
Laid out head to toe,
He's all dressed up,
With no place to go."
"Beneath this stone my wife doth lie,
Now she's at rest and so am I."
"Here lies a miser who lived for himself,
Who cared for nothing but gathering wealth,
Now where he is and how he fares;
Nobody knows and nobody cares."

In the Mexican tradition, on this day death is looked at not to be feared but to be embraced as an old friend. For those who live a faithful life there is nothing to be feared in death. In fact, this is even a day of fiesta, a day to celebrate, to laugh at the *Calaveras* (skulls) poems that make fun of people who are alive, especially *politicos* (politicians) and celebrities, as if they were dead. Candied skulls speak of the sweetness. Decorating tombs and leaving the favorite food of the departed lifts the spirit as we remember fondly those who are on the other side. There is a tradition that they actually cross over that day and are present in a special way among us. The day is a celebration that lifts the spirit and connects us to those who have gone before us. The church asks us to reflect on life as well today, but more to be sure we live it with our eternal life always in mind.

Today's gospel story of the rich fool is a strong lesson. One's life does not consist of possessions. At the same time, having riches is not sinful. Rather, it is what one does with them that determines virtue or vice. There are numerous heroes of the Scriptures who were rich and at the same time lived faithfully, like Abraham, Isaac, and Job. Zacchaeus, the tax collector, is touched so much by Jesus coming to his home that he immediately gives away half of his fortune.

In this parable, found only in Luke, the rich man is isolated. He is not necessarily a criminal, but oblivious to God or others around him, especially his workers and those in need in the community. Notice how he speaks only to himself, not to anyone else. There are numerous singular first-person "I's," as well as many first-person possessive ("my") words in the story. His dilemma is that he has abundance. His solution to having so much, namely, to build more storage space and keep it all for himself, would have been shocking to the listeners at that time. In the first century, Palestinian people believed there was only so much. Goods were limited, and if I have more, someone else has less or none. To hoard was the worst vice since it destroyed community life. In many ways it still does.

This is the only one of Jesus' parables where God actually appears, to emphasize the importance of this message. "You fool!" The word "fool" here refers more to an unbeliever than to stupidity. All the blessings around him should make him more of a person of faith in God, who blesses us so we can share. The fool is one who does not live his life with the constant awareness that everything he has comes from God and it all might end at any moment.

The key question in the parable is: "All these things, to whom will they belong?" The answer is in Psalm 24:1: "The earth is the Lord's and all it holds . . ." What this says is that everything we have is on loan: "*la vida prestada"* (life on loan to us), as my *abuelita* (grandmother) always told us.

In this reading, Jesus gives the interpretation before he gives the parable, which is common in Luke. We work to meet needs. The issue is what we need versus what we want. We need God. This comes at the beginning of a section on the attitude of disciples towards possessions. It is interesting that Jesus does not answer the issue given him about brothers sharing an inheritance or even engage the one asking, but rather he gives a teaching. Jesus will engage if they ask how to inherit the kingdom, but not if they want money.

There is a difference between what one has and who one is. Covetousness seemed to be a problem in the early church, and it also violated the law of Moses. Sometimes it is the desire to possess what belongs to another, or to continue to accumulate when one already has enough. Security is found in God, not goods. The parable does not show the rich man stealing, mistreating others, manipulating, or anything else bad. He is a fool because he lives only for himself, not talking to others, thinking of others, or thinking of God. The key for Luke's message to his community is the voluntary sharing of goods, which is the response of faith Luke wants.

I count myself among those to whom this parable is aimed. I know I have enough and it has all come from God. When I visited West Africa, India, Central America, and Palestine with Catholic Relief Services, I came home asking myself why I was born here with so much while they were born there with so little. I can't change what happened, but I can do something about my obligation to share and think of others who have much less.

Spiritual freedom means true generosity. Making friends with death in the way we live so that the afterlife simply becomes an extension of this life is the moral of the gospel and the lesson of *Día de Los Muertos.* The sweets of candied skulls, the laughter of funny poems, and the fun of a fiesta, all in the Mexican tradition, make sense on a day remembering we will die, if we are living in the grace of thanksgiving to God for what we have.

Jesus was born poor, lived poor, and died poor. Yet, no one in history gave others more.

This year, with the constant specter of COVID deaths, we are all too aware of the fragility of life. Jesus is the source of hope in the midst of despair. He is the reason for hope. Jesus broke the chains of death.

He understood death and embraced it for us, because despite having no wealth, his gift of life made all the difference. In his sufferings and his death we have hope. He did it first. With faith we can follow.

36

11/8/20 Thirty-second Sunday

. . . keep your eyes open . . .

Wis 6:12–16; 1 Thess 4:13–18; Matt 25:1–13

SIXTY-FOUR-YEAR-OLD DR. JOSE LUIS Linares did medical consultations in a poor *barrio* (neighborhood) in the south of Mexico City charging $1.50 per visit. His story was in *The Express* earlier this week.[1] When the pandemic began to spread there, his wife asked him not to go to work for fear of becoming ill. He simply told her, "Then who is going to see those poor people?" Even though he took precautions, he fell ill and died May 25th, after being hospitalized at the peak of infections there. This past Monday, on *Día de los Muertos*, Mexico honored more than 1,700 health workers known to have died from COVID-19. This year has been a devastating loss for the health care system south of the border.

Every November we end another liturgical year with gospels that speak of the end times and the Lord's coming. We are reminded to think about our own end, when we will be called to give an account of our lives. The focus for us is diligent watchfulness. We don't know when Jesus will come, just as we don't know when we will be called to give our lives back to God, so we must be always ready. The question is: What does it mean to be ready?

In this part of Matthew's Gospel, Jesus is finishing his public ministry and will now focus on his close friends and followers. This is aimed at us! Jesus talks about how to end our life. Matthew felt he needed to reflect on

---

1. "For Mexico's Doctors, an Especially Mournful Day of the Dead," para. 4.

this as the Jewish Christians struggled with the fact that most Jews did not convert to Christianity. They also felt disappointment with the delay in the return of Jesus. Many of the recent gospel stories were symbolic of those who did not or would not recognize Jesus.

Once again, in today's parable, we have a banquet; this time it is a wedding banquet. A banquet symbolizes heaven, and this is God's marriage with his people. This time the Jews are the foolish bridesmaids who are not going to be ready when Jesus returns in glory. Even the gentiles, often shunned by Jews as unbelievers but who accepted Jesus, will be admitted. Matthew is trying to tell his people that no matter who criticizes them for following Jesus and doing the right thing, they need to stay prepared by how they live their lives.

The delay is the issue. We don't know the day or the hour of our death or of the coming of Jesus. In those times, the groom would go and get the bride from her home and take her to his. The delay was because the groom and his father were often bargaining with the father of the bride for his daughter. The ten bridesmaids were probably teenage relatives of the couple. They would light the way for the groom on the journey to get the bride. The lamp's light represents what we do with good works during our life. We accompany each other to the banquet of the Lord with the light of our life, our good deeds.

There are wise and foolish people in life, as we see in the bridesmaids. Wisdom is listening to the word of God and putting it into practice every day. The good deeds are the proper preparation, the proper clothes for the feast, the light for the darkness. Remember a few weeks ago the person not dressed for the feast? We clothe ourselves in good deeds. This story says we light the way with our faithful deeds.

In the story, the foolish bridesmaids ask the wise ones to share their oil for the lamps. The fact that the wise ones did not share is not the point, since for Matthew we can't do the preparation for others. The foolish have to see for themselves that they need to live prepared in the midst of uncertainty.

It is not so much constant alertness, since all the bridesmaids fall asleep, but it is preparedness that counts. It is about carrying enough oil, and being sure they are ready. Maybe the only way is always to have excess, always do much more than you think is required. You can never do enough. It is with our lives, our works, our concern for others, especially those most in need, that we prepare. Through our daily living, preserving our faith, practicing forgiveness, and compassion, we show we are ready to be called by God.

The foolish bridesmaids were indifferent, not really evil. They thought it would just happen. How do you live your life? Pope Francis calls it "The false culture of indifference," or the attitude of, "If it is not bothering me or in front of my face, then I don't care."

How we live in the long run, how we day by day look for Jesus, especially in those in need, and do what he wants, that is what counts. It is how we will be prepared when he returns to call us. Final salvation is not guaranteed. The fact we are baptized or have received sacraments, even though they help, is not enough. It is the living our faith on a daily basis that keeps us prepared for the final coming. Otherwise, the door is shut and will not be opened.

Dr. Linares did not know he was going to die, but he knew it was possible and was prepared. His lamp was well lit. He was called home after serving Jesus in the poorest. He had accompanied many of his patients on that final journey. That made him ready in every way to walk the final journey himself.

A couple of weeks ago I anointed my cousin, dying of cancer, with the Sacrament of the Sick. She was lucid, and during our conversation she told me confidently she was ready to go back to God. She had lived a long life with family and friends, and felt blessed and grateful in so many ways. She was prepared. To be in the presence of someone so ready to return her life to God has always been a moment of grace for me. This is true even when there is struggle and pain. It makes me always ask: What more do I need to do myself? I need to be sure I have enough oil in the lamp with the time I have left.

Every Mass is a reminder of Christ's second coming and our final call. We are reminded to live our lives in constant preparedness. You cannot buy yourself an extra minute. You will be called to return your life to your maker at a moment you do not yet know. Listen to God's word. Respond by living your life, by making room in your life, for Jesus, always. Doing that, you are ready.

One of the lessons we have learned through COVID-19 is that we are not in charge of our lives totally, nor can we control all that happens. This global tragedy has caused sickness and death, but also affected the economy, families, and schools, and disrupted life in general. This again shows us it is not a perfect world. We are not perfect and things are generally not under our control. Yet, St. Paul in the second reading tells us, "Do not grieve like those who have no hope." He was reminding us that God is in charge. God's power and imagination go far beyond ours.

Sometimes we get complacent, especially when everything seems to be going well. However, the Christian lives expecting the unexpected. COVID is a clear example. The lives of many of the saints we celebrated on November 1st were surprises. They had no idea what their lives were going to entail, but they prepared themselves through faithfulness and living Christian virtues. Even the suffering we are all going through now in different ways calls us to remember we are united to the sufferings of Christ. At the same time, we are united to his resurrection. If we are not prepared by listening to what God is telling us daily, we will miss the surprise and miss the banquet.

Faithful listening, faithful living, faithful service. Keep your lamp lit!

37

11/15/20 Thirty-third Sunday

Come, share your master's joy!

Prov 31:10–13, 19–20, 30–31; 1 Thess 5:1–6; Matt 25:14–30

I RECENTLY READ THE story of Myrna, from California, who celebrated her seventy-fifth birthday last Spring by giving seventy-five dollars to seventy-five of her family and friends, with one twist. She asked them to find a way to give it to someone outside their family or a charity needing help, encouragement, or appreciation. She heard back from seventy-two of the seventy-five, who vastly exceeded her expectations, even matching or pooling to have a greater impact. Some told her they will copy her idea in the future. Even though she risked giving away $5,625 with no guarantees, Myrna feels it was her best birthday ever.

Today's parable of the talents is not just about money, but about risking ourselves. It is a judgment parable, as are the recent ones which will end next week with the final judgment. They are meant to make us think deeply about life and death. What are we doing with our lives? With what God has given us. Have I done what God sent me to do on this earth? Have I done enough? Have I just played it safe?

Every Mass remembers the life, death, and resurrection of Jesus and the waiting for him to return. The early Christians thought Jesus would return quickly so they sold things and just hung around, waiting. This parable says the master was delayed a long time, but it also says we need to persevere and not stop doing what we are called to do.

It seems interesting that here the term for their money is "talent." Talent is something we all have in varying amounts and in different ways. We are all given talents and then the work of our lives is to develop them, put them to good use and make them benefit not only ourselves, but others as well. That is why God gave them to us.

A talent was 12,000 denarii (Roman coin). It was worth maybe 1 million dollars in today's money, an unbelievable amount for any servant. Yet the master says it was "little" because money is not the important thing, but simply the key to the "larger things" of the kingdom. Money is insignificant when it comes to God. What is much more important are the things related to the reign of God. Gifts are to be shared and multiplied no matter how large or small we think they are. However, if we have been given more, then, as Scripture tells us, more is expected of us. Love of God, not fear, must be the motivation. We don't know how much time we have, but we do know what God expects, so we need to get to work.

In the parable the super-rich master entrusts all his money to three servants, according to their ability. The whole story sounds incredible. Everything is a total exaggeration, as often happens in parables, in order to make a point. However, what is not an exaggeration is that each of us has been given an incredible amount of talent in our lives. We never fully realize all we have or can do, but the purpose of life is to discover, develop, and share them. It is in the development, and especially in the sharing or giving, of our talents that we discover how much we can do, even more than we ever thought possible.

The master is gone longer than expected. Matthew's community expected Jesus to return during their lifetimes, but that was not to be. As some began to die, the others wondered why Jesus had not returned and were discouraged. Matthew is encouraging us to get on with life and do what Jesus asks us to do. That is why we are Christians, to follow the example of the Servant Messiah. Whether Jesus returns in our lifetime or not should not prevent us from using and sharing what God has given us.

The first two servants in the parable set to work immediately and doubled the money. However, the third one did not, due to fear as he himself admitted later. Paralyzing fear. He did not want to take any risk. He paid for this dearly. The parable seems to say doing nothing for the master was worse than losing it all in the attempt.

Life involves risk and those willing to take risks for the right reason are the ones who can change the world, or at least the world around them. The apostles risked their lives, changed the world and the course of human history. There was plenty to fear for them, but they moved forward always.

The master rewards the two who were faithful. It was really not the huge amount of money or even ability; it was faith, what we do with our faith. We have been given faith and talent, each according to our ability. We must risk faith in order to make it grow. We either go forward or backward. We can't just stay in place with what God gives us.

Jesus took risks. The master took a risk with his money. The first two risked a lot by working with it, since they could have lost it all. There are other parables that talk of risk. One example is looking for the one lost sheep and leaving the ninety-nine alone. The major themes of Christian faith, like caring, giving, witnessing, trusting, loving, and hoping, cannot be understood or lived without some risk.

The industrious servants in the parable are welcomed into the "joy of your Lord," which is better than any material benefit. The "small matters" are worth millions, which seems a lot. Jesus' point is that those millions pale in comparison with the future reward in the kingdom of heaven.

What happens when we are totally afraid of risking for the faith? The third servant, who was afraid to risk, is not just fired but is thrown out into darkness where there is "weeping and gnashing of teeth." Matthew uses this expression eight times, most recently as we saw in the wedding parable. This is not financial talk since Jesus is never interested in money. This is kingdom talk.

I have heard it said that the opposite of love is not hate, but fear. Fear is also the opposite of faith. Fear does not allow us to live love. Fear paralyzes. How do we overcome fear? Remember Jesus calming the storm on the lake, "Why were you afraid, you of little faith?" (Matt 8:26). The phrase "Do not be afraid," or its equivalent, is in Scripture 365 times, one for every day of the year. No excuses! Fear of failure, of judgment, of loss, paralyzed this servant. It also does the same to many people and even congregations.

My previous parish, Mission Concepción, was not a wealthy parish. The neighborhood was mostly the working poor and the elderly. Some people came from other areas. Over the course of the eight years I served there, the parish went over and above to help the most needy. We supported several poor parishes, annually adopted a refugee family, assisted the local food pantry monthly, helped Catholic Charities and Catholic Relief Services with their refugee and other programs, and assisted unaccompanied migrants, hurricane victims, and victims of the Mexico earthquake, as well as engaging in many other special giving projects. The people were extremely supportive, even though they were not required to contribute. After the eight years we had much more money than when we started. Like the first two servants, our funds had more than doubled. Did we do enough? Never enough! However, we took risks for the right reasons.

The COVID-19 pandemic has devastated many people. At the same time the stories of the medical personnel and other essential workers, who daily risk their lives in serving, have been nothing short of heroic. They have developed their own gifts and are risking to share them.

What about your faith? Are you willing to risk a lot? It could double as it did for the first two servants, but even if it does not, you do what you know the master wants. Will you risk something significant, more than you think you can afford, with faith that it will be OK?

"Do not be afraid."

38

11/22/20 Christ the King

For I was hungry and you gave me food.

Ezek 34:11–12, 15–17; 1 Cor 15:20–26, 28; Matt 25:31–46

I HAVE A RECURRING dream that plagues me often. In the dream I am in college again. It is the night before a final exam and I have not cracked a book or attended class, and now I have to cram all night in order to pass. It is scary! The funny thing is that in the dream after the panic, I tell myself I am not in school anymore. I passed everything years ago.

A recurring dream can be telling. Maybe there is more to do to prepare for the final exam, but not the one for school, rather the real final exam, the one for life.

I have always thought that today's gospel is the scariest in all of Scripture. It is the final exam, otherwise known as the final judgment. Matthew is the only gospel to include it. We have had a series of judgment parables in November, the month that calls us to reflect on life and death. This is not a parable, but an apocalyptic vision of the last judgment.

In Matthew's Gospel this is the climax of all Jesus wanted to say. The scene happens right before the events of the passion. This is the end of his public ministry. Matthew left the most important for last.

Jesus, who is about to be judged by others, is now judge, the Lord of all nations, the entire universe, not just Israel. This is the first time Jesus refers to himself as king. This reference is connected to the Epiphany story where three kings come to worship the newborn king.

"Come, you who are blessed by my Father." Jesus calls those blessed by the Father with a single word, "Come." It is the same word used when he began his ministry with the call of his disciples. It is the same word used to call those heavily burdened, to take his yoke which is easy and light. "Blessed" refers back to the Sermon on the Mount and the Beatitudes, where those called blessed are merciful, hunger and thirst for righteousness, and peacemakers. Many connections come together in this dramatic scene.

Holiness is deeds. It is doing the will of the Father, love in action. The surprise for those listening to this description of the final judgment is that Jesus identifies with the needy, not just those who look like us—all the needy. This is a theophany, namely, telling us how God is manifested. Jesus identifies himself with the poor and suffering of the world. When we see them, we see Jesus.

What is clear is that the judgment is not based on sinful versus nonsinful conduct, or even on a Ten Commandments-based morality, but rather on how we each pursue the authentic good of the other. Love of neighbor becomes explicitly love of God.

It is the least of these that stands out. Jesus goes to great lengths to describe them. Jesus lives in them. They are everywhere. The kingdom of God is expressed and realized in the hungry who have been fed, the oppressed freed, the imprisoned released, and the stranger welcomed. Christ's reign is not only realized, but it continues. The criteria for this are love, service, and hospitality, which are the measures by which we will be judged. If we do these things we are already living in God's reign. We are beginning our heaven.

Here we have two images of Christ: the Shepherd who cares for the sheep and the King who judges. They seem to be contradictory. Yet that is who God is. God loves us deeply and provides for us. Like a loving parent, God calls us to accountability for our actions, for what we do or fail to do.

The final criteria is hospitality. How do I live a spirit of welcome in my life? How am I a person of welcome by what I say and do? Hospitality was key to life in the first century. It was critical. If you did not help travelers, foreigners, or other strangers passing through, they might die. This happens regularly to migrants in the Southwest of our country today. Hospitality to strangers is the ultimate hospitality. Even pagans will be judged by this standard.

Today, with the pandemic, we see a broad base of suffering in the world. Yet, even before COVID there was much suffering in many places. However, if it did not touch me, I often did not pay much attention. With COVID it is now front and center to us all. It is always on our minds. This week we are changing holiday plans. We are being warned that the worst is coming over these winter months before we get more widespread access to the vaccines. It is really terrifying.

How do we live in a world so full of suffering, a suffering that may touch me at any moment? The world meets Christ through those in need. The world also meets Christ through his disciples. The Christ of the poor teaches us, while the Christ of the disciples responds in charity and compassion. In both, Christ is proclaimed. Our primary function is to look for and represent Christ to the world. This coming together in Christ is revealed at the *parousia*, the final coming. The surprise for the good and the bad is that in everyday actions they see Christ and can earn their salvation if they so choose. It is in the normal things, the little things, that we live in and with Christ.

The Office of Readings is part of the prayers that clergy and the religious recite each day. Recently one of the readings was from a homily written in the second century, reflecting on the theme of judgment. The following lines jumped out at me: "Therefore, a very good way of atoning for our sins is by being generous to the poor. Fasting is better than prayer, but almsgiving surpasses both, for 'love covers a multitude of sins.' . . . Happy the man who is found rich in these virtues; by relieving the poor, he himself will be relieved of his sins." Wow!

What are we willing to learn from this time of suffering? What can we learn from those who suffer, whether it is sickness or poverty or violence or so much more?

We in the church are blessed, especially in times like these. We have the support of the praying community, the reflection of the gospels, the sacraments, the example of so many responding to the Christ in need, and solidarity with others that assures us we are not alone. There is a superabundance of gifts to do what Christ calls us to do and for which we will be judged.

I have been inside the Sistine Chapel at the Vatican many times. I am always overwhelmed by it. Of course, it is one of the most spectacular pieces of art in the world, but that is only a part of the experience. As I stare at the ceiling, I try to grasp not only what Michelangelo wanted to tell us, but more than that. The power of the painting is to experience what those around Jesus heard and felt from him in today's gospel. It is powerful and scary. It makes you ask if you are ready. Are you?

In the *Confiteor* at the beginning of Mass, we say we are sorry for "what I have done and what I have failed to do." It works both ways. That makes me think of the holidays, traditionally a season of spending, often for things we and others don't need. These words should give us pause.

Yes, the final exam comes for us all. The issue for us is that unlike college, we will never know what day we will take it, so thinking that we will have time to cram right before it is not an option. What is an option, even an obligation, is to look for and learn from Jesus in everyone I meet, every day, especially the most needy, and to respond as I can.

The final exam: You have the questions. You have the answers. What more do you need to be ready?

39

11/26/20 Thanksgiving

…your faith has been your salvation.

Deut 8:7–18; 1 Tim 6:6–11, 17–19; Luke 17:11–19

So, WHAT DO WE have to be thankful for in November of 2020? Things are dark with the virus raging out of control, family gatherings cancelled, hospitals starting to be overwhelmed, and our lives put on hold again. There is the news that even though vaccines are on the way, they are still many months off from reaching the majority of the population.

A few people are actually happy that they don't have to sit at the table with the proverbial drunk uncle who spouts off about politics every year! Not sure if he exists for most families, but if it is my family, I'm the uncle, just not drunk and just not talking politics at table! My family has made the good decision to cancel our gathering, so the uncle will not be at any table this year. At any rate, it will be a bit of a lonely holiday trying to find new ways to give thanks.

Some time ago I read an article on the fact that expressing gratitude, even when we don't think there is a lot for which to be grateful, will actually not only make us grateful, but happier. The article also said some people are more naturally grateful than others, which comes from having a particular gene. We can actively choose to practice gratitude and that very fact will make us happier. The brain takes that grateful attitude, even when you can't see a lot for which to be thankful, and processes it into happiness. Choosing to focus on good things makes us feel better than focusing on the bad. It also brings out the best in others around us. There is one downside, however. In some people, gratitude can make them fat . . . they begin to crave sweets! Careful on the pumpkin pie!

How do we make gratitude a routine, something that is part of our everyday living? We start with interior gratitude, which then becomes exterior expressions to others. The author of the article concluded by saying he felt gratitude because I read the article.

Gratitude is the main point of the gospel on this Thanksgiving Day. This gospel story appears only in Luke as he stresses the theme of universalism. All can be saved, which was not the belief of the Jews at that time. Luke has already told the parable of the good Samaritan. Remember how Jews despised Samaritans as not being really faithful. Now there is another good Samaritan. This one is good not so much for what he did, but because he realizes what God has done and so he responds in gratitude.

The lepers at that time were outcasts. Their sickness was considered punishment for sin. They were expelled from the community. In effect they had to quarantine far from others, similar to what we are seeing today with COVID-19. However, their illness was never over in fourteen days; it was often for life. The only way to return was to have a priest certify they were well. When Jesus healed it was not only the physical cure but it also meant a return to the community, which was equally important. Those healed from COVID today know exactly what that feels like.

Notice how Jesus treats the ten lepers as if they were already healed, simply sending them to the priests to fulfill the law. They act in obedient faith. They asked Jesus for the healing, so they must have had some kind of faith he could do it. Yet, he tells only the Samaritan, the one that Jesus' hearers would not have expected, the foreigner, the one who came back to give thanks, "your faith has saved you." It seems that Jesus is speaking about some blessing other than the cure, namely, the next level: faith leading us to salvation.

Ten were healed, but the story tells us one was saved. The incident is about how the healing gratitude became the moment of salvation. Samaritans were not considered saved like Jews, so the story shows how powerful gratitude can be in one's life. The grateful Samaritan took action to believe in Jesus and returned to give thanks. This saved him. Luke wants us to see how Jesus' mission was to all, even those not like us.

Thanksgiving is at the basis of faith in God. It is the profound realization that all I am and have is from God and my whole life must be lived as a response to that in order to attain my salvation. When we really think about it, we all have much for which to be grateful. We are incredibly blessed.

The story is very clear. To be saved is to acknowledge God for blessings received and to respond in faith and action. There is a difference between healing and salvation. Salvation is taking healing to a deeper level where it is not just about us. When we reach that point, we can then respond with a continuing relationship with God, and thus with my sisters and brothers. That is when we truly are happy.

The good Samaritan now becomes the grateful Samaritan. The other nine did not see in the healing the coming of the Messiah. The Samaritan came to faith in Jesus as Messiah, which was remarkable for a non-Jewish person. Jesus recognizes his faith and his gratitude. One can be healed without coming to faith and thus being saved. The experience of healing does not necessarily save. It can move us to faith, which expresses itself in thanks. Those who have recovered from COVID or any other serious illness should take note.

To be thankful is to be a person of faith, because we recognize where everything comes from. It is expressed in how we live our lives and in how we recognize God's gift to us. We then become gifts to others.

I have been asked by many people who have been affected by COVID or other serious health issues to pray for their healing. I always assure them I will and add them to my prayer list each morning. They always are grateful, which is the movement towards salvation. That is certainly worth praying for!

Thanksgiving is essential to the life of a Christian. Giving thanks is giving of ourselves, putting our gratitude into action. In Spanish, today is "Día de Acción de Gracias." Notice the word "acción," which indicates giving thanks is doing something, taking action, living that thanks. How do you live your thanks?

The Eucharist is the ultimate moment of giving thanks, when we actually experience in a real way God's presence and Jesus inside of us. These months where many have not been able to physically assist at Mass and receive communion have been very difficult. Missing the Eucharist has made us appreciate what a great gift we have in the body and blood of Jesus offered at each Mass. Those who are attending Mass can make a point of reflecting on what you are grateful for each time you are there. As we leave Mass, we are called to take that thanks everywhere we go.

Live a eucharistic life. It will be a life of thanks. It will be shown in the action of giving of yourself. If you do, you will know you are happy.

40

11/29/20 First Advent

Be constantly on the watch!

Isa 63:16b–17, 19b, 64:2–7; 1 Cor 1:3–9; Mark 13:33–37

ALMOST EVERY EVENING SINCE March, Mayor Nirenburg, County Judge Wolfe, and other local government officials hold a press conference here in San Antonio concerning the latest developments in the coronavirus pandemic for our community. The message is usually the same: "Be vigilant! Be careful! Watch out! Keep your eyes open! You can help slow the spread. Wear your mask, keep your distance, don't congregate." We hear those and similar words over and over. It is urgent.

The leaders are warning us to be aware of our actions, of where we go, and how we interact with others. What we do today will have consequences for ourselves and others tomorrow. The virus numbers are now surging in San Antonio and all over the nation. It is a difficult time, especially as we enter the holiday season. If we are not vigilant, it could cost us our health or even worse, our life, or the life of a loved one. It affects many others, even our whole community.

At the same time, as we get these strong warnings, we are also experiencing a virus fatigue. This has been going on for almost ten months. We have done many of these measures—masks, social distancing, avoiding large crowds—and it still seems things are very bad. We are worn out and worn down.

The gospel is good news. That is what "gospel" means. There is good news! Help is on the way. There is hope in the midst of such darkness and fear. While we are being warned so strongly of the disaster around us, there are constant notices of the vaccines that will help end this nightmare. They are coming, we are assured. We can't wait!

The other good news is the fact that so many medical personnel, first responders, and people in essential services have not given up. They are there for us every day. They are showing us what it means to care and put ourselves on the line for others. That is truly good!

In the gospel today, we hear similar words from Jesus, the last ones before he begins his passion: "Keep awake!" This phrase is very important as it is repeated three times. These days we hear it repeated constantly as we try to contain the virus. Jesus' words were not about a virus but they were nevertheless about how we live life and care for others.

Today we begin the season of Advent and the beginning of a new liturgical year for the church. Advent is a time of expectation and waiting, a totally positive type of watchfulness and hope, unlike the pandemic problems we anticipate over the next weeks. Advent offers only hope. It points to the three comings of Christ. We remember the first coming of Christ that was highly anticipated by the Jews in the long-awaited Messiah. We Christians look forward to the second coming of Christ at the end of time with confidence. And in between, Advent calls us to be alert to the Master coming among us at any time, right here, right now. That needs to be our focus as we enter Advent, especially this year.

The parable in the gospel a few weeks ago, with the three servants who received different amounts of talents, tells us that waiting for the Master's return is an active process. The patron/client model then was the dominant model of employment. It was more familial than the employee-and-employer model in existence today. The patron protected, but was usually absent. There is a sense of both the now and the not yet. We are feeling that today.

This story becomes a farewell discourse by Jesus before his death. It is an inspiration and a warning to live every moment as if Christ were coming then. The warning is to be vigilant at night, which was when the passion began and when the body lay in the tomb. The warning not to be caught sleeping is related to the disciples in the garden of Gethsemane the night Jesus is arrested. They not only fell asleep when he needed them the most, but they fled and Peter betrayed him a few hours later. Not to be vigilant is directly related to a disastrous response on the part of the disciples. They did not understand the call to the cross despite the fact that Jesus had clearly told them if they wanted to be a disciple they would need to carry the cross and follow him.

Can we understand our cross today? Our call is part of what we are going through now with the pandemic. We must pick up our cross and do our part in following Jesus. The sacrifices we are being called upon to do are part of what it means to be awake and vigilant. They are mostly not a huge request, but accepting them is responding to those in need and to the wider community. It is being ready to meet the Lord however he presents himself.

I recently celebrated a Mass for former Congressman Henry B. Gonzalez on the twentieth anniversary of his passing. Henry B, as he was known to people in San Antonio, was a congressman for many years representing our area. He had broken many barriers in the political field as a person of Hispanic origin, beginning with the local level, then state, and finally national. He was known for his fierce support of social justice for the poor, especially the Mexican and Mexican Americans of South Texas. He was not afraid to speak out even when this would upset many powerful people.

Henry B.'s funeral card had this quote: "What I care about is what you care about . . . decency, justice and an abhorrence for what is wrong . . ." He was proud when attacked for fighting segregation and unprincipled privilege. He was always alert to how the vulnerable were being treated in society.

I was at the congressman's hospital bed with the family the moment he died. We prayed for him and stayed close around his bed as he gave his last breath. I remember so clearly seeing that he had expired, yet his eyes were fully open. As I think now about that moment, I realize how appropriate it was that he went back to his Creator with his eyes wide open, alert, always looking out for those who struggled, those discriminated against, those who only wanted a decent and fair chance at a good life. Maybe that is the message of today's gospel for all of us. Never stop being vigilant, looking for Jesus, who can be found in others, especially those on the margins of society.

The work is urgent! Stay awake. Life is fragile, especially in the face of a terrible virus. Anything can happen which will change your world. We have certainly learned that this year. Inaction is not an option for the follower of Jesus. Mark did not want Christians just to endure or put up with whatever was happening at the time. Rather he wanted an active presence, active working, doing the Lord's will, never letting down their guard, never stopping.

The gospel message is clear. It is not for you to know when Jesus will return; you just need to continue to be faithful. Look at everything with the eyes of faith, not the eyes of the world. If you do, you will see signs all around of hope breaking though, of Jesus in others. You will see Jesus in people, especially the vulnerable, the sick and the poor. You will see Jesus in those who daily are serving others, risking their own lives, going the extra mile. He comes to us through them.

The only thing that is always true is God. God is always faithful. We do not know many things! Even though people are fearful this year because of the pandemic, the Christian is never without hope. The Christian must proclaim the hope that says Jesus is among us, Jesus comes now, Jesus is in our brother and sister. This world needs the message of hope, especially this year.

Keep awake! Keep vigilant! You are that hope!

41

12/6/20 Second Advent

Make ready the way of the Lord.

Isa 40:1–5, 9–11; 2 Pet 3:8–14; Mark 1:1–8

RECENTLY POPE FRANCIS INVITED a group of NBA players, including Marco Belinelli of the San Antonio Spurs, to the Vatican to discuss the league's social and economic justice efforts. The pope wanted to highlight what the players were doing, especially about racism, since the killing of George Floyd by a policeman in Minneapolis last May. Pope Francis told them, "You are champions. But always giving an example of teamwork, you've become a model . . . always remaining humble . . . and preserving your own humanity."[1] The pope affirmed the power of sports to affect change in society. The players were inspired by the visit with the pope and moved to continue to fight racism and social injustice.

Our country, and many others, have had to face the sin of racism in our history. This is a time to decide that things do not have to be as they have been and take serious steps to change. Yet a change in society can start only with a change in each of us, especially in our hearts. That is what Pope Francis is calling us to do. That is what Advent is all about.

If John the Baptist were alive today, and in this country, I think he would be marching in the Black Lives Matter protests, carrying a simple sign with one word on it: Repent! He would be urging us all to repent for our original sin of racism. He would be asking us to rethink in our hearts a new way of seeing others, or interacting with those different from us.

---

1. The Associated Press, "NBA Players Meet with Pope Francis," para. 6.

He would tell us to look for so many things we take for granted that we could change in order to make the world better. He would say that is how we find the way to welcome Christ.

That is the message in the gospel today. John called for change in the people, a complete change of mind and heart called *metanoia*. He demanded that the people embrace repentance for the forgiveness of sins. They needed to see things differently and act upon that. This is how they would prepare for the coming of the Messiah.

John is the one who connects all of salvation history together. He comes out of the desert, just as Israel did after leaving Egypt and wandering for forty years. The prophets come out of the desert. The story of Jesus begins by his coming out of the desert by the River Jordan, where Israel crossed into the promised land. The desert is the place for encounters between God and the people. It is also a place of retreat, to go away from the world and enter into God's presence. The desert is the place where people begin a new way of life. It is a place that demands change of life. It is also a place of hunger. People hunger for the Lord.

Where is our desert? Where are we called to change? The desert today is at the margins of society. That is where we find Jesus. The margins are where the poor and powerless live and move. It is where we also begin. The desert symbolizes our need to change, to confront our sinfulness and seek a way to be different, to follow the call of God in our lives. This year we see the desert most starkly with so many people suffering from COVID and its effects on the economy. When we enter into the suffering of others, as much as we can, we see that things do not always have to be as they have been in the past. It is a call to help make a change. We can create a new world. That is how we prepare for the coming of Jesus.

Mark writes for first-century Palestinian Christians who were afflicted by poverty, disease, and marginalization, much like many people today in our world whose lives have been worsened by the effects of the pandemic. Many people today feel as if there is no hope, as if they are powerless. John promises something new. Things can be different, but the change must begin with each of us.

Advent is that time for us. It is a time of hopeful expectation, of preparing to receive the Lord, to see and recognize Jesus whenever and however he comes. Hope is confidence in the promises of God. Things will be better, but it challenges us to make that a reality by who we are and what we do. Make yourself ready!

In order to be ready, we must also eradicate from our lives whatever hinders us from seeing the greatest promise. Jesus is that promise, especially as he comes in those who are not like us, not of our race or ethnic group, the neediest, the sick, the stranger. We must eliminate the thinking that we are superior to others, not judge others as being less because they are different from us, or other quick ways we condemn others. Advent tells us Jesus comes in all of these on whom we look down. We must prepare to see and receive him. Something must change to allow us to do this.

This year, between the disastrous effects of the pandemic, where the poorest have again suffered the most, as well as confronting our racist history and its terrible effects on people of color, we have seen much bad news. Jesus is good news because he shows how in loving and serving others, especially the least, we can truly change the world. Jesus is the beginning of the mission to spread that good news to the world. We are the ones to continue that mission.

I met him at a Catholic school in Albuquerque a few years ago. I was speaking to about 250 children about Catholic Relief Services, the official international humanitarian agency of the US Catholic Church, and our work with the poorest people on earth. He was a boy about ten years old. He raised his hand while I was speaking and insisted he wanted to tell me something. He had learned on the internet that every minute a child in Africa dies of malaria. He also learned about a program, "Nothing But Nets," that donated treated sleeping nets to guard against the mosquitos that carry the sickness and bite at night. He told his parents that instead of spending money on his Christmas presents he wanted to help buy nets for kids in Africa. He estimated that he saved the lives of twelve children, twelve children he would never meet, twelve children who could never thank him.

That young child decided things do not always have to be the same. Privileged children do not have to receive so many gifts while others in another part of the world are dying. He had to rethink how things had always been and change himself. He did not need to receive gifts so that he could help other children have a chance at life. He could change the world a little by changing himself, his thinking, and his actions. Christmas was now not just what he was going to get, but what he could give. That is *metanoia*.

Mark opens his writing by saying it is the beginning of the gospel, the good news, of Jesus Christ, Son of God. Genesis 1:1 starts, "In the beginning when God created the heavens and the earth . . ." Therefore, Mark is telling us that with Jesus, God is beginning something new, a new creation. Jesus and the gospel are one. Jesus is the gospel, the good news.

The good news is born in those who take the mission of Jesus to others. Be good news, especially for those most in need. Make this Advent a new day for you. Look into your heart now and ask what needs to change this Advent. It will allow you to recognize Jesus as he comes and to share him with others.

Advent is a call to new beginnings. That is why it is a season of hope. Things do not always have to be the same. What new beginning do you need to make this year? Do it now!

42

12/12/20 Our Lady of Guadalupe

Blest are you among women . . .

Rev 11:19a, 12:1–6a, 10a–b; Luke 1:39–47

LAST YEAR AT THIS time, I was asked to lead *Las Posadas* at the Pearl. *Las Posadas* is a Mexican tradition celebrated on the days leading up to Christmas. It was a huge event, with over 3,500 people, including many children. Some children came dressed as angels or shepherds to really get into the story. I am sure they will remember it better than any candy they got that night. Why? Because it was an experience, not something that was bought for them.

The genius about *Las Posadas* is that we enter into the story with our bodies by walking with Joseph and Mary, trying to find room at the inn and being consistently rejected at every stop. That bodily experience can stay with us and teach us how Jesus was rejected from the womb on; therefore, we should not be surprised when we experience the same for doing something we feel is right.

In this country, the average amount per child spent by parents for Christmas gifts is $330, according to a study last year.[2] Often that prized gift is old by the next day. In contrast to receiving things, kids who communicate with parents do better in school, and teens who spend more time with parents have fewer behavioral problems. How about presence instead of presents?

2. Santoro, "Average Amount Parents Spend," para. 4.

Many parents have now turned Christmas gifts into experiences. Some cost money, many do not. This year it might be challenging with the pandemic cautions, but creativity could help make happy moments. Take a trip together to a local park or lake, a long drive in the country, or outings in the city to see the lights. How about each getting a gift card that promises a trip to the zoo or museum, or a family vacation when it is safe to do so in the New Year?

I remember our family outings from childhood, yet remember very few Christmas gifts. Children will talk about these experiences for a long time. Maybe some gifts are important, especially to those who have very little. Volunteering time at a food pantry or similar place to help others is a good start. If it is possible, take children along to experience and see many other children who are struggling this year just to get by and actually need food to stay alive. That memory might stay with them and give them a perspective of how blessed they are and their responsibility to give back.

Those who do not have children in the home can be a presence to others in many other ways. How about phone calls, internet Facetime, Zoom calls, and even old-fashioned written notes to let them know they are remembered during this time of pandemic? There are many options for reaching out today, but it can mean so much.

The gospel today on the Feast of Our Lady of Guadalupe is the story of the visitation of Mary to her cousin Elizabeth. It shows us Mary and Elizabeth believed in something much greater and deeper than giving each other gifts. Mary did not take Elizabeth any gift. Mary was a poor person, so she gave what she had, her presence. Both believed that what God said would happen to them would happen, even though it was improbable. They were believing in God's plan of salvation through Jesus.

Elizabeth salutes Mary for three reasons: Being chosen, saying yes to that choice, and acting on that yes. Two miracles meet, a woman who conceived in her old age and a woman who conceives without a man. Mary goes to Elizabeth, not vice versa, showing the poor of God proclaim the Messiah. Mary carries Jesus in her womb to proclaim good news. John the Baptist responds from the womb. The stories begin even before either child is born.

Believing is just the first step. We are meant to be companions to each other. Hearing the voice of one we love gives us delight, brings back memories, refreshes the soul. Elizabeth is affirmed by the presence of her special cousin.

This is a rare story of two women speaking to each other in the Scriptures. This is not necessarily an accurate account of what happened. It does not all make much sense. Mary went on a 100-mile journey alone. Mary leaves Elizabeth when she was needed most, right before her giving birth. It is theology, not history. It is not intended to be a logical story. Rather, it is a theology of God's plan of salvation through Jesus.

The two women praise God for what God is doing in and through them. Mary and Elizabeth are agents, faithful to God, obedient. Mary leaves in haste after her encounter with the angel, a sign of the desire to do God's will with zeal.

Mary is the model disciple, the first disciple. Acting on her belief is what the disciple does. The faithful one responds to God's call and takes action. The annunciation shows Mary's call comes during ordinary life. She was not in the temple, not praying like Zechariah or Simeon or Anna. Our call comes in everyday living. We need to be listening.

The two women exchange reflections on the actions of God in their lives. Elizabeth prophesies about the child in Mary's womb. Mary responds with recognition of the great things God has done for and with her.

Mary and Elizabeth celebrate what God has done—an elderly woman becomes pregnant and a virgin becomes pregnant. Both women were in some sense the forgotten, the rejected, the poor, the unnoticed, until they heard God's call. They accepted God's will and acted on it.

Both women also proclaim that with God things are different. Elizabeth gives a blessing, and says "Mother of my Lord," (Luke 1:43) meaning Jesus is Lord and Savior. The emperor is not the lord and savior, which was a clear revolutionary statement. Mary responds with the Magnificat, saying that with God the world is turned upside down, the poor are rich, the lowly are lifted up, and the mighty are deposed from their thrones.

The story we celebrate today of Guadalupe speaks of the apparition of Mary to a simple indigenous person. Again, as in the gospel, the emphasis is on presence. Her presence is what was important. "Am I not here who am your mother?" She wanted a church built where the people come to receive consolation and strength from their mother. It would be a symbol of God's presence, a house of God. It would be a place of welcome. Even though the basilica honors Mary of Guadalupe, her image on the tilma is not front and center over the altar, but placed at the foot of the cross, where Mary stood while Jesus gave his life.

The presence of *La Virgen* gave Juan Diego extraordinary courage to do what he felt he could not do, namely, to go to a place of power and speak to the bishop to carry out her message and desires. It is typical of the song of the Magnificat Mary sings with Elizabeth. The world turns upside down.

Las Posadas tells us that Mary's role in bringing Jesus to the world was difficult, with much rejection and sacrifice. She carries her cross right away. *Las Posadas* poses the question to us: Who is rejected today? How can we turn the narrative around with our presence and be people of *posada*, be people of welcome? It might mean helping to carry a cross with others, especially during this time of suffering through a terrible virus.

Christmas and Guadalupe, especially this year, challenge us to see gift-giving as secondary to companionship. Being for and with each other is what is important. Presence can be a bigger gift than anything else, especially during a pandemic when people feel alone, afraid, and powerless. You can't buy loving care. You can't buy the presence and support of that special other.

Many of us remember our mothers, whether alive or deceased, during this time of year. *La Virgen de Guadalupe* is our mother. This feast asks us to be Mary to others: carry Jesus inside, proclaim what God has done for you, and simply be a presence for others.

43

12/13/20 Third Advent

...in my God is the joy of my soul.

Isa 61:1–2a, 10–11; 1 Thess 5:16–24; John 1:6–8, 19–28

FRIDAY I WAS INVITED by former Mayor Phil Hardberger to see the new land bridge at Hardberger Park in north San Antonio. I was with several others who had been instrumental in both establishing the park and securing the land bridge which will allow wildlife to cross over a busy thoroughfare in the middle of the park to get to sources of water. While on the tour, I heard the untold stories of the hard work and sacrifices it took to acquire the land for the park and pay for the bridge. It was years of work with considerable opposition at times. However, all those involved said the struggle was totally worth it. They now see how happy the park has made so many thousands of people who use it. It is one of the largest parks in the city. This has been a joy for the people and will be so for the generations to come. Joy often comes with sacrifice.

Today is *Gaudete* Sunday, Sunday of Joy. The church asks us to be aware of the joy of the coming of Christ we will commemorate at Christmas.

This year is there any reason for joy? The worldwide pandemic continues. There is not only medical suffering, but many are struggling just to live, to eat, to have a roof over their heads. Millions of migrants and refugees throughout the world are escaping violence and impossible poverty in their home countries, and their journeys are compounded by the threat of the virus wherever they go. Even though the vaccinations have begun, it will be many months before things will be safer, and many people have to be convinced to take the vaccine for their own good and that of the community. In the midst of all this how can we be joyful?

"The joy of the gospel fills the hearts and the lives of all who encounter Jesus. . . . With Christ joy is constantly born anew."[1] With these words in 2013, Pope Francis began his apostolic exhortation translated, *The Joy of the Gospel*. The pope urges us to become missionaries of joy, the joy we have received from encountering Christ.

The gospel today challenges us to identify who we are. As Pope Francis tells us, we are called to be missionaries of Jesus. We carry Jesus to others because we have been touched by him. We have been transformed in Christ. Christ's love accompanies us in all we do. That is who we are. That is the cause for joy.

In the gospel today, John the Baptist is asked who he is. He says he is a voice crying in the desert. Remember last week the image of the desert as the place to encounter God, where there is no place to hide, where God sees us as we are and loves us. When we accept this, we can take God to others.

John also says who he is not. He is not Elijah. He is not the prophet. He does not fall into the trap to present himself as someone more than who he is, as tempting as that would be. We often are tempted to pretend that we are someone we are not, just to impress others or make ourselves feel better. We often try to hide our faults and failings instead of confronting them so we can learn and grow. People of that time did not understand what kind of Messiah was coming. They thought the Messiah would be a warrior-king, a great political ruler to make Israel a powerful state. Yet Jesus came as a Suffering Servant, a humble Savior, which was why so many did not recognize or accept him.

"There is one among you whom you do not recognize," John says. His words remind us that only with repentance, with admitting who we are and who we are not, can we see the Lord. Only then can we be missionaries for Christ. This means we must be honest with our failings and understand how much we need God.

The Scripture today tells us that witnessing to Jesus is to be a person of joy, to radiate happiness that we know Jesus is here with us. It is to be a witness to Jesus' life, namely, to bring good news to the poor.

I remember one Christmas Eve before Mass at the cathedral. I was in the back of church getting things ready and noticed a young woman

---

1. Pope Francis, *Evangelii Gaudium*, para. 1.

sitting alone, crying. I took a moment to see if I could help and found out she was going through what many people feel so deeply at this time, a profound loneliness and disconnectedness. The great Christmas expectations of joy were far away from her. I listened and assured her she was not alone, especially in the community of faith. Her story I have seen many times in people at Christmas.

During this season, when it is traditional to exchange gifts, we often try to decide what she or he would like or need. We try to match the gift with the person. Yet, repeatedly we hear that money does not buy happiness. We are not the things we have. There are countless stories of people who left high-paying jobs to use their talents in a lesser-paying position to help the disadvantaged. They sacrificed a high income, but became much happier.

It is said that with age comes a certain wisdom. People I know who are getting older begin giving things away, and start becoming donors to good causes. They see having so many things as a distraction from the simple pleasures of spending time with family and friends and appreciating the beauty of life. They see that helping others gives them more happiness than having many things.

Who are you? Can you ever be happy? What would it take?

John the Baptist says he is a voice crying in the desert, not in Jerusalem, not in the temple, not with the authorities and powers. He did not have to be the important one. He was the witness, a lesser one, but passionate about getting people to repent and prepare. He did what he was supposed to do, even though he was killed for doing it. John says over and over again who he is not. In contrast, Jesus later states who he is: "I AM," "I am the Good Shepherd," "I am the Bread of Life," "I am the Way, the Truth and the Life" (John 8:58, 10:11, 6:35, 14:6).

Like John, we are not Jesus, but are called to witness to him, to announce him. The Lord is coming. This is our joy. Today tells us that witnessing to Jesus is to be a person of joy, to radiate happiness that we know Jesus is here with us. God has blessed me so abundantly. I need to say and live my thanks. I must be a witness to Jesus' job description, namely, to bring good news to the poor.

Happy people spread happiness. So, we are people called to witness to Jesus by doing what Isaiah in the first reading says is good news, healing the brokenhearted, bringing liberty to captives—including those captured by consumerism—and release to prisoners. How many people would just love to be forgiven, to be listened to, to be reconciled, to be set free of so many things that hold them down and drain the life out of them? That would be all they want for Christmas. Can you help others experience that kind of joy at Christmas? If you are a person of joy, you can!

Today asks us the question: What is joy? The gospel is telling us that joy is to look at Christ and know he is there for us. It is to tell his story to others by how we speak and how we act. It is to take the focus off myself and put it on the joy of living the gospel.

People all around us are poor today because they struggle economically, but also because they feel alone, unsupported, isolated, and fearful. The pandemic has greatly multiplied this. We bring good news by our constant joy, a joy that comes from our encounter with Jesus and our mission to bring his joy to others.

Happy people spread happiness. Be a person of joy today!

44

12/20/20 Fourth Advent

Let it be done to me as you say.

2 Sam 7:1–5, 8b–12,14a, 16; Rom 16:25–27; Luke 1:26–38

AS THE PREDICTED WINTER surge of coronavirus cases affects our country, the pressure on many people is growing. I was listening to a story on the radio about an emergency room nurse who had to leave her position for something much less stressful. She is one of many who are making that decision, which multiplies the pressure for those who stay on the job. Many are saying they could handle the work, though challenging, up to now, but these last nine months were not what they ever imagined would happen when they first made the decision to do nursing.

People are making tough decisions now as this pandemic continues. Some have lost their jobs and are draining their savings just for basics. Others have taken a job at lower pay with longer hours. Still others have moved in with family or friends to share expenses. Many have no safety net.

What decisions have you made that had challenging, unanticipated consequences? Commitments like marriage and family are part of these. How did you handle the tough results?

Today's gospel is the story of a young woman who faced a huge decision. She said yes to something she never imagined would happen. She had no idea what would follow in her life because of that decision. It was a yes that brought her joy, but also tremendous sacrifice and suffering, even rejection.

The gospel today on this last Sunday before Christmas is the annunciation story. Last year, in Matthew's Gospel for this Sunday, we saw the role of Joseph and how he was conflicted about marrying Mary once he discovered she was pregnant and he was not the father. A dream convinces him to move forward. Matthew highlights Joseph, a descendant of the house of David, as his gospel is directed to Jews and Jewish Christians. Matthew's genealogy of Jesus begins with Abraham, father of the chosen people. To prove Jesus was the Messiah he cites Scripture and people familiar to Jews.

This year we have Luke's Gospel and we see Mary's role as prominent. This annunciation follows immediately on the one in the temple to Zechariah. There are also several other annunciation stories in the Hebrew Scriptures, the Old Testament. Usually they involve a miracle, in that a woman was old or barren and becomes pregnant, such as Sarah, Abraham's wife. This one to Mary is different. It is the first one where a man is not involved. God does not take the place of a man, but creates in her womb. She remains a virgin.

Luke is directing his gospel to gentiles, so he does not worry about the Jewish background of Jesus so much. He is a master storyteller and what a story he has to tell! Luke's genealogy of Jesus begins with Adam, the first man created by God. Mary's "yes" is contrasted with the "no" of Adam and Eve, who refused to obey God in the garden. With this "yes," God begins something new, and reverses the sin of the first parents. Mary is the new Eve, beginning the human race all over.

Just before this story in Luke we see the angel Gabriel announcing the future birth of John the Baptist to Zechariah in the temple. Notice how Elizabeth is not part of this dialogue. However, when Mary and the angel dialogue, we learn the theology of Jesus, which is the story Luke wants to tell. It becomes clear that Jesus was already God's Son, so this shows the conception was through the Holy Spirit. Joseph is not mentioned in this telling. This is a work that is completely God's action. God is the chief character in this story.

As with so much in our lives when God calls, Mary faces a tough choice: What does this all mean? She is disturbed by the greeting, which is a typical part of scriptural reaction to angelic announcements. Should I do it? Is it scary? Why me? Can I do it? Mary's life is turned upside down and so is the world because of her response.

This is the most important decision in the history of the world. God becomes a human being, but a "yes" is needed. What ultimately assures Mary are the angel's final words, "Nothing is impossible with God." Listen to those words from the angel. When things seem so bleak, as they do now in this dark winter of virus, we must remember with God nothing is impossible. God is still in charge. Working with God, miracles happen. Our faith is needed now more than ever. We need to console each other with these words.

The angel says Mary is favored, also translated as "blessed," which puzzles and startles her. Yet Mary is the prototypical Christian; she accepts and activates God's word in her, for which she is and will be blessed. The key is that Mary's relationship with Jesus is first of all by a word of acceptance to God's will, more than blood ties. Jesus will later say, whoever does the will of my heavenly Father is brother and sister and mother to me (Matt 12:50). How do you see God's will for you?

The Spirit overshadows Mary, the same word used in the transfiguration, when a cloud of glory overshadows his disciples. Mary believes the words of the Lord to her, which was required since it was a virginal conception. Mary is the first disciple. The Word of God becomes part of her, grows within, and is brought to life. She becomes an icon of faith.

A disciple is one who hears the word of God, acts on it, and makes it alive in one's life. In the process one is totally transformed. However, "yes" does not mean it will be easy, just possible. How many yeses have you given that were very difficult to live out? What made the difference in fulfilling that yes?

At this moment people are making another decision: what to do for Christmas. Health officials are urging us not to travel if possible and to keep gatherings small and safe. These and other decisions are not only for us but for the wider community as well. They may seem like little decisions but the consequences could be larger and even dangerous. We need to dig deep for the faith we have in God to make the right choices. Mary's faith was complete: "I am the servant of the Lord. Let it be done in me as you say." Mary looks at her life and gives it totally to God with the faith and the trust that God will work in and through her to accomplish the gift of his Son to the world.

Christmas is the time to think of decisions I make that help bring Jesus to others, decisions about the words I use, the actions I take, the thanks I give, and the generosity and compassion I share. People realize

Christ is alive through the faith of his followers, especially a faith that is lived despite hardship. This time of virus is that moment for us.

In the story that follows this one, Mary visits Elizabeth and the exchange with her results in Mary being overwhelmed with what has happened to her and what will happen to her. Mary gives all the glory to God, as we hear in her canticle, called the Magnificat. It is a song of the world being turned upside down beginning with her yes.

Mary said yes, and in that act of humble acceptance of God's will she gave herself as a gift. She opened her body to receive the Son of God and change the world. She was fearful, but faithful. Through the rest of her life she would learn what her yes meant, beginning with the rejection of there being no room at the inn when she was ready to give birth, and all the way to the foot of the cross.

What is your angel calling you to do? How can you help bring Jesus into the world this year when many are discouraged, depressed, and struggling? Nourish him in your body and share his life.

This Christmas, dig deep, make an act of faith, say "yes," and change the world!

45

12/24–25/20 Christmas

She gave birth to her first-born Son ... and laid him in a manger ...

Isa 9:1–6; Titus 2:11–14; Luke 2:1–14

RECENTLY I HEARD THE story of a Syrian refugee woman who had fled her war-torn country, and with much difficulty crossed Turkey and Greece, where she boarded a huge train with a thousand other refugees in North Macedonia to travel to the Serbian border. All of this happened, of course, in the midst of a pandemic. She had left her country at the beginning of a pregnancy with almost nothing, and as she was on the train she went into labor. Imagine this: in a crowded train with a thousand strangers, she began to feel birth pangs. Fortunately, the train arrived at the border in time for her to be taken to a small clinic that Catholic Relief Services had set up to help refugees on their way north. CRS is the agency of the United States Catholic Church for overseas relief and development. It has been helping thousands of refugees from Syria, Afghanistan, and other strife-filled countries for some years now. Along the way, the migrants have often faced hostility and rejection in the countries through which they traveled. She was welcomed at the clinic and had a safe delivery.

Christ is born.

The story in Luke's Gospel read at Midnight Mass is of Joseph and Mary desperate for a place to welcome the birth. They were migrants too, far from their home village, in the midst of many strangers. The gospel tells us they are a poor family, on a long journey, with much uncertainty as to how they will manage. They experience rejection over and over as no one will give them a room. It must have been a huge crisis for this young couple. Imagine the stress level!

Then, the baby is born. The gospel does not talk about a stable, just a manger, which was where animals were fed. Jesus, the Bread of Life, food for our own journey, lies in a food trough. No one saw this coming.

Luke's emphasis is on the poverty and simplicity of the birth and life of Jesus. Poor towns are the key locations in the story, like Nazareth and Bethlehem, not Jerusalem. The parents are poor. The first to hear the news are poor shepherds, considered the outcasts of society. Jesus is a spiritual, not a political king as most Jews imagined the Messiah would be. He comes for the rejected, those on the margins. From Mary's womb Jesus is also rejected as we commemorate in *Las Posadas*. Jesus' self-proclaimed job description will be, "I have come to bring good news to the poor" (Luke 4:18). The Christmas story tells us clearly that the poor are the first recipients of salvation. The whole narrative is not what anyone thought would happen.

We have all been poor this year. Few thought the world would experience a pandemic when 2020 began. In one way it has not spared anyone. We have all, rich and poor, been affected. It has made us all poor together. Many things are out of our control and this is so difficult. We feel vulnerable. Yes, the rich have not been affected as negatively as others, but we all have suffered uncertainty, fear, and life changes we cannot control. These kinds of things usually happen to the poor all the time, pandemic or not. However, when all of us are impacted, we begin to see better how others live every day.

It is through the eyes and experiences of the poor that we are saved. We are all poor in the sense that we share one small, vulnerable planet. We are understanding that more than ever this year. Climate change seems to be affecting all parts of the earth in different ways. Storms are more frequent and stronger. Artic ice is melting faster. Deserts are expanding. The years are warmer.

We are getting a perspective of the limited resources we have. To respond to the pandemic, vaccines are being produced, but it will take months and globally years before all are reached. There is a poverty in this moment we all share. Yet, all of us need to understand that it is from our poverty that we find Jesus most clearly, because fewer things get in the way.

We are all poor. When we identify with those who have less—not only less money, things, or resources, but less health, relationships, or opportunities to participate in society—we can then begin to understand and respond. Yet, from our poverty we give more. I have always seen that in the poor areas of San Antonio and the poorest places in the world I have visited with CRS. The poor give a much larger percentage of what they have to family, to others in need, and to charity. Less becomes more in Jesus.

The first part of the nativity story in Luke is simply the reality of what happened: the place, time, and who was in power. The second part is the significance of the event. Again, Luke is not writing for historical, but rather religious, purposes. The angel speaks to the shepherds, but not to Mary at this point. Mary could have used an angel's help as her birth pangs grew sharper and there was no place where she could give birth. Isn't that true for us at many desperate moments of life? That is where faith comes in. Mary is left to think about this in her heart, a good model for us all.

Jesus was born to die. All the signs were there from the beginning—the rejection of Joseph and Mary, being placed with animals, vulnerability, the poverty, the shepherds, the outcasts coming first. The story gets more desperate. Some days later the family has to flee to escape Herod's murdering intention and they become refugees in Egypt. Later they lose Jesus in the temple. It is not exactly a reassuring start to the life of the Savior of the world. Think about that as you stare at those peaceful, beautiful nativity scenes.

Jesus is not just one of us as a human being, but he shares in all our struggles, all the contradictions of life, the poverty, the rejection, the massive family problems. At the same time, Luke sets the stage for a world-shattering event by putting the birth in context of the Roman Empire. Jesus, not the emperor, is the Savior. The angels announce him as Savior, which was a title reserved for the emperor. A revolution is happening.

There was another story in the paper, similar to the Syrian refugee mother, that happened last month here on the Texas border. A pregnant Honduran woman walked alone in the South Texas brush after being pushed across the border by smugglers in a tire. Her labor pangs became intense and she fell down, screaming. Border patrol agents found her and helped deliver the baby girl on the spot. She was taken to a hospital and later mother and newborn were brought to Catholic Charities of the Brownsville Diocese. I was struck by the desperation of a woman who risked her life and that of her baby. Another mother, another birth under duress.

Christ is born.

Christmas gives us perspective: it is not about the gifts, it is about seeing things differently at the end of a year, seeing people differently, seeing ourselves differently. And what a year we have had! Seeing God differently in a baby, in poverty, in the rejected, and in those sick with COVID. As we see ourselves differently in the perspective of this small, poor child, we have hope for the future.

It is a small and vulnerable planet. We are so small in the grand scheme of things. Maybe this Christmas, as difficult as it might be for many because of the pandemic, is an opportunity to learn the lessons of poverty from a small, poor child, lying in a food trough for animals. That birth repeats itself today in so many ways and in so many places. We also, imitating Jesus, can be food for others both physically and spiritually this year.

Touch your poverty, recognize Jesus, and be food for others by sharing him. Tell the story. Christ is born.

46

12/27/20 Holy Family

He who reveres his father will live a long life;
he obeys the Lord who brings comfort to his mother.

Gen 15:1–6, 21:1–3; Heb 11:8, 11–12, 17–19; Luke 2:22–40

THE MOST DIFFICULT PART of the Christmas season this year was limiting our contacts with the family. Growing up I was blessed with wonderful parents, close family life, and lots of contact with the extended family. Both parents came from large families, so Christmas as a child involved grandmothers, aunts, uncles, many cousins, and lots of memories. For myself now, being a priest with no wife or children, I have always looked forward to special moments in the year when I can see the next generations, nephews, nieces, their children, and of course my sisters. Since the days and weeks go by rapidly, it is always a joy to have some moments during holidays to take time and be family.

COVID has been a gut punch this year for family. It hurts not to be able to have the traditional large gatherings, with great food and time to catch up and just be family. It hurts not being able to visit an elderly loved one in the nursing home and hold their hand or hug or kiss them. It hurts that we have to forego seeing close friends during the holidays. It all just hurts. Of course, we are telling each other that if we make the sacrifices now, hopefully we will all be here next year to return again to traditions, friends, and family time.

Faithful patience must be the theme of the Christmas season 2020 and into the New Year. Faithful, because even though there is much uncertainty and also some fear, God is always faithful to us and never abandons us. We are confident of that, even as the whole situation in which we live still hurts this year.

The gospel today speaks to us of the presentation of the child Jesus in the temple by his parents, Joseph and Mary. It is a powerful scene as two old people, Simeon and Anna, known mostly for their patient faithfulness to God, get a chance to see the salvation of the world almost at the very end of their lives. They are the models of Old Testament faith and waiting in God, many times not understanding what was going on, but accepting and continuing to do what they knew they needed to do to be faithful to their calling. Abraham, in the first two readings, is also a model for this kind of faithfulness. An old man, who had all but given up having his own child to pass on his inheritance, is finally rewarded by God with a son.

Simeon tells Mary she will still have many challenges to face, including much sorrow with this child. Therefore, there is joy, yet woven throughout the story of family joy is challenge, struggle, uncertainty, fear, and, ultimately, acceptance of God's will and faithfulness to God's promises.

Isn't this what is happening to you this year? In effect these stories give us a taste of the lives of all families and of this year's pandemic living. Ultimately, Simeon and Anna do what we all need to do in front of the mystery of the incarnation. They see, give praise, and tell others. The elderly have much wisdom, acquired from living, to share with us. We need to take the time to appreciate, pay attention, and learn.

Today is the Feast of the Holy Family. It celebrates relationships. Israel was in a covenant relationship with God. This demanded faithful patience since life was often very difficult. Love for each other flowed from the love of God. The first place where these relationships were to be lived was the family. Children were to respect their parents, and there was a special respect due to the elderly. Living in harmony with each other and in harmony with God's creation were expected. We see in the gospel how Joseph and Mary took their responsibility seriously to care for the future of this child. Their clan, the extended family and close relations, was also responsible in different ways for the next generation. Everything they did was for the future of the larger family. They wanted to create a world where the future generations would flourish in right relationship with God, others, and their environment. They were close to each other, their faith, and the earth.

How many of us will be here with our families next Christmas? We cannot guarantee it. All we have is time, and usually less than we think. Family life is about dreams, dreams of the future for our children, dreams of a happy family, dreams of success, dreams of a better year, dreams of a future of love, family, hope, and peace in the world. Dreaming is fine, but enabling dreams to happen with and for others is what life is all about and what ultimately satisfies us most.

We cannot control the future completely. What we can do is continue, in good times and in bad, to have the patient faithfulness of Abraham, Simeon, and Anna, and the acceptance and faith of Mary and Joseph. All of these set the context for the coming of Jesus and for his message to the people of his time and to us.

Today think of how much you still need to do with and for your family. If you have accomplished some of your dreams in life, tell someone else how you did it so they can know. If you lead your life the right way, in faithfulness to God, the dreams will come to you. Jesus was the best of all dreams to come true. It is up to us to make the Jesus dream come true for others as well. Our responsibility extends from our immediate family to the wider community. The Catholic Church teaches that we must all work for the common good. We are all responsible for all. Faithful patience means we never give up trying to make things better, and never give up sharing our experience of Jesus with others.

I was uplifted by reading recently about the United States Postal Service program called Operation Santa, which is 108 years old. Letters from children to Santa are posted online. People can choose one and send gifts anonymously through the Post Office, in many cases giving to a child who might not otherwise receive anything. Twenty-three thousand letters were received this year, often with many children asking for a cure for COVID or a job for a parent, along with the usual toys. The Postal Service was overwhelmed this year by the generosity of donors. So far, all letters posted have been adopted. It takes a village to raise a child. What a powerful example of caring for the next generation and faith in action! A Christmas story of faith and love!

Today is a good day to ponder the future of our children, the next generation, and the ones to come. What kind of world are we leaving to them? All parents have to sacrifice for their children. Maybe the lesson of the Holy Family, especially this year, is that we are all family and in a way all parents of the next generation. What example are we giving them? What kind of people are we forming to live in and lead the world? What will we leave them of creation, the planet, our common home?

Last week we were thinking of how small this earth is and how critical it is that we have to figure out how to live in it together. All of us have to sacrifice, especially in the midst of a pandemic, so that we and others will have what is needed to live in dignity as children of one Father: God.

Today we look at three elderly people, Abraham, Simeon, and Anna, faithful to their God to the end, always living their lives in the hope that God is present and God will respond. Look around. There are other Abrahams, Simeons, and Annas in our midst. What a blessing, example, and inspiration they are in living a faithful patience in action. They have much to teach and we have much to learn!

47

1/1/21 Mary, Mother of God

Mary treasured these things and reflected on them in her heart.

Num 6:22-27; Gal 4:4-7; Luke 2:16-21

I RECENTLY READ THE story of Ben Breedlove of Austin, who died a few years ago at the age of fourteen. He was born with a defective heart and came close to death several times. Shortly before he died, he did a video of his life which ended with a story of almost dying and seeing in a white room his favorite rapper and feeling very good. He concluded with, "Do you believe in angels and God? I do!"

Despite Ben's own sickness, he gave encouragement to many and in the process, to himself. He cared enough to share in such a positive way with others even as he was in his final days of life. At a moment when most people are cared for by others, he reversed the narrative.

I am remembering this remarkable young man as we all end a difficult pandemic year. So many have suffered. We have also seen incredible instances of heroic caring for people in desperate need. His example of faith, courage and especially care for others, despite his own sickness, is a great story to reflect on and maybe an important lesson with which to end our year.

Today, as we begin 2021 in the midst of the worst surge of the virus, the question might be: Did we care enough for each other this past year, and how can we care more this new year? How did 2020 leave us? This is a time for reflection that can lead us to a better 2021.

In the gospel we have the visit of the shepherds to see the child and also the naming of Jesus. We hear especially of Mary's reaction, a reflection on all these things in her heart, an attempt to see what God is wanting of her and to follow it. How will she care for this child that has been entrusted to her? Her responsibility as parent of this special child weighed heavily. The name given the child means "God saves." That name is the beginning of the responsibility of Mary for Jesus, namely, to help bring the saving love of Jesus to all. The peace that the angels proclaimed to the shepherds is what Jesus brings, a peace where we are in right relation with God and others. Peace, as Mary, Joseph, and the shepherds show us, comes with listening to the word of God and responding. It comes if we care enough to act.

This year, as with Mary, the education of our young has been a major challenge. Some children, especially in low-income areas, have fallen far behind where they might normally be in their studies as they are not in the classroom. Virtual learning is difficult for these families. The high dropout rate in this city might be made worse this year. Young people will not get decent jobs without education, which leads to intergenerational poverty. We need to think seriously about this and act. Raising children is all our responsibility and something we need to care about in 2021.

Today, on this feast of Mary, Mother of God, Luke in his gospel wants us to set Mary apart from all the others who are involved in the birth of Jesus. They come and go. We see the shepherds who hear from the angels; they come, see the baby, return glorifying and praising God, and then tell others who are amazed. The magi come, visit the baby after a long trip, give gifts, and return to their lands. Joseph also is present, but we do not hear anything from him nor is he seen beyond the childhood of Jesus. Simeon and Anna, in the story last Sunday, are elderly; they fulfill their role and are gone as well. All these who were part of the birth of Jesus disappear soon after their visit and we do not see them again in the gospel, even though each was important in some way to naming who Jesus was.

In the gospel, the only one who stays is Mary. She not only gives birth, but she is part of the story throughout Jesus' public life, including her agonizing presence at his death on the cross. We are told she is also part of the disciples at Pentecost to receive the Holy Spirit at the birth of the church. Mary is the mother; she also becomes the disciple of her son, whereas the others, important as they might be to the birth story, are not heard from again. What is the difference?

Today's gospel gives us a hint. It says Mary kept all these things and reflected on them in her heart. We also saw the same words about Mary after finding Jesus in the temple. The gospel is stressing the reflection of Mary as key to going beyond the initial amazement about Jesus to actually becoming his disciple and forming the church.

This feast is named for Mary, Mother of God. However, the celebration today is really about Jesus and how we must follow him. It is about deepening our own reflection on who Jesus is for each of us. Mary has always been honored by the church, and not only for her role as being chosen to be the mother of Jesus. She is also honored as the first of the disciples, a role model for all of us in faith. She is open to God's call even when she was unsure of herself. She accepted the role she had, even though it involved suffering. And she reflected on the meaning of Jesus over and over in her heart. Maybe it was this taking time to reflect and keeping things in the heart that made her strong enough to endure the difficult moments of following her son, even to the cross. This made her the model for all disciples.

Have we reflected enough on all that has happened this year and what it has meant to us as well as the community and even the world? Or have we just endured and said "good riddance to 2020?" If we do not follow Mary's example of reflection, we will miss an important opportunity. Her reflection led her to a life of caring love despite sacrifice and suffering.

We are beginning a new year. We have had time in 2020 to slow down our busy lives and be more sequestered at home. Has it made us more reflective, let things go to our heart and have greater awareness of people, events, and issues in our life?

Today is World Day of Peace. Pope Francis called on the world to learn the culture of care so as to confront the culture of indifference, waste, and confrontation. He speaks of care as the protection of the dignity and rights of each person, the common good, solidarity, and creation. He says educating people to care begins in the family, and is then promoted in schools, religious communities, the communications media, and in public service. The challenge is to form a community of brothers and sisters who accepts and cares for one another. The culture of care, the pope notes, is the privileged path to peace. He calls on all of us, this first day of 2021, to be peacemakers by becoming more caring each day.

Our reflection must also include, according to the pope, a wider reflection of care for the poor in the developing world. We are invited to read more, learn about new things, and to think more often about others, our community, and the world. We have the time now while homebound.

We have more special once-in-a-lifetime challenges as we begin 2021. How are you called to be a disciple in the new year?

Look at this incredible woman, Mary. She calls us to stop, reflect, care, and make the heart our guide this year. When we do this, we become people of peace. Jesus says "love your enemies, do good to those who hate you, bless those who curse you and pray for those who abuse you" (Matt 5:44). Mary lived this out all her life.

In 2021, look to Mary. Take time to reflect. Take time to care more.

48

1/3/21 Epiphany

Then they opened up their coffers and presented him with gifts . . .

Isa 60:1–6; Eph 3:2–3a, 5–6; Matt 2:1–12

RECENTLY, PALO ALTO COLLEGE received a 20-million-dollar, unexpected gift from MacKenzie Scott, the ex-wife of Amazon CEO, Jeff Bezos. The LiftFund, a local, nonprofit, small-business lender, also received $10 million, as did several other San Antonio nonprofits. It was part of more than 4 billion dollars in donations she distributed over the last four months in this country for pandemic relief and other causes. It was fairly unique in that the donations were unsolicited and came with no stipulations. The recipients could use the money where it was needed the most. As a former fundraiser, I know this is a rare kind of gift, really remarkable, a Godsend! It will be transformative for many of those who will benefit from it. What I hope it does is spur others to also consider giving more to worthy groups, no matter at what level.

Today's well-known gospel story of the three magi or astrologers is also a story of unsolicited giving. It shows what happens when we give and share what we have with others, especially those who have much less.

We know them popularly as the three kings, yet most probably they were not kings, but rather well-learned people. They were wealthy, as represented by the kinds of gifts they gave. They came from the east, representing the place of wisdom. They were not Jews, meaning they represented the whole world coming to bring gifts to Jesus. Matthew, writing for a Jewish audience, is referring to the first reading today from Isaiah which says all nations and riches will come to Jerusalem to praise the Lord. Matthew's underlying theme is also clear: The Messiah is born. Gentiles accept him, while Jews reject him.

Epiphany is meant to describe a divine manifestation. In this case the Son of God is shown to the world, represented by these foreigners, who also are depicted as diverse. We usually portray one of the magi as a person of color, although from where they come, they are all people of color. The theme is universal. Everyone is included in this gift from God for the salvation of all.

The visitors were overwhelmed with joy to see the baby. However, others were not and did not want to share. Herod was threatened. All Jerusalem was disturbed by him. Even though the Messiah was not to be a political king, Herod was afraid. For those who should have seen but were blinded by fear, jealousy, or threats to their power, they could not see, nor did they want to see.

The Jewish-centered theme continues. Herod's threat to the life of Jesus parallels Pharoah's threat to Moses, where he orders the killing of all Jewish male babies. Herod does the same for the male babies of Bethlehem. Jesus is the new Moses. The fact that earthly rulers feel threatened is a sign of divine intervention, which Mary's Magnificat celebrates. The world is overturned. Moses was saved and lived among the rich and powerful. Jesus is seen by the rich in the form of the magi. Herod reacts with violence and death, while the magi react by giving gifts. This is not the Messiah story anyone expected.

The magi change direction to return home after sharing their gifts with the child. This is to avoid Herod, and to avoid enabling the evil he wants to do. It clearly shows that a new direction in our lives happens when we encounter the child. We give our gifts, even though it requires difficulty and sacrifice, as it did for the magi. A transformation of mind and heart (*metanoia*) takes place that changes our direction in life. Giving our gifts, despite sacrifice, difficulty, and even threats, not only changes those who receive, but ourselves as well.

All of us have gone through shared sacrifice, struggle, and even threats this year. We know the virus could affect us at any time. Following mask and distance protocols helps, but these are not guarantees. At the same time, we have a two-sided coin. On the one side is threat, while on the opposite side are opportunities to reach out, to give what we can of our support, care, compassion, and resources. What gifts do I have to share in this new year?

Perhaps it was appropriate that this year we saw what many labeled the star of Bethlehem a few days before Christmas, when Jupiter and Saturn seemed to converge to create one brilliant star, visible to many. The convergence might have been exactly what we needed to finish the year and welcome the birth of Jesus. To many it was a moment of hope and faith following a very difficult and painful year. It also connected with the beginning of vaccinations that we hope will contribute to ending our common global nightmare of the pandemic. We are at that moment of hope now. Supporting each other as we move into this new phase of conquering the pandemic is one of the gifts we all can give.

The magi followed a star, because they wanted to pay homage to the new king and bring him gifts. In the giving of these gifts they themselves were affected; they changed direction to return home. When we give of what we have, something changes in us. We are forced to change direction and thus become different, better people because we overcome sacrifices and threats with gifts. We even discover many good things about ourselves we did not know we had. That is the life transformation that comes from giving.

The magi were able to keep focused on the star despite the length and hardships of the journey. They did not have the GPS systems we have today, although, despite using GPS I sometimes get lost! To follow a star you need to travel in the darkness of night. This makes for a good metaphor of our lives of faith: often in darkness, not knowing exactly where we are going, yet somehow reaching out in faith and trust to try to see where God is leading us to the light.

The magi brought gifts to *the* Gift that God gave us all. Because of baptism we not only receive the gift of Jesus, but also become co-partners in giving that gift to others. We can be that light the magi saw, a light to guide others by how we move through life. They had to move and leave their comfort zone to see something even greater. There is nothing in the gospel story that says they were religious at all. They just wanted to pay respect to this newborn king. Searching for something outside of themselves, something special, big, new, different, was what they did. It was something in which to believe.

Like the magi, we need a change of direction as we begin this new year. We don't want to go through another year like the one we just endured. Living in uncertainty and fear, and suffering through restrictions, sacrifices, grief, illness, and even death contributed to creating a year like no other in our lifetime.

What is our star? What is different, special, outside our comfort zone that we are being called to do this year? What gifts do I have to give and how can I give them now? Maybe it will require stretching myself to give what I am unsure I can give. Maybe it will require discovering new gifts I did not know I had to give.

MacKenzie Scott is not necessarily a saint for what she did. However, she stepped forward with an outstanding gift that will change and uplift the lives of many who might have struggled the rest of their lives. For that she deserves thanks and praise. She also deserves to be imitated by all of us, at whatever level we find ourselves. That spirit can make 2021 a year of hope, of faith in others, and can produce a real change in direction that we desperately need.

Can you follow your star? Give your gifts. Discover what more you have to give. Like the three astrologers today, you too can be truly wise!

49

1/10/21 Baptism of the Lord

You are my beloved Son . . .

Isa 55:1–11; 1 John 5:1–9; Mark 1:7–11

THE VACCINES IN TEXAS have begun for the general population over 65, and for younger people with some health conditions. The response here in San Antonio has been very good. The vaccine is designed to train the immune system to recognize the virus that could hurt the body and to resist and attack it. It is critical to be vaccinated, not just for ourselves but for the community. COVID has caused much suffering and death, disrupting and at times dividing families and society in general. The vaccine is finally helping inoculate us against this scourge. Thank God it is here!

In our spiritual lives we also need help to resist threats to following Jesus. We have experienced so much conflict and division this past year, not only with the pandemic but also racial unrest, political and economic strife, and more. The sacraments are the spiritual support we need to counter the hurt these threats cause the community. In effect they inoculate us and help us train ourselves to seek and do good over evil as we go through life. Our sacramental life begins with baptism, the first step on our journey following Jesus. We could say it is the first dose of spiritual vaccine.

The gospel story we read today of the baptism of Jesus comes from Mark, which is the gospel we are following mostly in this church year. Mark does not have any infancy narratives, as we see in Matthew and

Luke. He starts with John the Baptist and quickly follows that up with Jesus at his baptism. Jesus is an adult, ready for his ministry. There are no angels, shepherds, or wisemen. No presentation of the baby at the temple. No story of being lost in the temple as a young boy. Mark bluntly begins by saying his gospel is of Jesus Christ, Son of God. It could not be any clearer than that in his first line. We will see as we go through Mark that he wants us to read or listen to the gospel always asking ourselves two questions: 1) Who is Jesus? and 2) What does it mean to follow Jesus? Even though, in effect, he has answered the first question with his opening line, he wants us to keep inquiring. He will add to the first answer as the gospel unfolds. Each story in Mark has different ways to answer the two questions. Keep that in mind as we move through this year.

Mark quickly introduces John the Baptist, who in turn introduces Jesus. The Baptist preaches a powerful message attracting many to the desert to listen, confess sins and be baptized. It is important to remember that John's baptism is not the sacramental one we received, but rather a moment of visible repentance. The confessing of sins and the desire to repent of them is the starting point to recognize the Messiah. When too many bad habits and offenses against God and others remain in our lives without admitting and repenting of them, we simply cannot see Jesus. These could be anything from gossip to selfishness to anger to revenge, or other sins. We need to target them just as the immune system targets bad actors in our bodies. What's blocking your vision now?

John begins his preaching by emphasizing that Jesus is greater and will baptize with the Holy Spirit, as opposed to John's symbolic baptism with water. The comparisons and contrasts between the two are clear for Mark. John emphasizes repentance, while Jesus is baptized to affirm to others their need for a change of life. John comes from the wilderness. Jesus enters the wilderness and is tempted by Satan, after which he comes out and begins his ministry. John points to Jesus. Heaven points to Jesus as God's Son. John is soon arrested and his public ministry ends, while Jesus begins his ministry shortly thereafter by calling his disciples.

The story of Jesus' baptism is simple, but the important part is the heavens are torn open. Jesus starts doing what he was sent to do, namely, to connect heaven and earth. The Spirit, like a dove, descends as a sign of divine affirmation. We are reminded of the dove that returned to Noah with an olive branch, signaling the end of the flood and a new beginning for people of the earth. Jesus is that new beginning for us.

The next moment of the story is a theophany, a clear divine revelation. Jesus is named. A voice is heard, "You are my beloved Son. On you my favor rests." For Jewish people, the father had to acknowledge his son to make the son legitimate. Joseph, in the Gospel of Matthew, is instructed by the angel to take Mary as his wife and thus accept her child as his own and give him the name Jesus. The naming of the child was always by the father. Jesus, in today's gospel, has left his home of Nazareth and is now proclaimed by God the Father as Son. Later, Jesus will be named by others. Evil spirits will name him as he expels demons. Peter will name him the Messiah in the middle of the gospel. The centurion at the foot of the cross will call him the Son of God. Even the high priest will use the term "messiah" at his trial. Mark is answering his first question as clearly as possible: Who is Jesus? The answers are everywhere for those who want to see.

With the baptism, the heavens are open, showing that with Jesus there are no barriers between us and God. Jesus then goes from his baptism to confront the devil in the wilderness and continues the epic struggle throughout his ministry.

The first part of Mark is a constant battle with evil. Jesus cures people of various diseases. In those times sickness was often associated with being in the possession of demons. Also, it was thought the sick person was being punished by God with the illness because they had sinned. As we go through this long struggle with COVID it is tempting to see it as some kind of evil, maybe even as some divine punishment for the sinful acts done by all of us. Certainly, bad things have happened before and as a result of the pandemic. Illness, death, hospitals overwhelmed, jobs lost, people struggling to find enough food and to pay rent, essential workers exhausted—all of these are bad results. Viruses and other illnesses are part of the human condition, not part of the work of demons. God is a loving Father who does not punish sinners in this way; rather, as Jesus showed us, God is always seeking out the sinner with the call to return home. We also must overcome this and other evils in our world with the weapons of Christ, namely, love, care, compassion, generosity, self-sacrifice, cooperation, and unity. This terrible moment can be defeated. It is up to all of us to do that together.

Jesus returns from the wilderness to society, as Israel did from the desert. He goes to Jerusalem to proclaim his mission. It is not political but truly transformational. Peoples' lives will change. We may be feeling like we have lived in a wilderness in 2020, but will we be different, transformed, better because of this?

With this Sunday of the baptism of Jesus, the Christmas season concludes. However, it does not end with the baby Jesus, whom we have celebrated these past weeks. Rather, it continues with the adult Jesus, and what he began to do after his baptism, the reason he came.

This Christmas season needs to end for us as well, as adults. We are not babies brought by our parents to our baptism and dependent on them to grow and learn. We are now responsible for living the good news of Jesus, God with us, in the new year. We take our place in combatting the hurts of society by naming Christ in our lives. That is how we live our baptism, which inoculates us to recognize evil threats against us and strengthens us to help each other in the struggle for good.

Today think about your baptism. It has not only vaccinated you. but also empowered you. Live it!

50

1/17/21 Second Sunday

What are you looking for?

1 Sam 3:3b–10, 19; 1 Cor 6:13c–15a, 17–20; John 1:35–42

"I've looked over, and I've seen the promised land. I may not
get there with you, but I want you to know tonight that we as a
people will get to the promised land. So, I'm happy tonight. I'm
not worried about anything. I'm not fearing any man. Mine eyes
have seen the glory of the coming of the Lord."
—Martin Luther King Jr., "I've Been to the Mountaintop," the
night before he was assassinated.

MARTIN LUTHER KING JR. knew what he was looking for. He had fought
for it for so long and he had the vision to see it, even if at a distance. It was
in his heart and in his dreams. As we celebrate him this week, can we see
that vision and look for ways to help bring it about?

What are you looking for? With the events of the last year and those
of the last few weeks, especially January 6th, this question might be on
our minds. We are certainly looking for health and protection from the
virus. Also, we desire racial justice in our society. Lately, it is clear we
need to seek national reconciliation and unity in order to move forward
together. There are so many things we look for in the new year.

The one asking us this same question today is Jesus. In this Sunday's
gospel from John, we begin Ordinary Time and take a short break from
Mark. John the Baptist points out Jesus, naming him the Lamb of God, to

two of his own disciples. The two begin to follow Jesus. At that point Jesus asks them the question that is really a constant in all of our lives, "What are you looking for?" It is not a simple question. John's Gospel is always deeper and theological. What are we looking for? Do we even know what we are looking for in life? Will we even know it when we find it? This is a good question for us all now.

The two disciples respond by asking Jesus where he is staying, which again has a deeper meaning. The word they use is not just a place but also where Jesus abides, as in abiding in God. Jesus stays with the Father. "Come and see" is mentioned twice here, by Jesus and then by Phillip. Jesus responds to them and to us with "Come and see." "Staying" is mentioned three times. To stay in Jesus for John's Gospel is not just a location, but to really listen, and to be transformed. To stay with Jesus is to stay with the Father, in a communion brought about by the Spirit. This is not just a visit, rather it is a homecoming. It is where we belong, where we need to stay. We are created by God and will only be back home when we are with God. Listen to Jesus tell you, "Come and see."

In this gospel the disciples are slowly transformed as they identify Jesus in a deeper and deeper way. They start by calling him "Rabbi," which means "teacher," showing their openness to learn from him. Later in the gospel they will call him Messiah, Son of God, King of Israel, and finally the link between heaven and earth, where Jesus describes that they will see angels ascending and descending on the Son of Man. This progression is only possible through faith. To go through these stages of faith they need to go to school with the teacher. They need to be not only willing students but also disciples who go deeper into themselves.

The two disciples stayed with Jesus and began a relationship, a time together that creates the friendship that leads one to know Jesus, and then to invite others to get to know him. They brought Peter. When we discover something great, very special, we tell others, and keep spreading the message.

Sometimes when I listen to what has affected or impressed my friends, I come to know things better for myself. A good example is the experience of the ACTS retreats, which have deeply affected and changed many people. If I am impressed by you, maybe it will lead me to imitate what I admire in you. Until we simply come, see, and meet Christ, whether through others, prayer, Scripture, or sacraments, we will not know him. To know him is to be changed, transformed. To know him and stay with him is to have a new life, to be home.

John does not use stories of fishing, boats, nets or their fathers to recount when the disciples started following Jesus. His story is more theological, a post-Easter reflection, to stress what it means to be a disciple. The key here is to be a witness to Jesus, even if you cannot prove everything about Jesus to someone. You witness by your words and deeds. Whom do you know who really witnesses to Jesus?

John the Baptist witnesses to Jesus. His disciples also witness to him to their friends. Nathaniel later interrupts the invitation with skepticism and even prejudice, when he questions Jesus' credentials because of his origin in Nazareth. "Can anything good come from Nazareth?" (John 1:46). Does this kind of thinking sound familiar today? Martin Luther King Jr. Day is a time to root out prejudice. The immigration debate is questioning who we want in our country. Some look at certain countries as undesirable, yet the history of immigration shows that if people get an opportunity to improve their lives, they can contribute greatly to society.

I saw the immigration story while at Mission Concepción when we adopted a refugee family each year, assisted them with rent and food, and visited them. In the course of their first year, the children learned English and thrived at school while the parents often worked very hard and slowly got better jobs. They just needed to be secure, have some initial support and encouragement, and the rest would happen. Nathaniel meets Jesus and becomes a follower immediately, calling him Son of God. When we really know Jesus, our prejudice melts away, like when we take time to know others who are different from us. Tell that to white supremacists who loudly proclaim to be followers of Jesus, a total contradiction.

St. Basil the Great defined sin as the misuse of power given us by God to do good. We are created for good. We need to seek how to do that every day.

Do we know how to look? In reality, it is God who is seeking us. We do not find God; rather we let God find us. It was not Jesus asking the disciples, but simply inviting them. God does that for us. We need to be open. We need to take some action. The gospel has many action words today: see, stay, hear, believe, come, watch. All are ways we ultimately are found by and follow Jesus.

There are other important details in this story. The gospel makes a point to note it was four in the afternoon. We often remember the hour when something important happened to us. We remember an important event, what time it was, where we were, that might have changed our lives. 9/11 is an example. Meeting Jesus is a huge, life-changing moment for the disciples.

In John's Gospel, the call comes through someone else: John the Baptist sends Andrew and another disciple to Jesus. Andrew calls Peter. Philip calls Nathaniel. The Samaritan woman calls townspeople. Jesus often calls us through others. Who has helped Jesus call you? Is it your turn to call someone?

Take time to stay with Jesus, to listen, to see what he is all about. Creating a home is more than just buying a house. It is a growing in love and listening, a commitment to each other, an anticipation of needs, being thankful and generous, a sharing of values and faith, that goes beyond the walls. Our home with Jesus, staying with him, becomes the way we live life.

Take time to look for and stay with Jesus, to listen, to see what he is all about. Take time to create a true home this year. Then invite others. *Mi casa es su casa!* My house is your house!

51

1/24/21 Third Sunday

They immediately abandoned their nets and became his followers.

Jonah 3:1–5; 1 Cor 7:29–31; Mark 1:14–20

THERE WAS A COMPELLING op-ed piece in the *Express-News* this week by Mandy Stewart, a professor at Texas Woman's University.[1] She challenged us all about the events of January 6th at the Capitol to ask ourselves if we were complicit in the horrible violence of that day. Calling out those who incited and carried out the violence is important, but how about our own daily actions? Do they contribute to creating an atmosphere of intolerance, anger, fear of others, hate, or dehumanization of people with whom we disagree? She included the "little actions" we do online of sharing or liking a post that spreads lies, anger, or unrest. Words matter and little actions do too. Social media can be a great way to stay in touch and an equally great way to hurt others. She listed other actions in our lives that can also help or harm.

I was wondering. Lent begins in a few weeks. Might this year's Lent be a time to "fast" from social media? Maybe not all of it, but could we stop what makes us resentful of and angry with others, demonizing our brothers and sisters, making them inhuman? We are not only hurting them, but also tearing down our community, our nation, and our world. There are many positive ways to use the internet, but many harmful ways as well. What is it doing to me? What kind of a person is this making

1. Stewart, "Commentary."

me? Now might be the moment to ask if I could spend my time more positively. In effect, is this the call for me to change?

Change is always hard for us. The pandemic has changed the way we live. The loss of a loved one is a dramatic change, but others have seen the long-lasting effects of being sick, losing a job, having less income, and experiencing family conflict. So much has been out of our control, but making changes like wearing masks has protected us in many ways and limited what could have been a greater disaster.

The gospel today is about the call to a change of life to follow Jesus without conditions. In this liturgical year we will follow the gospel of Mark. Mark always wants us to be asking two questions as we read the various stories and accounts of Jesus in his gospel: "Who is Jesus?" and "What does it mean to be his disciple?" In effect, if I begin to know Jesus, how do I have to change to follow him?

Mark, in today's gospel, introduces Jesus simply as from Galilee, a humble origin. Jesus teaches dignity and respect. Even when he challenged the religious leaders of his time, he did it by engaging them with the respect owed to every human being. Can we do the same when we disagree? In Jesus' origins we see that one does not need to be rich, famous, or important in society to make a difference. We can all do something, even in small ways, to change the world for the better.

Today, in the gospel, John the Baptist is now gone; he was arrested. Mark means this to be a sign of the coming cross for Jesus as well. It is also a sign that we, his disciples, will carry a cross as we follow Jesus. However, before the cross, it is Jesus' turn to proclaim the message and call people to conversion and repentance. His message is "The kingdom of God is at hand. Repent and believe the gospel." It is a call to constant change as we live the good news.

Jesus begins in Galilee, where there are many different people, not only Jews, to show that his message is for all. Galilee was a crossroads for various nationalities and races. On the northern edge of Israel, the people there were often looked down on as a kind of half-breed by those in Jerusalem. In this gospel Jesus starts his ministry here and ends his stay on earth here after the resurrection. This is such an important aspect of who Jesus is and what our faith entails. It is not just a personal piety, although we need that to help ground us. It must always be an outward looking to others, especially those who are different from us. We must see the people of the world, no matter what color, nationality or religion, as Jesus saw them, namely, with dignity and respect. This applies to those who differ from us economically and politically. The dignity of the person means we never dehumanize another, which has happened frequently in our recent civic discourse. Who are the Galileans today for you? Can you see them as Jesus saw them, namely, as worthy to be disciples like you?

Jesus comes to proclaim and inaugurate the kingdom of God. He calls us to repent. The disciples heard his call, abandoned nets, family, and their way of life immediately. The repentance Jesus calls for is a change of life, whether it means a different occupation, leaving family, or any other radical change. The disciples heard the voice of Jesus and responded at once. It was a complete conversion.

The reign of God comes to life in us through a change of heart. It is ongoing. It is lifelong. Jesus' call is urgent. The time is now. All three readings point to the need to act now to change. We must look at what we need to do now to respect the dignity of all people, even those with whom we disagree.

The disciples became students of Jesus and began a new way of life. As followers of Jesus, we also are forever learning, forever students. To be a disciple is to always be in a state of conversion. It is not just a one-time event. It is a total, day-by-day change of life, making decisions based on following Jesus today, to see others as Jesus sees them. Our words, our attitude, our actions can help attract people to Jesus. Will you respond? Will you change?

This week we pray for the right to life of unborn children. This right to life extends also to all people from conception to natural death. We pray that all people will adopt a culture of life in our world, to embrace human life with dignity and respect.

What needs to be changed in our society and in our country also needs to be changed in each of our lives. What are the small ways you can respect life? How can you be more respectful of people with whom you disagree, or people you do not especially like? What changes in your life will help you respect the dignity of all? The unborn are vulnerable. Many others in society today are also vulnerable and disrespected, especially refugees, immigrants, the homeless, people of color, and many more. We can change that. It begins with little thoughts, little actions.

There are many faithful people, like those at our own Seton Home, who support pregnant women bringing their babies to term, even under difficult conditions. Catholic Charities helps feed and house vulnerable families, especially those affected by the pandemic. They follow Jesus' call. They are helping change the way people in difficult circumstances see themselves. They help them understand they are also people of dignity, worthy of respect, even if they have not been treated as such.

It is never too late to look seriously at ourselves, admit where we need to change and begin to take steps in that direction. Olympic swimming gold medalist Klete Keller was charged with being in the Capitol unlawfully on January 6th. He faces serious consequences. He also has expressed remorse to people close to him, saying "I let you down."[2] This can be a good first step to the repentance and change he needs to lead a positive life. Hopefully others who violated the Capitol will follow this example. It is never too late.

This week, respect human life. What change brings you to being the disciple Jesus calls you to be? Look at how you use social media, your words, deeds, or your attitude toward others.

Choose little daily actions. Change your life to follow Jesus.

2. Crouse, "'I Let You Down.'"

52

1/31/21 Fourth Sunday

What do you want of us, Jesus of Nazareth?

Deut 18:15–20; 1 Cor 7:32–35; Mark 1:21–28

SAN ANTONIO SPURS COACH Greg Popovich recently got the COVID-19 vaccine and was featured on an NBA public service announcement receiving the injection. He also endorsed mask-wearing as the right thing to do now. He was quoted as saying, "It's a no-brainer . . . Let's do this together." One of the Spurs' team members said that watching the coach get the shot made him more receptive to receiving it.

Sojourners Magazine recently featured an article on religious leaders of San Antonio who were publicly receiving the vaccine and urging congregants to do so as well.[1] I was interviewed for the article. Over eighty local faith leaders signed the pledge to participate.

"What do you want of us, Jesus of Nazareth?"

This is the first question in the Gospel of Mark. There will be many more questions in this gospel. Mark plants questions in all kinds of characters in the gospel: demons, his disciples, religious leaders, the people, and others. What Mark wants is to implant the question in you and in me, the listeners or readers of the gospel. All of those people are asking questions Mark wants you to ask and then to try to find the answer in his gospel.

I believe Coach Popovich and the eighty local faith leaders answered the question. They made a decision to do something simple yet powerful

1. Russell-Kraft, "Can Faith Leaders' Vaccine Selfies?"

199

to help protect the health of the community and defeat this horrible affliction. This is what they and I felt Jesus is asking of us now.

Jesus' question is an important one that we need to keep asking ourselves. The answer we give evolves and changes as circumstances evolve in our lives. Make it personal to you: "What do you want of me, Jesus of Nazareth?"

Previously we noted that Mark encourages us to go through his gospel with two constant questions on our minds: "Who is Jesus?" and "What does it mean to be his disciple?" At the end of today's gospel, people ask each other, "What is this?" It is another planted question meant for the reader, and it should be our question also.

What is strange is that the first of the many questions about the identity of Jesus in Mark comes not from a disciple or a person listening to Jesus, but from a demon, the evil one, the one spreading sickness, division, and hate. Yet, amazingly, the demon speaks the truth in this episode. It identifies Jesus as the Holy One of God. It has been said many times that even the devil quotes Scripture, though of course it is for an evil purpose. Words can have power, for good or bad. The lesson is, be attentive to who is speaking, what they say, and how it affects you. Always judge what is said by what Jesus asks of you.

We have gone through so much with the coronavirus. Death, sickness, isolation, exhaustion, despair, division, and loneliness have all been part of this demon that has possessed us for what seems like a long time. Yet, through it all, we have seen the truth as well. We have experienced extraordinary human love, commitment, caring, and generosity. The truth is that the human person has great capacity for good, even when under great duress and in the midst of a dark time. The darkness has actually helped identify the holiness that has always been there. We just needed to call it out of ourselves. That is what Jesus' questions do.

Today's gospel, however, is more telling. The people's question is not about the expelling of the demon, but about the teaching of Jesus with authority. They are more amazed by his teaching even though they comment on the miracle of the healing and exorcism. What is different is that Mark sets the exorcism in the context of teaching. This illustrates the power of Jesus' teaching. Jesus' words have power. He lives what he says.

In Mark we see Jesus' teachings are short and powerful, not like the lengthy Sermon on the Mount in Matthew or the Sermon on the Plain in Luke. In Mark, Jesus, in effect, practices what he teaches, which is where the power is shown. How often we hear, "Practice what you preach, since your actions speak louder than your words." Jesus demonstrates this idiom by example!

Through this healing, Jesus reaching out to someone suffering, the people heard the word of God. Perhaps this might be what we should look for as we slowly struggle with and overcome the virus. Where is the word of God in this moment? Where do we see Jesus in what we are experiencing? What is it asking of us? Are we allowing ourselves to be amazed, touched deeply by its power and authority in our lives?

Jesus is seen as doing battle with forces of evil from the beginning of his ministry, even in a synagogue. Evil is crippling, alienating, distorting, and destroys life. Jesus' word has the power to heal, help, give life, and restore. The battle between good and evil, truth and falsehood, life and death, God and Satan, is a major theme in Mark, as it is also in our lives today.

Jesus' power with words was different. It touched those who needed healing and inspiration. It was a threat to those who abused their power. This part of Mark is Jesus' early ministry. Mark wants to establish Jesus' authority and power right away. This authority and power come from the fact he is God's Son. He speaks with authority, then expels demons who know who he is. Amazement is the reaction, since no teachers then had that kind of authority. Most teachers quoted others, repeated the laws or other teachings. Jesus is teaching who he is. Again, who we are and how we act teaches more about us than our words can.

Jesus' preaching was about good news, rather than about laws or rules. God was seen as terrifying to the Israelites at that time, because they had been taught that they would be punished or cursed by God if they broke any law. Often, they did not know all the laws since the religious leaders were the ones who studied them, not the common people. The leaders used their knowledge of the law to control and scare people. Jesus, however, comes healing and teaching with authority. His authority involves responding to the needs of people, especially their health. It shows the power of Jesus' teaching, as well as the content.

Jesus teaches and Jesus himself is the sermon. Teaching and healing together are the sermon. Our words and our actions together are who we are.

The demons resist and fight back. They name Jesus, "The Holy One of God." Here is one answer to the question "Who is Jesus?" People thought that to gain mastery over a demon, you needed to call them by name, which is what the demon tried to do to Jesus, but it did not work. Evil fights hard to continue in our lives, which is why we must continue to root it out by naming it, recognizing it is there, in our own lives or in the community, and taking steps to defeat it.

This week I read about a group of public health workers in Oregon who were returning from administering COVID vaccines in a rural area and were stranded in a snowstorm. There was a jackknifed tractor-trailer ahead and they knew the remaining doses they had would expire before they could arrive at the next site. They decided to walk from car to car among others also stranded to offer them the vaccine on the spot. Some people politely declined, but others accepted immediately and the doses were quickly given. This is a good example of "What do you want of me, Jesus of Nazareth?"

What does Jesus want of you today? You speak with authority not only by your words but by naming the demons and overcoming them with healing and compassion. You are this homily.

53

2/7/21 Fifth Sunday

She immediately began to wait on them.

Job 7:1–4, 6–7; 1 Cor 9:16–19, 22–23; Mark 1:29–39

WHY DOES GOD ALLOW suffering? This question bugs us, especially when we see something like this pandemic affecting so many innocent people. It is not a new question. I asked it over and over when I traveled to some of the poorest areas on earth with Catholic Relief Services. I read it again recently in an article written by a Jesuit novice who was ministering in a juvenile detention center. He was told by a veteran guard that many of the young people there, predominantly Black, would spend their lives in and out of prison. There are so many cases we could point to of suffering. Why?

"So, I have been assigned months of misery . . . I shall not see happiness again." Job in today's first reading sounds like many of us going through these last eleven months. Will this pandemic ever end? Is there any hope we will return to any kind of happiness in life?

The story of Job in the Old Testament is a somber reflection on bad things happening to a good person. Job had everything in life and was faithful to God. Yet in an instant it was all gone, including all his children, who die in a tragic windstorm, as well as losing his own health. He can't understand it. The book details his lamentations and struggle to keep faith. In the end he realizes God has always been present, even in misery, and God cares for him. There is a happy ending despite the intense suffering and feelings of abandonment he undergoes.

The gospel today shows us this lesson through the ministry of Jesus. Mark presents part two of a day in the life of Jesus, teacher and healer. Last week he fights demons with power, and as we move forward in the story Jesus heals the sick with power.

Sickness in first-century Palestine was associated with sin, as we have noted before. People feared God more than loved God since God to them was a punisher, a vengeful God who would inflict sickness and other bad things on those who were unfaithful. When someone was sick it was understood they had sinned and were suffering the consequences. The community did not tolerate the sinner and often expelled the sick, furthering their misery.

Jesus comes presenting another face of God: the compassionate healer who shows love, especially to those most rejected and vulnerable. Jesus calls God Father, which was not a term the Jews used for God. It was a whole different way of looking at God.

Mark shows that people were healed by interaction with Jesus, but not all were cured. The healing Jesus restores wholeness. Meaning was renewed to their life. They were restored to the community. Healings were a sign of God's reign. Jesus in this gospel understands the pain of illness and the lack of hope, and he goes directly to confront the pain.

In today's story, as soon as Jesus enters the home he is told about the sickness of Peter's mother-in-law. He grasps her hand and helps her up. The translation of the phrase could also be "raised her from the dead," which is a foreshadowing of the resurrection we will all share. The fever leaves her. She immediately waits on them. No recuperation for her! Her being touched and lifted up by Jesus results in her service to the community. She was truly cured. That is our call. We have been touched by Jesus. We must serve.

It is key that the Greek word used here for her service was *diakoneo*, which is only used three times in Mark. The title "deacon" comes from it. The word is used here, and also when Jesus speaks of himself coming to serve and not be served. Finally, at the cross we hear about the women who were there and had been the ones "who had followed him in Galilee and ministered to him." Mark is affirming the essential service of women following the example and ministry of Jesus.

The lifting or raising up of Peter's mother-in-law prefigures resurrection, where we are raised up in baptism to serve and share in the resurrected life of Jesus. Jesus' miracles prove his authority, which challenges all that enslaves and holds people down. It is the key to the good news.

In Mark, the ones who seem to know Jesus are the demons, which he silences. Others only slowly recognize him. This in Mark is the messianic secret, namely, Jesus not wanting to be known as Messiah until the end. Much of this was the misunderstanding by the Jews of who the Messiah was supposed to be, namely, a warrior king destined to make Israel the greatest and most powerful country. Yet, for Jesus, the ultimate recognition of the Messiah is to follow him to the cross. In suffering we see the ultimate service to others. We can see that today in people of faith and good will sacrificing to serve those suffering in the pandemic.

The sick in Mark are a symbolic reference to the wider issue of social exclusion. People are always finding ways to exclude others for whatever reason. Jesus broke through the barriers of exclusion. Jesus is the compassion of God. Jesus reaches out and touches the excluded, the suffering, those who feel no one cares, and returns them to the community. He shows that God does not forget our pain.

In the gospel Jesus' healing aims at the illness and exclusion so that people work out a new meaning in life. Peter's mother-in-law is healed for service. The miracles of Jesus are more about a comprehensive healing because he often challenges religious and political powers and structures that oppress, exclude, and enslave. It is holistic healing that goes beyond a biomedical function. Jesus has to break barriers to heal and restore people to the community. It often puts him at odds with the leaders and rules of society. Mark shows this a lot.

Jesus' first full day ends in his withdrawing in prayer. This is important as he does not want to be lauded for his miracles, for his confronting the demons and overpowering them. Prayer is what grounds him, just as it does for us, if we are willing to put time into it. Prayer helps us put things into perspective. We are not God's gift to the world, better than others. We are simply servants who need God's mercy and compassion to do what we are called by God to do, namely, be instruments of God's love to others.

People flock to Jesus, but he keeps his focus on movement, mission, and preaching. He does not want to be a celebrity miracle worker, nor does he want to have demons identify him. He withdraws in prayer to keep his focus. He wants to simply be the one announcing the kingdom of God.

Jesus is looking for followers, not fans. The healing is aimed at a deeper message. Jesus responds by keeping his balance: prayer and reflection and missionary outreach to others. Jesus returns to the desert.

The apostles find him and tell him of his popularity, making it another temptation in the desert. He resists by going to others rather than returning for accolades.

There is much in the way of misery and feelings of hopelessness in our community and in our world. The virus has taken a huge toll on us. Many people need healing in the midst of this pandemic. How does a follower of Jesus respond? We can contribute to the healing that is needed in people and in the community, even though we might not be in the medical field. We can affirm in others the feeling of being part of society, of helping them work out a new meaning in life. How do we do that? If we look at the model of Jesus in this gospel we will see that it usually involves some service and even suffering on my part to take the time and effort. Our words and actions can bring healing, inclusion, and compassion. People need that so much.

In the end, there is not an answer to why there is suffering in our world. However, there is a response. God is present, and so must we be.

54

2/14/21 Sixth Sunday

I do will it. Be cured.

Lev 13:1-2, 44-46; 1 Cor 10:31—11:1; Mark 1:4-45

DR. RICARDO CIGARROA, A Laredo cardiologist whose brother Francisco is a surgeon in San Antonio and former Chancellor of the University of Texas system, was featured lately in several national and local stories about COVID-19 in Laredo and along the border. He is being called the Dr. Fauci of South Texas. At a time when Dr. Cigarroa could have continued his thriving cardiology practice, he responded to the greater need. He converted his practice into a makeshift COVID clinic. Last month Laredo had one of the worst outbreaks of the pandemic in the country. It continues today to be very critical. The doctor regularly does house calls all over the city and across the border. He himself contracted the virus in July and was hospitalized in San Antonio. He feels that having survived the disease, he now can more sensitively understand and serve others.

Dr. Cigarroa is adamant about how the system is not working for the people of Laredo. He feels fighting the coronavirus has been more difficult in Texas because the city and county political authorities were stripped by the state of their ability to enforce local mitigation measures. This week it was also announced by the state that San Antonio would not be a super site to receive enough vaccines to administer 5,000 doses a day, even though we have demonstrated the capacity to do that. Our mayor, county judge, and local health authorities have complained that their hands are tied when more can be done to contain the virus. Dr. Cigarroa especially feels the system is not helping Laredo or the border area which is overwhelmingly Hispanic and poor. Many suffer multiple health issues. He is speaking more forcefully against the current system.

The gospel today tells us that Jesus also faced a system that was stacked against people who were sick and powerless. We hear the story of a curing, this time of a leper. Jesus has pity when the leper asks to be healed; however, the word "pity" can also be translated as "anger." Jesus is moved with compassion, from the depths of his body. The feeling of Jesus here is more accurately translated as a "gut response" against a system where the sick were expelled from the community just for being ill. As has been noted previously, people were seen as sick due to punishment for sin, and thus they were not allowed to remain in the village or city. They had to live away from others, which compounded their situation and made their illness even more painful. Often without any support, they died alone.

Leprosy was the name for any number of skin diseases. Since whatever skin affliction was visibly evident, the person was said to be unclean. They were considered a threat to others, as their illness was thought to be contagious. To be able to return to the community one needed the priest to examine and declare the person free of sickness and make a payment. How could they have any money for the payment if they were excluded from any chance to work in society? The exclusion was worse than the disease, since the person was effectively given a death sentence. The system especially affected the poorest who lacked any kind of a support system. This is what angered Jesus.

Jesus rejects a system which fails the sick. He touches the leper. This would have horrified the people watching, since it was strictly forbidden to do so. Jesus breaks the rules of the system, and then cures and instructs the former leper to go to the priest and follow a ritual law, which entailed inspection and a declaration that the person was now clean. Jesus adds that complying with the ritual will be proof for "them," a word that also carries the idea of a hostile audience. In effect, this is Jesus' protest against a system where the weakest people are forced to make payment for restoration to the community when they should not have been excluded in the first place. The religious leaders controlled the system, and received money offered for their declaration of the cure.

Jesus tells the cured man to keep this a secret. Last week he tells the demon to be quiet. This is Mark's messianic secret. Jesus does not want others to know he is the Messiah at this point. His ministry is to be the Suffering Servant and must be understood in the context of the cross. Only then will people understand the Messiah. All this will come much later. However, as much as Jesus tries to tell others to keep the miracles to themselves, they never do. Would you?

Jesus is forced to withdraw because he does not want to be seen only as a miracle worker, but as proclaiming the kingdom of God. He does not want people to think that with the Messiah there are no more troubles or difficulties, but rather with troubles and difficulties there is the Messiah. Now, Jesus trades places with the leper as Jesus is excluded from the community. He is a marked man for touching the leper and for challenging the system. He risks rejection and exclusion, which will ultimately and most clearly be shown by the cross.

Jesus takes on our infirmities. This shows that in our infirmities, in our isolation where we feel excluded and alone, Jesus is there. This is exactly how we need to see our struggles with the pandemic. In many ways, those with the virus are excluded from the community and told to quarantine themselves and stay away from any involvement with others. This is extremely painful, as they need the support of others precisely at this difficult time. People need to reach out to them in multiple ways through calls, emails, Skype, Zoom, notes, and other forms of support. Their exclusion cannot be rejection. We can show them by our words and actions that Jesus is there in the midst of their pain and isolation.

This is part three of the first day of Jesus' ministry. The question Mark plants is, "Who is this Jesus who speaks with authority, makes demons obey, and cures leprosy?" As we answer that question, we need to follow him, to speak out with the authority of our behavior, to expel the demons that try to control and divide us and our society, and to heal others with our support and compassion. We have been touched and healed by Jesus. We need to bring healing to others.

Years ago, when the Ebola crisis was happening in Africa, few people in this country were concerned. Five thousand died and there was very little reaction by Americans; however, when it was known that one person had died in Dallas from Ebola, it became a crisis here and got our attention. That is what Pope Francis calls the false culture of indifference.[1] Unless it is in front of my face, I don't care. Who are the stigmatized today and how do we exclude others? How can we be Jesus to them? When we

1. Pope Francis, "No the Culture of Indifference."

are the ones who are excluded or isolated, or who feel alone, we must see that here is the place where we meet Jesus. We must remember this as we continue to go through COVID.

Dr. Cigarroa may not be able to cure all the people in Laredo who are sick with COVID. However, he seems to be trying to let them know they are not forgotten or abandoned. He is sacrificing and advocating for them and working to help others avoid becoming infected. They deserve to be treated and not to be overlooked because they come from a mostly poor border town. There is something of last week's story of Job in Dr. Cigarroa and the people of Laredo; there is catastrophe on all sides, yet a steady, unfailing commitment to the healing needed to return to life as it was and as it can be. God is somehow present in all of it.

At times we need to challenge a system that keeps the most vulnerable at the greatest risk. There are many ways to do this. Perhaps now is the time to act!

55

2/17/21 Ash Wednesday

. . . your Father who sees what is hidden will repay you.

Joel 2:12–18; 2 Cor 5:20—6:2; Matt 6:1–6, 16–18

THE *EXPRESS-NEWS* HAD AN article by staff writer Rene Guzman on Lent this past Sunday with the title, "Jesus, Haven't We Given Up Enough This Year?"[1] It spoke about Lent and the practice of sacrificing or giving up things we like, such as a favorite television show, chocolate, soda, or other things. This past year we have all had to make many sacrifices in light of the pandemic. We carry and use our masks everywhere, keep socially distanced, wash our hands frequently, and follow every protocol. We did not go to the theatre, sporting events, receptions, and even family gatherings. So, the question is: How much more do we need to give up? Haven't we all done enough?

It would seem that the article had a good point, except that giving up things for Lent is not just about doing without, but rather to focus on doing more. The piece did quote several people who said they will do more praying and more giving, which is the reason for the season in the first place. I was happy it put Lent into the proper perspective. It is meant as an annual moment of refocus on what we are about as followers of Jesus. We prepare best for Holy Week by our actions, which hopefully will become ongoing habits for the rest of the year.

Matthew, in the gospel reading for today, is speaking to a Jewish-Christian audience who knew these penitential practices. He did not

---

1. Guzman, "Catholics Face 2021 Lent."

need to explain or urge the faithful to do these, but rather he wanted them to work on their disposition. The question Matthew wants us to ask ourselves is: Why do I do these practices?

This section is part of the lengthy Sermon on the Mount where Jesus lays out what it means to be a faithful follower. It is interesting the order in which Jesus puts these penitential practices: almsgiving is first, as if to show that if we are living charity in our lives, if we are really people who give generously, then prayer and personal sacrifice like fasting will flow from that. Prayer and reflection become the fruit of our encounter with those in need, with doing it for Jesus, with giving of ourselves.

When Jesus says to practice these in private or in secret, the idea is not so much not to let others know what you do, but rather not to seek others' approval rather than God's. Are we role-playing, or is it something we do from the heart? Do we fear rejection or are we just trying to please others? Hypocrites are condemned by Jesus later. Lent is a good time for an attitude adjustment!

What Jesus says here seems to contradict what he urged the disciples after teaching the Beatitudes in the previous chapter. He had called them "the light of the world" (Matt 5:14) and told them to "let your light shine" (Matt 5:16) but here "your" was meant for the whole community. It is the community of disciples giving and praying and sacrificing together that shines forth for all to see. We live our faith and follow Jesus, not as loners but as a community of faith. That is more difficult since we constantly deal with each other and try to figure out how we come together as disciples.

Prayer is the same, not to be done for other's admiration, but to God. Prayer is taking the time to just be there with God, even "wasting time with God," listening for what God wants to say to us. I have a special prayer spot in my home for morning and evening prayer. I know when I am there it is God's time to speak to me and my time to really listen. We will always hear something if we just take the time.

Fasting is challenging for us. We have so much food in our lives. Food is one of those wonderful pleasures which not only nourishes the body and provides such enjoyment in the taste; often it also becomes the moment to gather with others around a table for great fellowship. Fasting asks us to simply reduce the volume and to be aware when my stomach growls that I am reminded of how much I have while so many others have so little. It is a moment to be in God's presence and ask how to give back as well. Fasting is done with joy and life, in union with God.

Lent is a time to return to basics. True religion is to acknowledge that God is God and we are God's creatures, sent to this world to share God's love. We give form and substance to this in the way we practice our faith every day in little and not-so-little ways.

This Lent we are dispensed from attending Sunday Mass, even the Holy Week services. We are dispensed from abstaining from meat on Fridays of Lent. What we are not dispensed from is imitating Jesus in the way we live, think, and treat others. This special year with the pandemic should call us to be creative with our Lenten sacrifices. A few weeks ago, I suggested we all consider giving up social media, especially the type that angers us, or tempts us to strike out or to blame or to judge others. On the positive side, helping those suffering economically from the virus is a great way to live Lent. Reaching out with calls or emails to those quarantined or to a homebound loved one is another. Come on, you can think of many more ways!

Lent asks us to prepare to enter into the paschal mystery, the passion, death, and resurrection of Jesus. It confronts us with the one who gave his life for us as the Suffering Servant. We are called to figure out how we also give our lives in following him.

This Lent, instead of giving up, try giving. Do a work of charity each week. Find a way to reach out to others, then pray over it, fast, or do some personal sacrifice in union with those who suffer.

So, "haven't we given up enough this year?" Nope, not enough, never enough, when the one we follow gave his all.

56

2/21/21 First Lent

Reform your lives and believe in the gospel.

Gen 9:8–15; 1 Pet 3:18–22; Mark 1:12–15

As IF COVID WERE not enough, San Antonio went through an incredible and difficult time this week. In four days we had two snowstorms, sleet and ice, temperatures in the single digits, and outages of power and water. This has never happened in my lifetime (and that is a long time!). We still do not know the extent of the damage nor do we know of all the fatalities, which I fear will be discovered soon. What impressed me was the response of so many groups, agencies, civic officials, and individuals reaching out to those most vulnerable. Over forty-five years of active ministry, I served four parishes that were mostly low- and modest-income. In the winter, when I entered homes, often they were drafty, cold, and heated by one space heater. A time like we just had spells disaster. Yet, hundreds if not thousands responded to help with food, water, housing, and other needs. People checked on neighbors. San Antonio is known for this kind of response. The faith liaison for the city, Rev Ann Helmke, coordinates a program called Compassionate San Antonio.

The gospel story today was the moment of Jesus entering deeply into the human condition so that he could feel total compassion with us. Through his time in the desert he bonded with humans, as he felt their weakness, their hunger, their threats, and their temptations. He also allowed himself to be ministered to by God. As he overcame each of these tests he was more ready to proclaim the kingdom, show God's compassion, and ask all to repent. This testing of Jesus was key to his future ministry.

Lent is a time to test the depths of our faith. Every first Sunday of Lent we hear one of the accounts of Jesus' temptation in the desert. It is a great way for us to start Lent. Mark's is the most concise account and does not record the three temptations enumerated in Matthew and Luke. The focus is Jesus entering into battle with Satan, which shows us that we, his followers, also must enter into the fight against evil with him.

In the gospel today, Jesus has just come from his baptism, where the Voice from Heaven affirmed him as "Son." Mark wants to connect this moment with the temptation in the desert. Jesus, still wet from the Jordan River, enters the desert and is tested. We are reminded of Israel crossing through the waters of the Red Sea, entering the desert and encountering many tests and trials. Jesus spent forty days in the desert; Israel, forty years in the desert; and we begin forty days of Lent, our desert.

The language is harsh. Some translations say Jesus was driven or literally thrown into the desert. There are temptations by Satan, the adversary, while he is among wild beasts, which were also thought to be possessed by demons. The consolation in this fearful time was the angels, representing God's presence and power, who waited on him while he was in this contest with evil. Sometimes our desert time might feel similar: alone, with threats and disaster all around. At these times, think of the angels. We never can tell who might be an angel for us, not one with wings and a halo, but a person sent by God, whether we realize it or not. We had many of them this week here in this city. God's presence is here. Just look and know God sent them for you.

Jesus has the support of his Father as he enters into the conflict with evil. This is his first test, but the rest of Mark will show us that the battle will continue all the way to the cross. Just because we are baptized does not mean we have a free ride. We need to be aware of the many forces of evil around us, and they are everywhere! We must be ready to confront them, knowing that baptism gives us support for this task. Baptism is our commitment to follow Christ and God's commitment to be with us on our pilgrimage.

It is also important to note where Jesus begins his ministry. It is not at the temple or some palace in Jerusalem. Israel had expected a political, military Messiah. Mark wants us to change expectations and understand the Suffering Servant Messiah comes from the desert and from Galilee, a backward, suspect area. This forces us to ask: How do we follow this Messiah?

The desert was also considered by the people of Jesus' time as a place to meet God most intensely. Israel's experience showed that. It was a place for deep, abiding intimacy with the God of our ancestors. All distractions are gone. It is just God and me, a thought both exciting and scary.

The desert showed a provident God who provided for the people by giving them water and food for their journey. The prophets would remind the people of what God had done for their ancestors as a call to return to a desert spirituality. It was also a call to treat the stranger and alien as they would want to be treated since they once were strangers and aliens in Egypt.

For Mark, the issue in the temptations is loyalty. Will we follow this Jesus or will we follow the evil one? This will be what we are constantly asked through this gospel. This is really what constantly confronts us in our lives. What does it mean to be his disciple?

The ancient Mediterranean world believed that spirits were always trying to interfere with human life. For Jesus to be tested in the desert and throughout his ministry, confronting evil spirits to heal and free people, would have been a clear sign of God's favor. Mark will show us that Jesus entered into the great battle with the forces of evil. Often in Mark we see Jesus expelling demons as he struggles to show compassion for the weak and vulnerable. People throughout the gospel are always asking: Who is this who commands demons? Ask it for yourself.

Jesus' confrontation with evil was intended to show and live the compassion and love of God. Lent is a time for us to feel compassion as well. That is why we fast, pray, and give alms. It connects us with our own human weakness, vulnerability, and threats, along with Christ, who was forty days in the desert, and with those around the world who suffer. We enter into ourselves, and these practices help us find the capacity for the kind of compassion Jesus showed during his life.

Fasting helps us to prepare for the battle Jesus fought. Isaiah the prophet says,

> This, rather is the fasting that I wish: releasing those bound unjustly . . . setting free the oppressed; breaking every yoke; sharing your bread with the hungry; sheltering the oppressed and the homeless; clothing the naked when you see them, and not turning your back on your own. Then your light shall break forth like the dawn. (Isa 58:6–8)

Lent gives us an agenda which should be practiced every day, namely, to participate in the paschal mystery of Jesus, his life, passion, death, and resurrection. We do this by ongoing conversion, a constant turning of our minds and hearts to God, by repentance for our sins and a commitment to live our baptism. Lent shows us that pain, suffering, and death are realities in the experience of every human. However, by living our faith, we unite these as a sharing in the sufferings of Christ. It is a free and loving participation in Christ's passion so that we can show compassion.

Can Lent be for you a uniting of all your sacrifices, sufferings, and setbacks of the past year of COVID, as well as the recent sufferings due to the extreme cold weather? Can these be put in the context of a sharing in the total giving of life Jesus showed us in his passion and death? Can you be that compassionate?

This is our desert as Lent begins. This is the battle against the evil one. We in San Antonio did not anticipate it would be in our face on day one.

57

2/28/21 Second Lent

He was transfigured before their eyes ...

Gen 22:1–2, 9a, 10–13, 15–18; Rom 8:31b–34; Mark 9:2–10

LAST SUNDAY I READ an article in the paper about a remarkable man, Pablo Pedraza. He works part-time for a delivery service which contracts with Texas Children's Hospital's specialty pharmacy in Houston. Monthly they ship anti-rejection medicine via UPS to an eighteen-month-old toddler in San Antonio. The little girl needs the medicine after a recent heart transplant due to a rare condition. The transplant was performed at that hospital. The Wednesday of the big freeze, when UPS suspended deliveries due to harsh road conditions, Pedraza transported the medicine. Driving very slowly and carefully he made the dangerous trip to San Antonio passing numerous accidents and sidelined trucks along the way. The family of the young patient was overwhelmed by his tremendous and risky effort and tried to tip him, but was politely refused as Pedraza said, "I am just doing my job."[1] The parents called him a life-saver and a huge blessing. Pedraza, who also has a young daughter, rarely meets clients or knows their conditions. Yet that day he met the toddler and was very moved. He said, "It puts everything in perspective."[2] He returned

1. Davis, "'Just Doing My Job,'" para. 20.
2. Davis, "'Just Doing My Job,'" para. 24.

home to Houston slowly, arriving late that night to his worried yet grateful family.

There were many inspiring stories of people reaching out during
the deep freeze, despite the brutal conditions and threats to their own
safety, so that those who were at risk would receive the help they needed.
Delivery of food, water, blankets and rides to safe, warm locations
happened often out of the sight of anyone except the ones involved. There
have been equally inspiring stories of people doing similar acts of duty,
mercy, and compassion during the past year of COVID. We will never
know all the stories, but the few we hear about should give us inspiration
and strength to imitate their uplifting example. At difficult times we can
think of these heroic people as a shining light of tribute to the best of the
human spirit.

That is what the transfiguration story in today's gospel reading was
about, a moment of glory to overcome what was coming, the agony of the
cross. Jesus and the disciples are on a mountain. As has been mentioned
before, a mountaintop was always considered a place where revelations
from God happen. It is the intersection of heaven and earth. Something
very special will happen on this mountaintop. It will be a moment of
glory to strengthen the disciples for the future trial.

It is important to note where in the narrative of the gospel this
story takes place. This gives the context Mark wants. In this case the
transfiguration happens right after Peter's confession of faith in Jesus, and
Jesus' immediate prediction of his passion. This frames both the cost of
discipleship and the promise of *parousia*, the heavenly kingdom. It comes
after Jesus says to be a disciple is to take up a cross, one answer to the
question of Mark on what it means to follow Jesus.

For Jesus to speak of a cross was a sign of rebellion, since execution
by the cross was reserved for those who challenged Rome. There was
nothing private about this death penalty. It was designed for all to see
and to warn others that they could be next if they challenged the system.
The cross was carried in public to a very public place, after which the
condemned person was stripped naked in front of all and brutally
crucified. Those who heard Jesus say this would have shuddered to
think of the implications of picking up a cross to follow him. However,
Jesus wants to be clear that following him was and still is a very public
commitment. It was going against the status quo. It was risking one's life.

The transfiguration was intended for the disciples, to help strength-
en them to accept not only Jesus' cross but their own. The story also calls

us to accept our crosses behind Jesus. The message for believers was that if they shared the cross while following Jesus they would also share in the glory. Think of the crosses in your life. Certainly, we recently have shared several. The COVID pandemic has caused great suffering and death for so many and much sacrifice for the whole world. Many people in this part of the world suffered the harsh winter storms of the past weeks, and some are still feeling the after effects. Where is the glory? For me, as mentioned above, it is realizing how throughout the past year and past weeks we have seen the resilient human spirit reaching out to those most in need. It is people going beyond what would seem ordinary to do the extraordinary. They are truly most fully alive, really in their glory.

In this story Mark wanted to solidify the identity of Jesus after Peter's profession. Even though the disciples did not understand fully what Peter said about Jesus being the Messiah, they needed to understand what that title meant. They needed to change their expectations of a military political savior to a Suffering Servant. At the same time, suffering is not the end of the story. It is important that we always remember this when we are in the midst of sacrifices and sufferings. This moment on the mountain showed that God was with Jesus, despite the cross. "This is my beloved Son; listen to him." These are powerful words that answer the two key questions of Mark's gospel: Who is Jesus? Answer: My beloved Son. What does it mean to follow him? Answer: Listen to him.

There are paradoxes in the story on the mountaintop to connect this with the cross. Jesus is surrounded by the great heroes of Israel here, and by criminals on Calvary. His clothes are brilliant here, and torn from him there. God declares him Son here, and the executioner calls him Son of God there. Jesus' suffering is connected and was part of the glory. The cross is not suffering for the sake of suffering. The cross makes sense only with the glory of the resurrection.

God names Jesus Son here, and the disciples hear the voice. These are the same words as during the baptism where only Jesus heard them. However, the command of Jesus to the disciples not to tell anyone is so that they focus not on the glory, but rather on the teaching of the cross. Mark, by placing Jesus in the midst of the heroic figures of Israel's history, is saying all prophets are put to death. To challenge the injustices and suffering of innocent people often leads to the persecution of the one who does so. Yet the heroic actions are both part of the cross and part of the glory.

In the midst of the sufferings, sacrifices, and tragedies of the past year of COVID and the past weeks of the freeze, we need to speak with our actions and our words that this is not all there is. In the midst of the many hatreds, hostilities, prejudices, frustrations, and the pettiness of our current lives and our world, we need to reflect the glory of God as Jesus did in the transfiguration. We do that when we listen to Jesus. We do that when we choose the often-difficult path of loving one another, especially the one different from us. Jesus never said to love only those like us, but he showed that loving all and acting on that love was the sure road to share in his glory.

Pablo Pedraza will probably not receive any medals or awards for his heroic action. After all, he was "just doing his job." However, we all were rewarded by his inspiring attitude and spirit. He also got the prize of seeing a little human being, whose life he probably saved, and parents who could not express how grateful they were for his effort. He sacrificed and carried his cross that day.

We need to be extremely grateful that we can also see transfiguration all around us. Take time to appreciate and be strengthened by those extraordinary actions of others for others. Pablo Pedraza made it to the mountaintop, and just as Jesus promised, he and we saw the glory.

58

3/6/21 Third Lent

Destroy this temple . . . and in three days I will raise it up.

Exod 20:1–17; 1 Cor 1:22–25; John 2:13–25

WHEN COVID BEGAN LAST March and the lockdown affected almost every part of our lives, the churches closed as well. It was traumatic for many not to be able to attend Sunday Mass, and even more so not to celebrate Holy Week and Easter inside the churches we were accustomed to attending. Shortly after the lockdown I began riding my bicycle daily to get out of the house and get exercise. There are two homes next to each other in my neighborhood that posted identical yard signs close to the curb almost immediately. They read, "The church has left the building," then under it, "the people are the church." That has given me comfort as I pass almost every day. Yes, we love our church buildings and want to gather together, but our faith tells us the church is the people living our discipleship by following Jesus every day in all we say and do. Hopefully, soon we can all return to our communal worship; in the meantime, we take strength in our faith which makes us all church.

Today's gospel is somewhat troubling as it seems to be out of the norm. It is known as the Cleansing of the Temple. What is striking in the story is we never see Jesus physically angry in any of the other gospels. He actually becomes violent, whipping, overturning tables, and running people out. However, it was a different kind of anger, somewhat like the protests we have seen around racial injustice, economic disparity, and kids demanding safe schools free of guns.

Jesus was constructing something new. He had spoken forcefully many times, confronting especially those in power who abused the poor and vulnerable. However, he was never physically violent except here at the temple. One translation of his words in the gospel is, "You have made this a den of thieves" (Luke 19:46 KJV). The operative word is "thieves." People were being robbed. What Jesus saw was the robbing of the poor who were simply trying to be devout Jews. He substitutes himself for the temple. He is especially the place for those suffering, the poorest and most in need. In the Eucharist we receive Jesus, and we are called to see him in the poor and be committed to them.

Jesus cleanses the temple today precisely for the same reason. It was supposed to be sacred space, where all could come to access the divinity. However, some few had made it a profit center and even a place to cheat the poor. Jesus says from now on he is the temple, accessible to all. His priority is to focus on the people and their relationship to God, and not on the building. That is why he came, namely, to connect us to God so that we would see God in a different way—more accessible, close to us, a compassionate and loving Father. We are temples of God. We are the body of Christ.

The issue of justice in this action is a key factor of this story. Jesus is angry that the poor are being forced to buy animals in the temple for sacrifice with money needed for basics like food. They could have bought an animal for much less cost from the outside, but that was not allowed. There is a monopoly occurring in the name of worship. Doves are the only animals for sale in the temple that the poor can afford. The temple is sacred space, which is where people access God. Sacred actions are done there. Jesus objects to the attitudes where the money is first, not the disposition and heart and piety of the person. God wants justice and righteousness to be the offering, not the sacrifices of animals.

Another abuse of the poor in the temple was the changing of currency. The money-changers were the ones to exchange Roman coins, which the people were required to use for daily transactions, for Jewish coins. The reason was that the Roman coin was inscribed with the face of the emperor and the words, "Image of the Divine Caesar." This was blasphemous to Jews since they believed in only one God. Inside the temple, the religious leaders allowed only Jewish currency, so people coming to buy an animal for sacrifice had to change their money. If you have ever had the experience of changing currency at the airport when arriving in another country and feeling you were losing out on the exchange rate, you begin to get the picture of what was happening. Multiply that by ten! The temple money-changers were notorious for cheating the poor in the name of worship, and the poor had no option except to buy the animal at inflated rates and exchange their money at a loss. The poor lost out twice simply trying to be devout. Now, are you angry like Jesus? You get the picture!

This gospel story is a good reminder during Lent that we must remember the poor and sacrifice for them. Reach out; be committed. The poor have so many strikes against them in their daily lives. Often, they struggle against a system about which they have no knowledge or power to challenge. They often come out losing. Catholic Charities promotes Forty Cans for Lent in the parishes to collect food from each parish family for those in need. This year, because of COVID and the loss of jobs, especially in areas that employ the working poor, has been devastating. The winter storm made it worse.

We also need to keep aware of the poor throughout the world this Lent. Those of us who experienced power outages and water shortages during the recent big freeze now have a tiny taste of what the majority of the world lives with every day. I saw it with my own eyes traveling with Catholic Relief Services in Africa, India, and Central America. Billions live without power or running water in the home. Some walk hours to the nearest water source every day. CRS Rice Bowl is a Lenten program to remember and support the most vulnerable throughout the world.

Jesus came to give us a new way to approach God, a huge change. This gospel story was written at a time when the early Jewish Christians were being ejected from the temple for being traitors to the faith. They saw in this story a justification, a way to make the change of not going to the temple. Jesus was the temple, as he says in this gospel, and his followers formed his temple. Around this same time the temple in Jerusalem was destroyed by the Romans in retaliation for the Jewish revolt. It was a terrible collective shock to all Israel and all Jews. Yet for Jewish Christians it became the moment to make way for the new temple, which is Christ.

This story appears in the four gospels. However, in the other three it happens after Jesus' entrance into Jerusalem before his passion. It becomes one of the final reasons to kill Jesus. John does not present it in that context; rather, he shows it as a theological event. Here it happens at the beginning of Jesus' ministry as a sign. The temple has become the object of adoration, not God, so Jesus places things right. Jesus' body substitutes for the temple, a truly revolutionary act. It is a new form of worship centered in the relationship between God and believers, not just tied to one location.

Here in San Antonio, the archbishop this week asked that despite our governor's loosening of COVID mandates, those who attend Mass should continue with masks and all other virus protocols. The best way to be church is to be considerate of all who are church.

We are the body of Christ, the church, the new temple. Worship is in all we do, whether inside a building or anywhere. Our life, faithfully lived, becomes uninterrupted prayer. Lent is the time to imitate Jesus and see the poor and vulnerable as those deserving of our action. Be the hands of Jesus this Lent, but most of all be church by being the heart of Jesus.

59

3/15/21 Fourth Lent

But he who acts in truth comes into the light . . .

2 Chr 36:14–16, 19–23; Eph 2:4–10; John 3:14–21

POPE FRANCIS CONCLUDED AN historic visit to Iraq this past week amid
concerns for his safety, as well as fear of spreading the pandemic. He
reached out to the small Christian population that has suffered during
the various conflicts and persecutions of recent years. He also reached
out to Muslim religious and political leaders to show them his desire that
all peoples live in unity and peace. He made a special effort to visit the
spiritual leader of the Iraqi Shia Muslims, and spent time sharing how
religion can help bring peace and unity to a troubled area of the world.
At Ur, where God directed Abraham to go to the promised land, the
pope said, "We profane God's name by hating our brothers and sisters.
Hostility, extremism and violence are not born of a religious heart: they
are betrayals of religion."[1] The trip truly shed a beautiful light on what
could be if people lived out their faith in God.

Today's gospel is also the story of the meeting of two religious leaders with great differences. Nicodemus was part of the Pharisees who opposed Jesus, yet he risked his status by reaching out. John's Gospel was
written at a time when conflict between the early Christians and Jews
was high. John helps his community go beyond Jewish worship and see
Christianity as superseding it. However, there was an exception, namely,
the Jewish ritual and religious requirements regarding almsgiving to the

---

1. Wooden, "Update," para. 3.

poor. The early Christians placed a high priority on upholding care for the weak, the poor, and the marginalized. Nicodemus, a Pharisee and member of the Sanhedrin, a major council with political, religious, and judicial function over the people, represents the religious elite who, despite Jewish requirements, marginalize the poor. Remember last week, in the story of the cleansing of the temple, when Jesus was angry with the leaders because they defrauded the poor in their acts of worship.

Nicodemus begins his journey half-heartedly, afraid for his reputation. Sometimes to follow Jesus means others will reject us. We worry more about what others think than actually doing the right thing. Nicodemus had that dilemma. He slowly grows from one who participated in the systems of marginalization to one who, by believing in Jesus publicly, becomes himself an outcast from his class.

John wants us to know that this meeting happened at night. For John, light and darkness are important images to show how Jesus is the Light of the world and enlightens those who believe. The entire lengthy discourse is helping Nicodemus to go from darkness to light. He does not see Jesus for who he is yet, nor can he see him in the poor. Jesus' love goes beyond class or social standing. Nicodemus finally embraces Jesus as a disciple openly only at the cross. There he makes an act of faith. What matters is the ultimate giving of one's life and destiny to Christ. Nicodemus is at the cross publicly anointing Jesus' body with lavish oil only a rich person could afford. In effect he gives Jesus a royal burial. He offered this last tribute to Christ the King. Nicodemus was converted and unafraid to follow Jesus. He was now a true disciple, living in the light.

The words "believe" and "light" each occur five times in the gospel of John. For John, seeing is believing. He talks of the works of the one who lives in truth, works done in God. God's work is to die to self so as to live for others and fulfill what God wants of us. This is to shine our light, as Isaiah the prophet said of freeing the oppressed, sharing bread with the hungry, sheltering the homeless, and clothing the naked, "Then your light shall break forth like the dawn" (Isa 58:8).

Lent is a time to assess our lives and especially see and admit the dark areas that hold us back from being Jesus for others. Light can also expose the evil that people would rather keep hidden. What are your dark areas? Jesus, by his life and death, was the greatest gift God could give us. The only response to that love is faith. For John, faith demands action. The truth involves thinking, accepting, and doing concrete gestures in commitment and solidarity with those in need.

John's Gospel challenges readers to understand Jesus more deeply. Nicodemus risks, tries, and finally understands. John sees the world as hostile to Jesus, preferring darkness to light. There is much darkness on the web today. Anything can be said unverified and it is believed. It can and does promote hate, conspiracy, division, racism, anger, and outrage against another. It is dark because it thrives on hearsay, lies, stereotyping, and judging others as less than us. It cannot bear the light of truth; yet so many choose that darkness over the light. Why do people prefer to engage in such dark actions? For John, rejection of God's love is to prefer darkness over light.

John wanted early Christians to know that the church must be welcoming of all peoples, especially the poor, the vulnerable and those who were rejected by society. John shares the view of the other gospels that to be a disciple and to love God is to love our neighbor, especially those most in need. Certainly, the COVID crisis gives us all many moments to love God through our neighbors.

Today's second collection is for Catholic Relief Services, the official agency of the United States' bishops for assistance to the poorest of the world. I was privileged to work with CRS for ten years. We must always remember, as Pope Francis showed us this week, that the church is catholic, namely, universal, reaching out to all, even those not of our faith, and especially those suffering. We have the opportunity today to do works of light, to bring light to the darkness of poverty, hate, violence, and all the evil forces in the world. We are the blessed ones who can do this through the collection today.

Pope Francis also gave us an example this past week of reaching out in understanding and reconciliation to people from different cultures and religious traditions. In the process he was enlightened, and all of us with him. Those who met him were also enlightened. What does it mean to truly understand another person, especially one very different, so as to be enlightened? That seems to be the challenge today in our very polarized world, where we judge first and condemn quickly, rather than reach out, listen, and seek to put ourselves in the shoes of the other. We will never have peace unless each of us is willing to suspend judgment.

Amanda Gorman, the young poet who delivered her powerful poem for the presidential inauguration, had these lines which struck me and speak to this gospel reflection:

And so we lift our gazes, not to what stands between us
but what stands before us
We close the divide because we know to put our future first,
we must first put our differences aside
We lay down our arms
so we can reach out our arms
to one another
We seek harm to none and harmony for all.[2]

What was the moment when both Nicodemus and the disciples began to understand Jesus? It was the lifting up of Jesus on the cross, where he was willing to give his life, where he was unwilling to condemn those who crucified him, where he showed the ultimate love of a person for others. We begin to understand each other, to know the truth, only when we are willing, like Jesus, to give ourselves. When we sacrifice for others it puts so much into perspective. Things become different. When we suspend judging and condemning, then understanding and light come through. How many times a day are you judging someone else? How often will you condemn actions or words of others without taking time to try to understand? How can the world ever change if you don't start first?

Amanda Gorman ended the inaugural poem with these inspired words: "For there was always light/if only we are brave enough to see it/if only we're brave enough to be it."[3]

2. Gorman, "Youth Poet Laureate Amanda Gorman's Inaugural Poem," lines 28–35.

3. Gorman, "Youth Poet Laureate Amanda Gorman's Inaugural Poem," lines 108–10.

60

3/21/21 Fifth Lent

We would like to see Jesus.

Ezek 37:12–14; Rom 8:8–11; John 11:1–45

ONE OF THE EARLY homilies in this series touched on the many times in our nation's history when a crisis moment caused prejudice and bigotry to rise and show its ugly face. We in San Antonio had another one of those moments last week when an Asian restaurant was vandalized with racist graffiti and the owner's life was threatened. Mike Nguyen, a French-Vietnamese suffering from lymphoma, had spoken out publicly against relaxing the mask and safety protocols by the governor. He continued to require all virus precautions be followed in his restaurant. Despite the hateful act, many people gathered the next day to help clean up the damage, leave heart shaped cutouts with messages of encouragement in place of the graffiti, and purchase meals. The windows, previously filled with hate, were shining with messages of love. The owner continues to receive online threats but refuses to back down, both to fight the virus and the prejudice. He knows he is risking a lot, even his life, but he feels strongly he is saving lives with his actions.

Jesus, in the gospel today, reflects on his upcoming death. He knows he will give life by dying and that "this world's prince," the evil one, will be driven out. The giving or sacrificing of our lives is what all of Lent has been about. It is what is modeled by the penitential practices of prayer, fasting, and almsgiving that the church asks us to practice during this time. Each of these is a dying to self, so as to give and share life. That is exactly the point of Lent, namely, that something needs to die in all of us in order to produce more life, and to drive out the evil that continues to rear its ugly head. Otherwise, the evil one will continue to sow hate, division, and prejudice among us. Last Lent it was not as clear as it is today, having gone through this past year.

This is the last chapter of John before the passion. Jesus is preparing his disciples for the shock when he is arrested and executed. They still have no idea of what is coming. He asks them not to abandon him in his hour. The "hour" is what John has spoken about throughout his gospel. It involves the new covenant between God and God's people, which is mentioned in the first reading where God "will write it upon their hearts." It is also the definitive battle between the love of Jesus versus the unjust evil rejecting him. Jesus giving his life on the cross reveals the love that is God.

The story in today's section begins with a simple yet powerful request: "We would like to see Jesus." What a beautiful aspirational wish! It is in the heart of all believers in Jesus. We just want to see him. We just want to hear his voice in our heart. We want to feel his compassion and gentle touch healing us of so much that afflicts us. We just want to know he walks with us in this difficult time of immense stress. In a year when so much has gone wrong, when lies, so much tension, division, suffering, hate, prejudice, and death have been a big part of life, we just want Jesus! Is that too much to ask?

Jesus does not give the Greeks the answer we might expect, such as, "See me this afternoon." Instead, he connects their request to see him with another way of seeing him, namely, understanding that to see him is to accept the total giving of our lives for the other. To see Jesus is to see him in the suffering, sacrifices, struggle, anxiety, challenge, and even despair of others, and to see him in my response.

"Unless the grain of wheat dies it does not bear fruit" (John 12:24). This entire past year has been trying to see Jesus in so much that has happened with this virus, in the terrified faces of the sick, in the loneliness of the elderly in nursing homes with no visitors, in the despair of the medical staff holding the hand of a stranger at the last breath of their life. So much! "We want to see Jesus." This year has been spiritual as much as it has been medical.

There has been a lot of dying as well, over 540,000 Americans as of this writing, and 2.7 million worldwide. In this country, more Americans have died in the one year of COVID than in both World Wars and Vietnam combined. Almost everyone now knows someone who has died of the virus. We have seen death up close. Perhaps each of us needs to reflect on why we are not among the COVID dead. Any of us could have been fatalities. The virus spared no age group, no ethnic group, no area of the country. Have we allowed ourselves to be touched by others' pain? How can we be indifferent now after this experience? If anything, we have learned how much we are bound together.

To find life we must die to what we are now. That is how we need to see Jesus, by dying to ourselves. It is the process of conversion, which is what we do during Lent. Otherwise, too much can get in the way. I want to see Jesus. To see is to have faith. That is what the Greeks who asked Philip wanted. There was something inside drawing them. Is that same desire in us? How do we act on it?

Jesus' words are a prayer, as he is having an interior monologue with himself as his hour approaches. This takes the place of his struggle in the other three gospels at the agony in the garden. John does not include that, but simply has Jesus after the Last Supper in the garden being arrested. Here, Jesus is already at peace with what will happen.

This story of the Greeks seeking Jesus was John's way of appealing to Jewish Christians to accept gentiles, people not like them, into the church. This is a small part of the dying to self so that there is room for others in my life. Also, it helped them understand the persecution they were undergoing. Were they ready to sacrifice their lives for their faith? Giving life is our mission as well. It may not be suffering martyrdom but it always involves some sacrifice. Mike Nguyen had to close his restaurant one day this week out of caution for the increased threats he was receiving. Despite all the support he received, it was still clear that the powers of evil do not surrender without a fight.

"We want to see Jesus." Really? How do we see him? We die to self so that we see him in those around us, and in the everyday small acts of love and self-sacrifice. Lent has been a journey to see how we can avoid those things in our lives that hinder us from being the good persons we can be. It is a time to take inventory of how we may not have been as good as possible, even evil at times. Lent calls us to discover the good within and to die to whatever hinders that good from happening. The dying and rising are continuous. The struggle against the evil in us and in the world is never ending. Lent has been about "we want to see Jesus." With him we can truly be at our best. How have you seen Jesus so far? Have you even looked?

With this reflection we complete one year of homilies. It has been a momentous, historic year, one that shouted out for deep introspection about what was happening and how it was touching us all. Sharing these with you has been a gift for me as much as it may have helped you. For that I am grateful.

I cannot think of a better way to sum up what all this special year of preaching has been about than "we want to see Jesus." I hope in many little ways these writings helped in accomplishing just that!

Bibliography

Abrams, Jonathan. "N.B.A. Players Meet with Pope Francis on Social Justice Efforts." *The New York Times*, Nov 23, 2020. https://www.nytimes.com/2020/11/23/sports/basketball/nba-pope-francis-protests.html.

Andal, Elizabeth. "10 Famous Failures to Success Stories that Will Inspire you to Carry On." *Lifehack*, June 4, 2021. https://www.lifehack.org/articles/communication/10-famous-failures-that-will-inspire-you-success.html.

The Associated Press. "NBA Players Meet Pope Francis at Vatican, Hailed for Demanding Justice." *NBC News*, November 23, 2020. https://www.nbcnews.com/news/world/nba-players-meet-pope-francis-vatican-hailed-demanding-justice-n1248665.

Bell, Rob, et al. *Naked and You Clothed Me*. Princeton, NJ: Clear Faith, 2013.

Birmingham, Mary. *Word and Worship Workbook*. Mahwah, NJ: Paulist, 2000.

Boadt, Lawrence, et al. *The Paulist Liturgy Planning Guide*. Mahwah, NJ: Paulist, 2005.

Catholic News Agency. "Beware of the Virus of 'Selfish Indifference,' Says Pope on Divine Mercy Sunday." April 19, 2020. https://www.catholicnewsagency.com/news/44248/beware-of-the-virus-of-selfish-indifference-says-pope-on-divine-mercy-sunday.

"Covid-19 to Add as Many as 150 Million Extreme Poor by 2021." *The World Bank*, October 7, 2020. https://www.worldbank.org/en/news/press-release/2020/10/07/covid-19-to-add-as-many-as-150-million-extreme-poor-by-2021.

Craddock, Fred B. et al., *Preaching through the Christian Year*. Valley Forge, PA: Trinity, 1993.

Crouse, Karen. "'I Let You Down': Klete Keller's Path from Olympics to Capitol Riot." *The New York Times*, January 18, 2021. https://www.nytimes.com/2021/01/18/sports/olympics/klete-keller-capitol-riot.html.

Davis, Vincent T. "'Just Doing My Job' - Houston Driver Braves Icy Roads to Deliver Vital Medicine to San Antonio Toddler." *San Antonio Express-News*, February 20, 2021. https://www.expressnews.com/news/local/article/Just-doing-my-job-Houston-driver-braves-15963446.php.

Day, Jennifer Cheeseman, and Cheridan Christnacht. "Women Hold 76% of All Health Care Jobs, Gaining in Higher-Paying Occupations." *United States Census Bureau, August* 14, 2019. https://www.census.gov/library/stories/2019/08/your-health-care-in-womens-hands.html.

Dickerson, Caitlin. "Vulnerable Border Community Battles Virus on 'A Straight Up Trajectory.'" *The New York Times*, July 19, 2020. https://www.nytimes.com/2020/07/19/us/coronavirus-texas-rio-grande-valley.html.

Egnew, Thomas R. "The Meaning of Healing: Transcending Suffering," *Annals of Family Medicine*, May 2005. https://www.ncbi.nlm.nih.gov/pmc/articles/PMC1466870/.

Faley, Roland J. *Footprints on the Mountain.* Mahwah, NJ: Paulist, 1994.

Fazio, Marie. "An Italian Teenager Could Become the First Millennial Saint." *The New York Times,* November 6, 2020. https://www.nytimes.com/2020/10/12/world/europe/millennial-saint-carlo-acutis.html.

"For Mexico's Doctors, an Especially Mournful Day of the Dead." *The Express,* November 3, 2020. https://www.lockhaven.com/uncategorized/2020/11/for-mexicos-doctors-an-especially-mournful-day-of-the-dead/.

Francis, Pope. *Evangelii Gaudium. The Vatican,* November 24, 2013. https://www.vatican.va/content/francesco/en/apost_exhortations/documents/papa-francesco_esortazione-ap_20131124_evangelii-gaudium.html

———. "No to the Culture of Indifference." *The Vatican,* January 8, 2019. https://www.vatican.va/content/francesco/en/cotidie/2019/documents/papa-francesco-cotidie_20190108_notothe-culture-ofindifference.html.

———. *Urbi et Orbi. The Vatican,* April 12, 2020. https://www.vatican.va/content/francesco/en/messages/urbi/documents/papa-francesco_20200412_urbi-et-orbi-pasqua.html.

Fuller, Reginald H. *Preaching the Lectionary.* Collegeville, MN: Liturgical, 1984.

Gorman, Amanda. "Youth Poet Laureate Amanda Gorman's Inaugural Poem." *CNN,* January 20, 2021. https://www.cnn.com/2021/01/20/politics/amanda-gorman-inaugural-poem-transcript/index.html.

Guzman, René A. "Catholics Face 2021 Lent Asking, 'Jesus, Haven't We Given Up Enough?'" *San Antonio Express-News,* February 10, 2021. https://www.expressnews.com/lifestyle/article/Catholics-face-2021-Lent-asking-Jesus-15940295.php.

Howes, Lynn. "Food Banks See 623% Surge in New Donors During COVID." https://blog.rkdgroup.com/ food-banks-see-623-surge-in-new-donors-during-covid.

King, Martin Luther, Jr. "I've Been to the Mountaintop." The Martin Luther King, Jr. Research and Education Institute, April 3, 1968. https://kinginstitute.stanford.edu/encyclopedia/ive-been-mountaintop.

Kuruvilla, Carol. "Pope Francis: Helping Poor and Migrants Is 'Equally Sacred' as Fighting Abortion." *HuffPost,* April 9, 2018. https://www.huffpost.com/entry/pope-francis-poor-migrants-abortion_n_5acb6c76e4b0337ad1ea14fd.

Mares, Courtney. "Pope Francis: Economics should not 'sacrifice human dignity to the idols of finance.'" *Catholic News Agency,* September 4, 2020. https://www.catholicnewsagency.com/news/45711/pope-francis-economics-should-not-sacrifice-human-dignity-to-the-idols-of-finance.

———. "Pope Francis Says Blessed Carlo Acutis Is a Model for Young People to Put God First." *Catholic News Agency,* October 11, 2020. https://www.catholicnewsagency.com/news/46170/pope-francis-says-blessed-carlo-acutis-is-a-model-for-young-people-to-put-god-first.

O'Connell, Gerard. "Pope Francis: 'Globalization of Indifference' Contributes to Killing." *America,* March 21, 2016. https://www.americamagazine.org/issue/pope-francis-globalization-indifference-contributes-killing.

Reid, Kathryn. "Forced to Flee: Top Countries Refugees are Coming from." *World Vision,* June 18, 2021. https://www.worldvision.org/refugees-news-stories/forced-to-flee-top-countries-refugees-coming-from.

Richtel, Matt, and Reed Abelson. "Nursing Homes Confront New Covid Outbreaks Amid Calls for Staff Vaccination Mandates." *The New York Times,* August 4, 2021.

https://www.nytimes.com/2021/08/04/health/nursing-homes-vaccine-delta-covid.html.

Russell-Kraft, Stephanie. "Can Faith Leaders' Vaccine Selfies Rebuild Public Trust?" *Sojourners*, January 27, 2021. https://sojo.net/articles/can-faith-leaders-vaccine-selfies-rebuilt-public-trust-interfaith-covid-san-antonio.

Santoro, Alessia. "The Average Amount Parents Spend on Christmas Presents Per Child Might Surprise You." Yahoo.com, December 22, 2017. https://www.yahoo.com/entertainment/average-amount-parents-spend-christmas-123031742.html.

Stewart, Mandy. "Commentary: Consider Your Own Role in Political Division." *San Antonio Express-News*, January 20, 2021. https://www.expressnews.com/opinion/commentary/article/Commentary-Consider-your-own-role-in-political-15885278.php

"UN Report: Pandemic Year Marked by Spike in World Hunger." *World Health Organization*, July 12, 2021. https://www.who.int/news/item/12-07-2021-un-report-pandemic-year-marked-by-spike-in-world-hunger.

Wooden, Cindy. "Update: Hostility, Violence Are 'Betrayals' of Religion, Pope Says in Iraq." *Catholic News Service*, March 6, 2021. https://www.catholicnews.com/update%3A-hostility-violence-are-%27betrayals%27-of-religion-pope-says-in-iraq/.

Zimmerman, Joyce Ann, et al. *Living Liturgy*. Collegeville, MN: Liturgical, 2008.

CPSIA information can be obtained
at www.ICGtesting.com
Printed in the USA
LVHW010007161221
706129LV00001B/3

9 781666 730500